The SR Programming Language

Language

Concurrency in Practice

Gregory R. Andrews
The University of Arizona

Ronald A. Olsson
University of California, Davis

The Benjamin/Cummings Publishing Company, Inc.
Redwood City, California • Menlo Park, California
Reading, Massachusetts • New York • Don Mills, Ontario
Wokingham, U.K. • Amsterdam • Bonn • Sydney
Singapore • Tokyo • Madrid • San Juan

Sponsoring editor: John Carter Shanklin
Production coordinator: Megan Rundel
Copyeditor: Barbara Conway
Cover designer: Rudy Zehntner

Library of Congress Cataloging-in-Publication Data

Andrews, Gregory R.
    The SR programming language: concurrency in practice / Gregory R.
  Andrews, Ronald A. Olsson.
          p.   cm.
    Includes bibliographical references and index.
    ISBN 0-8053-0088-0
    1. SR (Computer programming language) 2. Parallel programming
(Computer science)   I. Olsson, Ronald A.   II. Title.
[QA76.73.S68A53 1992]
005.13'3–dc20   92-25056
                                                              CIP

ISBN 0-8053-0088-0

1 2 3 4 5 6 7 8 9 10–MA–95 94 93 92 91

The Benjamin/Cummings Publishing Company, Inc.
390 Bridge Parkway
Redwood City, CA 94065

To my mother, Ruth, and the memory of my father, George

GRA

To my parents, Dorothy and Ronald, and my siblings, Dorothy and Robert

RAO

Preface

SR (Synchronizing Resources) is a language for concurrent programming. It is an imperative language that provides explicit mechanisms for concurrency, communication, and synchronization. SR is suitable for writing programs for *both* shared- and distributed-memory applications and machines; it is, of course, also suitable for writing sequential programs. SR can be used in applications such as parallel computation, distributed systems, simulation, and many others.

SR supports many "features" useful for concurrent programming. However, our goals have always been keeping the language simple and easy to learn and use, while at the same time providing an efficient implementation. We have achieved these goals by integrating common notions, both sequential and concurrent, into a few powerful mechanisms. We have implemented these mechanisms as part of a complete language to determine their feasibility and cost, to gain hands-on experience, and to provide a tool that can be used for research and teaching. The introduction to Chapter 1 expands on how SR has realized our design goals.

The SR implementation executes on many UNIX systems, including most popular ones such as those from DEC, HP, IBM, NeXT, Silicon Graphics, and Sun. The implementation also supports true multiprocessing on the Sequent Symmetry and Silicon Graphics IRIS. The implementation is in the public domain and is available free by FTP or for a nominal charge to cover media costs (see the ordering information inside the back cover). The implementation includes documentation and example programs. Ports to systems other than those listed above are likely and encouraged; the implementation includes a porting guide. Contact us for the most recent list of systems to which SR has been or is currently being ported. There is also an electronic mailing list for discussions of SR topics (information on that too appears inside the back cover).

Content Overview

This book contains 18 chapters. The first chapter gives an overview of SR and includes a few sample programs. The remaining 17 chapters are organized into three parts: sequential aspects, concurrent aspects, and applications. In addition, six appendices contain language reference material, describe how to develop and execute programs, present an overview of SR's implementation and performance, and trace SR's historical roots.

The introduction to each part summarizes the key language mechanisms or applications introduced in that part and describes their relation to material in previous parts. Each chapter in Parts I and II introduces new language mechanisms and develops solutions to several problems. Some problems are solved in more than one chapter to illustrate the tradeoffs between different language mechanisms. The problems include the "classic" concurrent programming problems—e.g., critical sections, producers and consumers, readers and writers, the dining philosophers, and resource allocation—as well as many important parallel and distributed programming problems. Each chapter in Part III describes an application, presents (typically) several solutions, and describes the tradeoffs between the solutions. The end of each chapter contains numerous exercises, including several that introduce additional material.

Part I introduces the sequential aspects of SR. Chapter 2 describes many of SR's basic mechanisms: types, variables, assignment and other operators, elementary input/output, etc. This material is necessarily quite detailed (the rest of the book is much less so). It can be scanned on a first reading and referred to later as needed. Chapter 3 presents sequential control statements for alternation and repetition. Chapter 4 describes procedures, the simplest form of SR's operations. Chapter 5 introduces SR's modules: resources and globals. Finally, Chapter 6 covers input/output and shows how SR code can be used with code written in another language (e.g., C).

Part II describes the concurrent aspects of SR. Chapter 7 introduces the language mechanisms for creating concurrently executing processes. Chapters 8, 9, 10, and 11 show how processes can synchronize and communicate using semaphores, asynchronous message passing, remote procedure call, and rendezvous, respectively. All these mechanisms are variations on SR's operations. Chapter 12 describes how to distribute a program so that it can execute in multiple address spaces, potentially on multiple physical machines such as a network of workstations. Finally, Chapter 13 describes the classic dining philosophers problem to show how many of SR's concurrency features can be used with one another.

Part III describes several realistic applications for SR. Chapter 14 gives four solutions to matrix multiplication. Included are solutions appropriate for both shared- and distributed-memory environments. Chapter 15 describes grid computations for solving partial differential equations. It too provides both shared- and distributed-memory solutions. Chapter 16 presents solutions to the traveling salesman problem that employ two important paradigms: bag of tasks and manager/workers. Chapter 17 describes a prototype distributed file system. Finally, Chapter 18 shows how to program a discrete event simulation in SR.

The first four appendices contain material in quick-reference format. They are handy when actually programming in SR and when reading the rest of the text. Appendix A outlines the major syntactic forms. Appendix B gives the complete syntax of the language. Appendix C summarizes the operators and predefined functions. Appendix D describes how to compile, link, and execute programs; it also describes other tools for SR programs, including a UNIX Makefile generator, text formatters, and three preprocessors (described below). Appendix E gives an overview of the implementation and describes the performance of SR code. Finally, Appendix F gives a short history of the SR language and mentions other SR-related work.

Classroom Use

Drafts of this text have been used in a variety of undergraduate and graduate courses at The University of Arizona, the University of California, Davis, and several other universities. These courses cover topics such as programming languages, operating systems, concurrent programming, parallel processing, and distributed systems. The SR language and implementation have also been used as the basis for a number of undergraduate and graduate independent study projects, master's theses, and doctoral dissertations and in a number of other research projects.

This text can serve as a stand-alone introduction to one particular concurrent programming language or as a supplement to a more general concurrent programming course. For example, it forms a natural supplement for a course that uses Greg Andrews's text entitled *Concurrent Programming: Principles and Practice*, also published by Benjamin/Cummings. That text explores the concepts of concurrent programming, various synchronization and communication mechanisms, programming paradigms, implementation issues, and techniques to understand and develop correct programs.

The SR implementation comes with three preprocessors that convert notations for CCRs, monitors, and CSP (Communicating Sequential Processes) into SR code. These allow students to get hands-on experience with those mechanisms. Together with SR, the three preprocessors provide a complete teaching tool for a spectrum of synchronization mechanisms (corresponding to chapters in Andrews's book): shared variables, semaphores, CCRs, monitors, asynchronous message passing, synchronous message passing (including output commands in guards, as in extended CSP), RPC, and rendezvous. The preprocessors have been used in courses based on Andrews's book as well as in operating systems courses.

We have aimed this text at junior or senior level undergraduate students and at graduate students. Previous or concurrent courses in programming languages or operating systems are beneficial, although not essential, in understanding the material. The following is a typical use of this book: Read Chapter 1 to get a feel for the language; scan Part I to be exposed to SR's sequential aspects; read Part II carefully to understand SR's concurrent aspects; and then read Part III to see how to apply SR in a number of application areas. As noted, it should suffice to scan Part I and then refer back to specific topics as the need arises in reading the later parts. However, the pervasive concepts of operations and operation capabilities (Chapter 4) and of resources, globals, and resource capabilities (Chapter 5) warrant some extra attention before reading Part II.

Each chapter contains exercises dealing with the concepts and examples presented in the chapter. They range from simple to more difficult ones, including suggestions for a number of larger projects, especially in Part III. A number of other exercises and projects can be found in Andrews's concurrent programming book. To save readers typing for some of the exercises, complete programs that appear in this text are included online with the rest of the SR distribution; they are located in subdirectories of the `examples` directory.

Acknowledgments

Numerous people have read, commented on, and class-tested drafts of the text and have also used earlier implementations of SR. They have provided us with feedback that has helped us write a better book and provide a better language and implementation. We thank them and all the students who have studied SR and concurrent programming at Arizona and Davis the past few years. Three reviewers have also provided numerous helpful suggestions on content, organization, and technical points: Stella Atkins, Andrzej Hoppe, and Michael Scott. Michael Scott's comments were especially detailed and useful.

Mike Coffin, Irv Elshoff, Phil Kaslo, Kelvin Nilsen, Titus Purdin, and Gregg Townsend helped implement earlier versions of SR. Mike and Gregg contributed key ideas to this version of the language, and Gregg has done an outstanding job producing the current implementation, which has included a major rewrite of the compiler. Gregg also reviewed the text and gave us many useful suggestions and even some prose. Dave Bakken implemented the run-time support for the Sequent and Silicon Graphics multiprocessor versions of SR. A number of other people also contributed code that has been incorporated into the current implementation. They are listed in the `Authors` file that is part of the distribution.

The staff of Benjamin/Cummings has been a pleasure to work with. This book was first suggested and signed by Alan Apt when he was with B/C.

Subsequently, Dan Joraanstad and then Carter Shanklin took over the role of sponsoring editor. Vivian McDougal handled logistical aspects of reviews and schedules, Megan Rundel coordinated production, Barbara Conway did copy-editing, Lynn Sanchez supervised art work, Rudy Zehntner designed the cover, and Colleen Dunn has supervised promotion and marketing.

The National Science Foundation has supported the computing equipment used to prepare this book. The NSF has also supported our SR-related research for several years, most recently through grants CDA-8822652, CCR-8811423, and CCR-9108412 at Arizona and CCR-8810617 at Davis. The pages were generated by a Lintronic 300 phototypesetter in the Department of Computer Science at The University of Arizona. John Cropper and Song Liang did a superb job producing the copy and overcoming mechanical problems that arose in the process.

We would also like to thank the sponsors and developers of the Internet, which has greatly facilitated our long-distance collaboration both on SR and on this book. In fact there are more characters in our files of book-related electronic mail than in the book itself.

Jeff Andrews extracted the SR programs from the book text files. Amy Morgenstern tested the programs and packaged them for inclusion in the SR distribution. Amy also constructed a timing suite of test programs to produce the performance measurements reported in Appendix E.

Last, but far from least, we would like to thank our families and friends. Greg's wife, Mary, and sons, Jeff and Brad, put up with another year of long days and lost weekends. It's time for the Andrews family to enjoy more time together (and to spend a little royalty money!).

Ron's family and friends put up with him. They also helped by asking him "How's the book?," by "being there," and by making him play more.

Greg Andrews
Tucson, Arizona

Ron Olsson
Davis, California

Contents

CHAPTER 1

Introduction

Concurrent programming is concerned with writing programs having multiple processes that may execute in parallel. The topic originated in the 1960s when the invention of independent device controllers (channels) led people to organize operating systems as concurrent programs, even for single-processor machines. Since then, rapid developments in computer architecture have led to an increasingly large number of multiprocessor architectures, such as shared-memory multiprocessors, multicomputers, and networks of workstations. The operating systems for these architectures are all instances of concurrent programs. More importantly, multiprocessor architectures make it possible to write application programs that exploit the concurrency inherent in the hardware.

A concurrent program specifies two or more processes that cooperate in performing a task. Each process consists of a sequential program. The processes cooperate by communicating, which in turn gives rise to the need for synchronization. Communication and synchronization are programmed by reading and writing shared variables or by sending and receiving messages. Shared variables are most appropriate for concurrent programs that execute on a single processor or a shared-memory multiprocessor. Message passing is most appropriate for distributed programs that execute on multicomputers or networks of workstations. (Message passing can also be used on shared-memory machines.)

This book describes the SR (Synchronizing Resources) programming language and shows how it can be used to write concurrent programs for a variety of hardware architectures and software applications. One of SR's distinguishing attributes is its expressive power. It contains a variety of communication and synchronization mechanisms, including most of the ones that have proven popular and useful: shared variables, semaphores, asynchronous message passing, remote procedure call (RPC), and rendezvous. This makes SR suitable for writing concurrent programs for *both* shared- and distributed-memory applications and machines. As we discuss in this book, SR is also an interesting and useful language for sequential programming.

In addition to being expressive, SR is easy to learn and use. Its variety of concurrent programming mechanisms is based on only a few underlying concepts. Moreover, these concepts are generalizations of ones that have been found useful in sequential programs. The concurrent programming mechanisms are also integrated with the sequential ones, so that similar things are expressed in similar ways.

A further consequence of basing SR on a small number of concepts is good performance. SR provides a greater variety of concurrent programming mechanisms than any other language, yet each mechanism is as efficient as its counterpart in other languages. We have designed the language, compiler, and run-time system in concert to ensure that language features can be implemented efficiently. In addition, some of the expressiveness in SR has been realized by "opening up" the implementation. For example, SR provides several mechanisms for invoking and servicing operations, all of which are variations on ways to enqueue and dequeue messages.

Parts I and II of this book describe the sequential and concurrent aspects of SR in detail and give several examples. Part III develops complete programs for several larger applications: matrix multiplication, partial differential equations, the traveling salesman problem, a distributed file system, and discrete event simulation. These illustrate the use of SR for distributed programming using message passing and parallel programming using shared variables. Implementations of SR exist for a corresponding variety of architectures, including networks of workstations and shared-memory multiprocessors. SR programs can also be executed on single processor machines, in which case process execution is interleaved.

The remainder of this chapter gives a brief overview of SR. First we describe the main components of the language. Then we present complete programs that solve several familiar problems. The solutions illustrate the structure of SR programs and some—but by no means all—of the language's power and flexibility. Finally, we describe how to create and execute SR programs.

1.1 Resources, Globals, and Operations

The key components of SR—for both sequential and concurrent programming—are resources, globals, and operations. An SR program contains one or more resources. Each is a template from which resource instances are created dynamically. The programmer can control where a resource instance is placed, i.e., the machine on which it executes. Every program has one distinguished "main" resource. One instance of this resource is created automatically when an SR program begins execution.

The resource is SR's main unit of compilation and encapsulation; it corresponds roughly to modules found in many other languages. A resource has a specification part (*spec* for short) and an implementation part (*body* for short). The spec defines symbolic constants, user-defined types, and operations; these objects are automatically exported. An import statement is used to acquire access to objects exported by other resources (or globals). The spec also defines the formal parameters of the resource body.

A resource body gives the implementation of a resource. It contains declarations, statements, procedures, processes, and optional final code. The statements are executed when an instance of the resource is created; they are used to initialize the instance. The final code is executed if the instance is destroyed. A resource's spec and body can be written (and compiled) separately or as a single unit. Declarations and statements in the body can be intermixed; this supports dynamic arrays and permits the programmer to control the order in which variables are initialized and processes are created.

A global is a collection of objects shared by resources (or globals) in the same address space. It is essentially an instance of an unparameterized resource, and it can also have a spec and a body. Only one instance of a global is created per address space, and it is created implicitly the first time it is imported. A global can be used to declare types, constants, variables, and operations that are shared by resources. These objects are referenced directly by name, whereas objects in resources are referenced indirectly by means of capability variables.

Processes in the same resource can share variables, as can resources in the same address space (through the use of globals). Processes can also communicate and synchronize by means of operations.

An operation can be considered a generalization of a procedure: It has a name and can take parameters and return a result. An operation can be invoked in two ways: synchronously by means of a call statement or asynchronously by means of a send statement. An operation can also be serviced in two ways: by a procedure-like object called a proc or by input statements. These ways of servicing an operation support local and remote procedure calls and rendezvous. As we shall see in Part II, this variety of possibilities provides a great deal of flexibility and power for solving concurrent programming problems.

The SR language provides a variety of useful predefined operations. These include common math functions, timing functions, and a variety of input/output functions. The programmer can also declare external operations, which provide access to operations implemented in other languages, such as C.

SR contains several mechanisms that are abbreviations for common uses of operations; these can be used to simplify many programs. Abbreviations include process declarations, procedure declarations, receive statements, and semaphores. SR also provides a few additional statements that are useful for concurrent programming. The reply, forward, and concurrent invocation statements provide additional ways to use operations.

1.2 Two Simple Examples

One of the best ways to learn a new programming language is to start writing programs. To do so, it helps to look at examples.

A standard first example in a programming language text is a program that writes the message "Hello world" on the standard output file. In SR, the following program does the trick:

```
resource hello()
  write("Hello world")
end
```

It contains a single resource. The "shortest" SR program has an empty resource body; i.e., it omits the call to write above.

A more interesting example is the following interactive program, which computes factorials of positive integers:

```
resource factorial()
  procedure fact(v: int) returns r: int
    # v is assumed to be positive
    if v = 1 -> r := 1
    [] v > 1 -> r := v*fact(v-1)
    fi
  end
  var n: int
  writes("enter a positive integer: "); read(n)
  write("the factorial of", n, "is", fact(n))
end
```

This program first calls writes, which prompts for an input value and leaves the cursor positioned on the same line. After reading a value for integer n, the program prints n and its factorial. (In contrast to writes, write inserts one space between each pair of arguments, and it appends a newline character to its output.) Of course, in general it is best to check that the input is valid before using it.

The factorial is computed in the standard way by a recursive function. The procedure definition in the program declares an operation named `fact` and gives an implementation for the operation. The expression in the last write statement invokes `fact`. The body of `fact` contains a multi-armed if statement, with one arm for $v = 1$ and one for $v > 1$.

The line in `fact` beginning with the sharp character, #, is a comment line. The comment ends at the end of the line.

The factorial example also illustrates SR's punctuation style. A statement is terminated by a newline character or by a semicolon. Our conventions are to use a newline character to terminate a statement that is on a line by itself and to use semicolons to separate statements or declarations that are on the same line. (A declaration or statement can also span lines, as described in Section 2.1.)

1.3 Matrix Multiplication

Now consider the problem of multiplying two $n \times n$ real matrices a and b. We first present a sequential program to solve this problem and then show how to modify the program to compute all n^2 inner products in parallel.

The following program is executed with three command-line arguments: the value of n and the names of data files containing the source matrices. The program first reads its arguments, then reads the data files, then computes the matrix product, and finally prints the result matrix.

```
resource matrix()
  # read command-line arguments and open files
  var n: int; getarg(1, n)
  var namea: string[20]; getarg(2, namea)
  var nameb: string[20]; getarg(3, nameb)
  var filea := open(namea, READ)
  var fileb := open(nameb, READ)
  # declare and initialize matrices a, b, and c
  var a[1:n,1:n], b[1:n,1:n]: real
  var c[1:n,1:n]: real := ([n] ([n] 0.0) )
  fa i := 1 to n, j := 1 to n ->
      read(filea, a[i,j]); read(fileb, b[i,j])
  af

  # compute n**2 inner products
  fa i := 1 to n, j := 1 to n ->
    fa k := 1 to n ->
      c[i,j] := c[i,j] + a[i,k]*b[k,j]
    af
  af
```

```
# print c, one row per line
fa i := 1 to n ->
  fa j := 1 to n -> writes(c[i,j], " ") af
  write()     # force new line
af
end matrix
```

The program reads the command-line arguments by calling the predefined `getarg` function. Then it opens the two data files by calling the predefined `open` function. In the interest of keeping the program short, we have not checked the validity of the results from these function calls.

Next the program declares matrices a, b, and c. Since n has a value at this point in the program, the sizes of the three matrices are determined dynamically. The declaration of matrix c also contains an initialization clause, which assigns n rows of n zeroes to c. After declaring c, we use a for-all statement to read in values for a and b:

```
fa i := 1 to n, j := 1 to n ->
    read(filea, a[i,j]); read(fileb, b[i,j])
af
```

This statement contains two *quantifiers*: the first one assigns values to the new variable i, and the second one assigns values to the new variable j. The value of j varies most rapidly, so values are read into a and b in row-major order, i.e., first row 1, then row 2, and so on.

The program next computes n^2 inner products using nested for-all statements. The inner for-all statement computes the inner product of row i of a and column j of b and stores the result in c[i,j]. (Here we could have used just one for-all statement containing all three quantifier variables.)

Finally the program uses nested for-all statements to print matrix c. Each row is printed on a separate line of the standard output file; values in a row are separated by one blank space.

Since the inner products are independent of each other, we can compute all n^2 in parallel, as shown below. This program will not be very efficient, since each process does very little computation, but we could readily modify it to use fewer processes (see Exercise 1.2 and also Chapter 14).

```
resource matrix()
  # declarations and initialization, as above
  process compute(i := 1 to n, j := 1 to n)
    fa k := 1 to n ->
        c[i,j] := c[i,j] + a[i,k]*b[k,j]
    af
  end
```

```
        final
          # print c, as above
        end
    end matrix
```

This program reuses many parts of the sequential program. Only two changes are needed: (1) replace the outer for-all statement in the computational loop by a process declaration, and (2) embed the statements that print results in final code. The matrix multiplication itself is accomplished by the compute process, which has the following heading:

```
    process compute(i := 1 to n, j := 1 to n)
```

This heading contains two quantifiers, so n^2 processes are created, one for each combination of values for i and j. In fact, i and j are parameters to each instance of compute and are available in the body. Each process computes one inner product, as in the sequential program. The compute processes are created when the process declaration is encountered. At this point in the above program, arrays a, b, and c have already been initialized.

When inner products are computed in parallel, c should not be printed out until all processes have terminated. As mentioned in Section 1.1, a resource may contain optional final code, which is executed when the resource is destroyed. The main resource in an SR program is destroyed implicitly when the program terminates. Hence, if there is final code in the main resource, it is executed *after* the rest of the computation terminates. (The position of the final code in the body of a resource has no bearing on when it is executed.) In the program above, once the compute processes terminate, the final code in matrix is executed to print out c. By using final code, we do not need to add synchronization code to the rest of the program to determine when all the compute processes have terminated. This feature of SR makes many programs, including this one, easy to write.

1.4 Concurrent File Search

The programs given so far are very short, so they consist of a single resource. Often it is best to employ multiple resources and to use globals for shared declarations. The last two examples in this chapter illustrate how to do so.

The grep family of UNIX commands is commonly used to search for patterns in files. For example, the following command searches each of the named files:

```
    grep string filename1 filename2 ...
```

Each line containing `string` is printed on standard output. (If there is more than one file, each line of output begins with the name of the file.) The `grep` command searches each file sequentially.

The following SR program gives a concurrent implementation of the above command. In particular, it searches each file in parallel. The program has the same arguments as `grep` above: a pattern string and one or more file names. Like `grep`, the program prints all lines that contain the pattern string on the standard output. A string containing the file name concatenated with a colon is printed at the front of each line. Since searching and printing proceed in parallel, however, lines from different files will be interleaved.

```
global defs     # shared definitions
  const MAXPATTERN := 20
  const MAXFILENAME := 20
  const MAXLINE := 120
end

resource grep(pattern, filename: string[*])
  import defs
  var fd: file := open(filename, READ)

  procedure find(pattern, line: string[*])
    # if line contains pattern, write out line
    var i := 1, plen := length(pattern)
    do i <= (length(line) - plen + 1) ->
      if pattern = line[i:i+plen-1] ->
          write(filename || ":", line); return
      fi
      i++
    od
  end

  process search
    # find all instances of pattern in filename
    var line: string[MAXLINE]
    do read(fd, line) != EOF ->
      find(pattern, line)
    od
  end
end grep

resource main()
  import defs, grep
  # read command-line arguments and create instances
  # of resource grep
```

```
           var pattern: string[MAXPATTERN]; getarg(1, pattern)
           var filename: string[MAXFILENAME]
           fa i := 2 to numargs() ->
               getarg(i, filename)
               create grep(pattern, filename)
           af
       end
```

The program contains three components: a global and two resources. The global, `defs`, defines shared constants. Resource `grep` has two formal parameters: `pattern` and `filename`. Each instance of `grep` finds all instances of `pattern` in `filename` and writes them out; the file name and a colon are printed at the front of each line. Resource `main` is the main resource in the program. It reads the command-line arguments and creates one instance of `grep` for each `filename` argument. Again, the program does not check the validity of its input.

All instances of resources in the above program execute on the same machine. However, we can readily modify the program so that different instances of `grep` execute on potentially different machines. For example, suppose a file name is specified on the command line as `machine:filename`. Also, suppose that `main` separates `machine` from `filename` and stores the values in string variables with those names. Then `main` can create an instance of `grep` on `machine` by executing

```
       var vmcap: cap vm
       vmcap := create vm() on machine
       create grep(pattern, filename) on vmcap
```

A `vm` in SR is a virtual machine (address space). The first line declares a capability for a `vm`. The second line creates a new `vm` on the machine whose name is stored in variable `machine`. The third line creates an instance of `grep` on the newly created `vm`, and hence on a potentially remote machine. The effect of making the above changes is that each instance of `grep` will open `filename` on the machine on which it is executing.

1.5 Critical Section Simulation

As a final example, we present a program that illustrates a few of the numerous message-passing mechanisms available in SR. The program also illustrates how one can construct a simple simulation of a solution to a synchronization problem.

The following program contains `numusers` instances of a `user` process, each of which repeatedly executes a critical section of code and then a non-critical section. At most one process at a time is permitted to execute its critical section. If more than one process wants to enter its critical section at the same time, the one with the highest priority is permitted to do so. Each user process has an index i; the lower the index value, the higher the priority of the process. We simulate the duration of critical and non-critical sections of code by having each user process "nap" for a random number of milliseconds.

```
global CS
    op CSenter(id: int) {call}     # must be called
    op CSexit()     # may be invoked by call or send
body CS
    process arbitrator
      do true ->
        in CSenter(id) by id ->
            write("user", id, "in its CS at", age())
        ni
        receive CSexit()
      od
    end
end

resource main()
    import CS
    var numusers, rounds: int
    getarg(1, numusers); getarg(2, rounds)

    process user(i := 1 to numusers)
      fa j := 1 to rounds ->
        call CSenter(i)              # enter critical section
        nap(int(random(100)))    # delay up to 100 msec
        send CSexit()            # exit critical section
        nap(int(random(1000)))   # delay up to 1 second
      af
    end
end
```

The global, CS, declares two operations in its spec; hence these are exported. The body of CS contains an arbitrator process that implements these operations. It first uses an input statement to wait for an invocation of CSenter:

```
in CSenter(id) by id ->
    write("user", id, "in its CS at", age())
ni
```

This is SR's rendezvous mechanism. If there is more than one invocation of CSenter, the one that has the smallest value for parameter id is selected, and a message is then printed. Next the arbitrator uses a receive statement to wait for an invocation of CSexit. Receive is a special case of in that can be used when one just needs to pass a message or, in this case, simply a signal. In this program we could have put the arbitrator process and its operations within the main resource. However, by placing them in a global component, they could also be used by other resources in a larger program.

Each user process calls the CSenter operation to get permission to enter its critical section, passing its index i as an argument. After "napping" the process then invokes the CSexit operation. The CSenter operation must be invoked by a synchronous call statement because the user process has to wait to get permission. This is enforced by means of the operation restriction {call} in the declaration of the CSenter operation. However, since a user process does not need to delay when leaving its critical section, it invokes the CSexit operation by means of the asynchronous send statement.

The program employs several of SR's predefined functions. The age function in the write statement returns the number of milliseconds the program has been executing. The nap function causes a process to "nap" for the number of milliseconds specified by its argument. The random function returns a pseudo-random real number between 0 and its argument. Since the argument to nap must be an integer, we also use the int type-conversion function to convert random's result to an integer.

1.6 Executing SR Programs

To execute an SR program, one must first create one or more files containing the program text. In keeping with a common UNIX programming convention, the names of these files must end with .sr. For example, the "Hello world" program might be placed in a file named hello.sr.

The standard name of the SR compiler is **sr.** Assuming the directory containing the compiler is in a particular user's search path, the user can compile hello.sr by executing the UNIX command

    sr hello.sr

Unless the SR compiler detects fatal errors in the source program, executing **sr** as shown creates an executable file named a.out.

In addition to producing an a.out file, the SR compiler creates a new directory named Interfaces (unless it already exists) and creates several files in that directory. In particular, the Interfaces directory contains information about the specification part of every global and resource, and it contains intermediate object files. The programmer should have no need to be concerned with the contents of these files but also should not modify them. However, `Interfaces` is not needed to run a program, so it can be deleted after an executable file has been created.

The SR compiler has several command-line options. There are also several additional programs in the SR distribution, including the SR linker and an SR makefile generation program that facilitates compiling and executing SR programs. See Appendix D for further details on developing and executing SR programs.

Exercises

1.1   Copy the factorial program into a file and then compile it. Try executing the program. What is the largest factorial that can be computed on your machine without causing overflow? Also examine the contents of the `Interfaces` directory. Finally, try modifying the program so that it continues to read integers and print factorials until the user inputs a non-positive value.

1.2   (a) Copy the sequential and parallel matrix multiplication programs into files, compile them, and compare their execution times. Use the `age` function to time your two programs for various size matrices. Which is more efficient?

      (b) Modify the parallel program so that it uses only n processes, each of which computes one row of result matrix c. Compare the performance of this program to your answers to (a).

1.3   (a) Copy the concurrent file search program into a file and then compile it. Execute the program using different patterns and files. Compare the output to that of the `grep` command. Now try piping the output of your SR program through the `sort` command, and compare the output to that of `grep`. What happens if the file-name arguments to your SR program are given in alphabetical order?

      (b) Modify the program to create instances of `grep` on different machines, as described in Section 1.4. Experiment with this version of the program.

1.4   Copy the critical section program into a file and then compile it. Execute the program several times and examine the results. Also experiment with different nap intervals by modifying the argument to the `random` function. Modify the program by deleting the phrase `by id` in the `arbitrator` process, and execute this version of the program several times. How do the results compare to that of the original program? What if `by id` is replaced by `by -id`?

## PART I

Sequential Aspects

This part introduces the sequential parts of SR, which in fact constitute the bulk of the language. SR's sequential programming mechanisms are conceptually similar to those found in imperative programming languages, such as Algol, Pascal, Modula-2, and C. However, their form and many of their details are different, as the examples in Chapter 1 illustrate. These differences are largely to facilitate the integration of the sequential and concurrent components of SR. They also make it easy to program commonly occurring algorithmic patterns.

Resources, globals, and operations are the key components of SR for sequential as well as concurrent programming. SR's other sequential parts are statements, expressions, variables, and types.

The sequential control statements in SR include an alternative statement and a general repetitive statement. These are based on Dijkstra's guarded commands [Dijkstra 1976], mainly so their structure is similar to that of the input statement, which is used for concurrent programming. SR also provides a novel iterative statement—the for-all statement—that facilitates programming the common situation where the number of loop iterations is known in advance.

SR provides the usual kinds of basic types (e.g., integers, reals, booleans, and strings), and the usual kinds of structured types (e.g., arrays, records, and unions). In addition, SR provides three kinds of *capabilities*. Resource capabilities serve as pointers to instances of resources; they are needed since instances of resources are created dynamically. Operation capabilities serve as pointers to individual operations. Virtual machine capabilities, as described in Part II, serve as pointers to the address spaces that comprise a program. All three kinds of capabilities can be passed to resources and operations, thus permitting functions to be passed as arguments and inter-process communication channels to vary dynamically.

We describe the sequential aspects of SR in a bottom-up manner. That is, we first describe the "small" aspects of SR—declarations, types, variables, and statements—and then describe its "large" aspects—operations, resources and globals. Consequently, the programming examples in the first few chapters are just single resource programs.

The chapters in Part I are organized as follows: Chapter 2 describes SR's most basic mechanisms: types, constant definitions, variable declarations, assignment operators, and basic input/output facilities. Chapter 3 discusses sequential control statements. Chapter 4 shows how procedures are declared and invoked and how operation capabilities are used. Chapter 5 describes how resources and globals are declared, created, and destroyed and how their objects can be imported. Finally, Chapter 6 describes SR's input/output facilities in more detail and shows how to use external routines written in other languages.

## CHAPTER 2

Types, Variables, and Assignments

This chapter describes the mechanisms at the heart of SR programming. We first describe the basic and user-defined types. The basic types are built into the language; they are boolean, character, integer, real, and string. User-defined types are defined by the programmer. The type constructors are array, enumeration, record, union, and pointer; operation types and capabilities are defined in Chapter 4. For each type, we describe the values of the type and the operators and predefined functions that can be used on those values; Appendix C summarizes the operators—including their associativity and precedence—and predefined functions. We then show how variables and constants are declared, initialized, and referenced, and how they are assigned values; we also present the rules for forming expressions. We then examine the basic forms of input and output; these are covered in depth in Chapter 6. We then discuss type equivalence and present the functions for converting between values of different types. Finally, we conclude this chapter by examining SR's scope rules.

2.1 Vocabulary and Notation

We begin by explaining the notation and conventions we will be using in the remainder of the book. An SR program is constructed out of sequences of tokens. The tokens include identifiers, keywords, literals, operators, and separators. As illustrated in Chapter 1, we typeset SR tokens and programs in the Courier (typewriter) typeface.

- Identifiers are sequences of letters, digits, and underscores. The first character must be a letter. Case is important; e.g., CS, Cs, cS, and cs are all different identifiers.

- Keywords are special identifiers, such as if and do, whose meaning is fixed in the language. They will be introduced as we describe the various language mechanisms. The complete set of keywords is listed in Appendix A.

- Literals are specific values of different types, such as booleans, integers, reals, characters, and strings. Most of the different literals are defined later in this chapter.

- Operators and separators are keywords or special characters, such as <, <=, or []. They are typeset as they would appear in a source program.

White space—blanks or tabs—may appear between any two tokens. It is ignored unless it is essential to separate two tokens, such as a keyword followed by an identifier.

Newline characters, too, can sometimes be used as white space. However, they can also indicate the end of a declaration, statement, or expression. When a newline character is encountered, its role is determined by the following rule: If the previous token can legally terminate a declaration, statement, or expression—and if the following token can legally begin one— then the newline acts as a separator; otherwise it is ignored. For example, consider the following program fragment:

```
x := 10 +
    3
```

It consists of a single assignment, assigning 13 to x. In contrast consider

```
x := 10
    + 3
```

This consists of two expressions: the first assigns 10 to x, and the second just evaluates the expression + 3. To rewrite the original example with the + on the second line, an explicit line continuation, denoted by \, is placed at the end of the line to be continued, as in

```
x := 10 \
    + 3
```

In addition to newline characters, semicolons can be used to terminate declarations, statements, or expressions. Semicolons also appear in the SR grammar in a few places, such as between field definitions in a record (see below). Semicolons can *always* be replaced by newline characters. As mentioned in Chapter 1, our convention is to use semicolons only to separate declarations, statements, or expressions that appear on the same line in a program.

SR provides two different kinds of comments. In Chapter 1, we used a one-line comment, which begins with # and ends at the next newline character (or the end of file). The second kind of comment is a bracketed comment, which begins with /* and ends with the corresponding occurrence of */. Bracketed comments can appear within a line, or they can span more than one line. Bracketed comments can also be nested; otherwise all characters within a comment are ignored until the end of the comment is reached. For example, # is ignored within a bracketed comment.

We will present the syntax of SR programs in a "pictorial" form in which each syntax display conveys what an element of the SR grammar looks like in a program. For example, a record definition contains one or more field definitions separated by semicolons:

```
rec ( field_definition; field_definition; ... )
```

The keyword `rec`, the parentheses, and the semicolons are SR tokens, so they are typeset in Courier. The *field_definition* is a non-terminal in the SR grammar. When an item such as *field_definition* can be repeated, we will always list two instances and two separators and follow them with an ellipsis. We will also say whether there must be zero or more or one or more instances of the item.

2.2 Basic Types

SR has five basic types: boolean, integer, real, character, and string. They are represented by keywords `bool`, `int`, `real`, `char`, and `string`, respectively.

Booleans

The boolean type has two literals: `false` and `true`. The boolean operators are `and`, `or`, `xor` (exclusive or), and `not`. Each operator returns a boolean result.

Evaluation of boolean expressions is *short-circuit*: evaluation stops as soon as the final value of the expression can be determined. In particular, evaluation of `and` and `or` are short-circuit. For example, if `and`'s first operand evaluates to false, its second operand is not evaluated because the entire expression is known to be false. Similarly, if `or`'s first operand evaluates to true, its second operand is not evaluated because the entire expression is known to be true.

Integers

Integer literals are unsigned sequences of digits. Decimal numbers are sequences of 0-9. Octal numbers are sequences of 0-7 followed by q or Q. Hexadecimal numbers are sequences of 0-9, a-f, or A-F, followed by x or X; hexadecimal numbers must begin with a digit. All numbers specify the least significant bits of the literal; unspecified bits are set to 0. Some examples of integer literals are

```
11   4096   1333Q   0abcdefX
```

The integer operators include arithmetic operators, such as +, **, % (remainder), and mod; bit-wise operators, such as not and or; and bit-shifting operators, such as >> (right shift). Each operator returns an integer result.

The modulo and remainder operators are related in that they both return a result that represents the remainder from the division of their two operands. However, they differ in exactly what they return. The sign of a mod b is that of b, while the sign of a%b depends on how integer division is performed on the underlying machine. For example, consider a circular buffer of size n with slots numbered 0, 1, ..., n-1. The two slots adjacent to slot i have indices (i+1) mod n and (i-1) mod n. When i is zero, the value of this last expression is n-1, whereas the value of (i-1) % n can be either n-1 or -1. Accordingly, the modulo operator is generally more useful than the remainder operator.

A number of predefined functions—such as abs and max—can be applied to integers. See Appendix C for details.

Reals

A real (floating-point) literal has the general form

integer_part . fraction_part exponent_part

The three parts and decimal point are optional, subject to the following rule: Either the integer or the fraction part must be present, and either the decimal point or the exponent part must be present; the decimal point must be present if the fraction part is present. The integer and fraction parts are sequences of decimal digits. The exponent part starts with e or E, has an optional sign, and ends with a sequence of decimal digits specifying a power. Some examples of real literals are

```
11.2       3.1415927   0.0      0.       .0
1.23e-45   1.23E-45    .123e-44  421e+3   421e3
```

`\n`	newline (NL)	`\a`	alert (BEL)
`\t`	tab (HT)	`\e`	escape (ESC)
`\b`	backspace (BS)	`\v`	vertical tab (VT)
`\r`	return (CR)	`\f`	form feed (FF)
`\'`	single quote	`\"`	double quote
`\\`	backslash		
`\ooo`	bit pattern where *ooo* is 1-3 octal digits		
`\xhh`	bit pattern where *hh* is 1 or 2 hexadecimal digits		
`\c`	character *c* where *c* is any other character		

Table 2.1. Special characters.

The real operators are the same arithmetic operators as for integers. Each operator returns a real result. The comments regarding the modulo and remainder operators on integers also apply to their real counterparts.

As with integers, a number of predefined functions—such as `abs` and `max`—can be applied to reals. Other predefined functions for reals include standard mathematical functions, such as `sin`, `log`, and `sqrt`. Again, see Appendix C for details.

Characters

Character values are represented using type `char`. Character literals are single ASCII characters enclosed in single quotes (apostrophes). In addition, character literals can contain the special characters shown in Table 2.1. Examples of character literals include

```
'a'   'Z'   '4'   '\''   '\e'   '\33'   '\x1b'
```

The fourth literal is a single quote. The last three literals are all the escape (ESC) character: as a special character, in octal, and in hexadecimal.

The character type has no type-specific operators, although characters can be concatenated to form strings.

Strings

Strings are sequences of zero or more ASCII characters enclosed in double quotes. String literals can also contain the special characters listed in Table 2.1. Examples of string literals are shown below; the first is the empty string.

```
""   "alpha"   "Z"   "44"
"I'm having fun"   "here is a \" in the middle"
```

The string type has one binary operator, ||, for string concatenation. Each operand is either a string or a character. The result is a string that is the concatenation of the two operands.

An implicit part of every string is the number of characters it holds. The declaration of a string variable must specify a maximum length, e.g., string[20]. The actual number of characters in a string variable can vary from zero up to the specified maximum. The predefined function length(s) returns the current number of characters in string s. The predefined function maxlength(s) returns the maximum number of characters in string s, e.g., the declared maximum length. For either function, s can be a variable or an arbitrary string expression. The following table gives some examples of the values of these predefined functions, assuming x is a string variable declared as string[20], and its current value is "oscar".

expr	length(*expr*)	maxlength(*expr*)
"abc"	3	3
x	5	20
"abc" || x	8	8

The values of length and maxlength on a given expression will differ only when the expression is a single variable.

2.3 Relational Operators and Ordered Types

Relational operators compare their operands and return a boolean value that reflects the result of the comparison. They are defined on reals, strings, and all *ordered types*. Of the basic types, booleans, characters, and integers are ordered types; that is, it makes sense to define an ordering among values in each of those types, *and* their successive values differ by a fixed amount. Reals and strings are not considered ordered types because adjacent values differ by a variable amount. However, orderings exist between their respective values so that reals and strings can be compared. Enumeration types, described later, are the only user-defined ordered types.

The ordering among boolean values is that false precedes true. Among character values, the ordering is defined by the underlying bit representation treated as an unsigned integer. (Thus the ASCII ordering is preserved, although all eight bits of a byte can be used in a character.) The ordering of integer values is by their numeric values; the same applies to real values. Strings are ordered lexicographically using their underlying character representation. The empty string is the smallest string. For example, the following strings are in increasing order:

```
""    " "    "12"    "123"    "A"    "a"    "alpha"    "beta"
```

The relational operators—which again may be used only on ordered types, reals, and strings—include the usual comparisons =, !=, <, <=, etc. Each operator is binary and returns a boolean result; its operands must be of the same type (though see Section 2.12). The precedence of relational operators is above that of the boolean operators but below that of all other operators encountered thus far. Thus, expressions involving multiple relational operators can be written without requiring parentheses (unlike in Pascal). For example, the following two boolean expressions are equivalent:

```
a < b and c > d      (a < b) and (c > d)
```

The relational operators = and != are also defined for pointers, as described in Section 2.4 below, and for capabilities, as described in Sections 4.6 and 5.6 and also in Part II.

A number of predefined functions are useful in dealing with ordered types and reals. The function min(x1,...) returns the smallest value among its arguments; the function max(x1,...) returns the largest. Both min and max take one or more arguments of the same type. For example, max('4','A','c') returns 'c'. For an ordered type T, the function low(T) returns the smallest value of type T; the function high(T) returns the largest. On a machine that stores integers in 32 bits using two's complement form, for example, low(int) is -2147483648 and high(int) is 2147483647. The values of low(real) and high(real) return, respectively, the smallest and largest representable positive real numbers. Finally, for ordered types (but not reals), the function pred(x) returns x's predecessor in the defined ordering; the function succ(x) returns x's successor. For example, pred(8) is 7 and succ('f') is 'g'.

2.4 User-Defined Types

So far in this chapter, we have considered only the basic types. We now look at four user-defined types: enumerations, records, unions, and pointers. (The others appear in later chapters.) We first see how types, aliases for types, and array types are declared.

User-defined types can be declared in type declarations and subsequently referenced by means of the type identifier. Such types may also be declared anonymously by simply being defined at any point a type is required. For example, a variable can be specified to have a record type either by using the name of a previously defined record type or by defining the record structure in the variable's declaration.

Type Declarations

A type declaration introduces a new identifier that is a synonym for the declared type. Its form is

> `type` *type_id* = *type_definition*

A type definition has several forms. It can define an enumeration, record, union, or pointer type as described in subsequent parts of this section; define a capability type as described in Sections 4.6 and 5.6; specify a string type, e.g., `string[20]`; or name an already declared or basic type optionally preceded by dimension information. This last form of type definition is

> *type_id*   or   *dimensions* *type_id*

Without dimensions, the new name is just an alias for the old name; with dimensions, the new name is an alias for an array of the old type.

The dimensions consists of a list, enclosed in brackets, of one or more ranges separated by commas:

> [*range*, *range*, ...]

There is one range for each array dimension. A range has one of two forms:

> *expr* : *expr*   or   *expr*

In the first form, the expressions specify the lower and upper bounds; these expressions must yield values of the same ordered type. In the second form, the single, integer-valued expression specifies the array's upper bound; its lower bound is implicitly 1. An array has no elements if the value of any upper bound is smaller than that of the corresponding lower bound.

The following are examples of the last two forms of type definitions—i.e., strings and aliases:

```
type age = int
type side = real
type box = [3] side
type name = string[20]
type point = [2] real
type score_array = [0:100] int
type grade_array = ['a':'e'] int
type address = [3] string[40] # name, street, city
type real_matrix = [10,10] real
```

Examples of type declarations for enumeration, record, union, and pointer types appear later in this section.

An array constructor is used to specify the value of an entire array. It contains a list, enclosed in parentheses, of one or more vector elements separated by commas:

   (*vector_element*, *vector_element*, ...)

Each vector element has one of two forms:

   expr   or   [*repetition_expr*] *expr*

The first form specifies a single value. The second form specifies zero or more identical values. All values in a constructor must have the same type.

Some examples of array constructors are

```
(0, 0, 0)   ([3] 0)
(1, 2, 0, 0, 0, 6)   (1, 2, [3] 0, 6)
([3] "")   ("smith", [2] "jones")
```

The two constructors on the first line have identical values, as do the two constructors on the second line. The constructors on the third line are assignable to three-element vectors of strings, such as variables of type `address`. Note that in both of these constructors, the strings are of identical length; this is required since otherwise the types of the values would not be identical. To initialize an array of strings to strings of different lengths, one should assign to individual elements, perhaps within a loop.

The following array constructors are assignable to 10×10 matrices of reals, such as variables of type `real_matrix`:

```
([10] ([10] 0.0))
([5] ([10] 0.0), [5] ([10] 1.0))
```

Each of these uses nested array constructors to build a two-dimensional array with ten rows and ten columns; the nested constructors here specify values of entire rows. The first constructed array contains all zeros. The second contains zeros in its first five rows and ones in its last five rows.

When an array constructor is evaluated, each repetition expression is evaluated once to yield a repetition count. If the count is positive, the following expression is evaluated and its value is replicated count times. If the repetition count is zero, no replication occurs and the following expression is not evaluated. A negative repetition count is an error.

Enumerations

Enumeration types define symbolic literals. Each enumeration type is an ordered type—the ordering among literals is the order in which they are declared. The definition of an enumeration type contains a list of one or more identifiers separated by commas:

```
enum ( id, id, ... )
```

Some examples of enumeration types are

```
enum(red, blue, yellow)
enum(ivy, holly, thyme)
```

These might be used in type declarations such as

```
type primary_color = enum(red, blue, yellow)
type machine_name = enum(ivy, holly, thyme)
```

The predefined functions `max`, `min`, `succ`, `pred`, `low`, and `high` may be used on enumeration types. For example, given the above type declarations, `high(machine_name)` is `thyme` and `succ(low(machine_name))` is `holly`.

Records

A record type defines a collection of data values. Its definition contains a list of one or more field definitions separated by semicolons:

```
rec ( field_definition; field_definition; ... )
```

Each field definition defines one or more field names of the same type:

variable_name, *variable_name*, ... : *type*

For now we will assume that a variable name is just an identifier; its exact form is described later in Section 2.5. The size of each field in a record must be determinable at compile time; i.e., array bounds and string lengths must be compile-time constants.

Some examples of record types are

```
rec( height, width: real )
rec( name: string[10]; grade: int )
```

The first record type has two real fields. The second has two fields of different types. These record types might be used in type declarations such as the following:

```
type dims = rec( height, width: real )
type person = rec( name: string[10]; grade: int )
type info = rec( p: person; m: dims; employed: bool )
```

The last type declaration defines a record type whose first two fields are records and whose last field is a boolean.

A record constructor is used to specify the value of an entire record. It contains an identifier that names a record type and a list of one or more expressions, one for each field in the record type, separated by commas.

id (*expr*, *expr*, ...)

For example, the following record constructors could be used for the above type declarations:

```
dims(3.8, 2.1)        dims(1.4, 20.2)
person("karl", 92)   person("gene", 90)
info(person("smith", 78), dims(7.3, 2.9), false)
```

The last example uses nested constructors for the two fields that are themselves records.

Unions

A union type is a collection of other types, each of which has a tag (name). Its form is similar to that for records:

union (*field_definition*; *field_definition*; ...)

Unlike a record, the value of a union is just one of its named fields; which field is the union's current value can vary as the program executes.

Two examples of union types are

```
union( radius, circumference: real )
union( name: string[10]; id: int )
```

These union types might be used in type declarations such as

```
type circle = union( radius, circumference: real )
type uperson = union( name: string[10]; id: int )
```

The first union type represents two alternate forms for describing a circle. The second union type represents two alternate forms for describing a person. In the second example, however, the types of the two fields are different.

A variable whose type is a union may be assigned to only by assigning to a field in the union. Thus, there are no special constructors for union types. The programmer must keep track of which field is the union's current value as the program executes. Section 2.6 describes how unions are referenced and dereferenced.

Pointers

Pointer types define references to data objects. They have two forms:

```
ptr type   or   ptr any
```

The first form defines a pointer to an object of a specific data type. The second form defines a pointer to an object of any type. Some examples of pointer types are

```
ptr int                ptr any
ptr rec(i1,i2: int)    ptr [7] int
```

The last example defines a pointer to an array containing seven integers. Aliases for these pointer types can be declared in type declarations:

```
type pint = ptr int
type ppint = ptr ptr int
type pp2int = ptr pint      # same as previous
type pr = ptr rec(i1,i2: int)
type pany = ptr any
type p7int = ptr [7] int
```

Mutually recursive record types are allowed, as illustrated by the following type declarations:

```
type r1 = rec(a: char; p2: ptr r2)
type r2 = rec(b: real; p1: ptr r1)
```

The declaration of `r1` uses `r2` before `r2` has been declared, which is an exception to the normal "declare-before-use" rule, as discussed in Section 2.13 (however, see Exercise 2.24).

The generic pointer type, `ptr any`, can reference a value of any type. Such a pointer can be assigned to and copied, but it cannot be dereferenced.

The pointer literal `null` is used to indicate a pointer value that points to no valid object. It can be used for all pointer types. The address-of operator, @, returns the address of a variable, which can then be assigned to a pointer; this operator is described in Section 2.6.

2.5 Variables and Constants

A variable holds a value of some specified type. Its value can change during its lifetime, as controlled by the program. A constant also holds a value. Its value, however, remains the same for its lifetime. A variable may be initialized as part of its declaration; a constant must be.

A variable or constant can be *simple*, in which case it holds one value of its type. Alternatively, a variable or constant can be an *array*, in which case it holds multiple values of its type. Arrays can have any number of dimensions. Individual elements of an array are referenced using subscripts, one for each dimension.

Variable and constant declarations have similar syntactic forms. These forms are a bit complicated so as to accommodate all the possible kinds of variables and constants mentioned above. A variable declaration contains a list of one or more variable definitions separated by commas:

> `var` *variable_definition*, *variable_definition*, ...

Each variable definition specifies either an initialized variable or one or more uninitialized variables.

An initialized variable definition specifies the variable's name, optionally its type, and its initial value:

> *variable_name* : *type* := *expr*

The type part can sometimes be omitted, as described below. An uninitialized variable definition specifies a list of one or more variable names, separated by commas, and their type:

> *variable_name*, *variable_name*, ... : *type*

A variable name has one of two forms:

> *variable_id*   or   *variable_id dimensions*

The first form defines a simple variable. The second form defines an array; the dimensions give a range for each dimension of the array. The form of array dimensions is the same as for type declarations (see Section 2.4).

Some examples of variable declarations are the following:

```
# three uninitialized integers
var i, j, k: int
# two initialized integers
var front: int := 0, rear: int := 0
# a string of 0 to 80 characters; initially empty
var line: string[80] := ""
# an initialized record of type person
var k: person := person("karl", 92)
# an array of 10 integers; indices are 1, 2, ..., 10
var a[10]: int
# an array of 128 ints; indices are 7-bit characters
var char_count[char(0):char(127)]: int
# a two dimensional array of booleans
var boolean_matrix[N,N]: bool
```

Note that the number of elements of `boolean_matrix` references `N`, which must be declared previously and given a value. An array with multiple dimensions should be thought of as a vector of arrays of one less dimension, and so on, with the last array being a vector of elements. For example, `boolean_matrix` is a vector of `N` vectors, each containing `N` boolean elements. A three-dimensional array is a vector of matrices, each of which is in turn a vector of vectors of elements.

The fact that a variable is an array can be specified with the variable's name, as in the above examples, or with the variable's type. The array declarations above can be written equivalently as

```
var a: [10] int
var char_count: [char(0):char(127)] int
var boolean_matrix: [N,N] bool
```

The last array can also be declared as

```
var boolean_matrix[N]: [N] bool
```

A small syntactic variation allows arrays or types with more than one dimension to enclose each dimension in its own pair of brackets. For example, each of the following is equivalent to the earlier declarations of `boolean_matrix`:

```
var boolean_matrix: [N][N] bool
var boolean_matrix[N][N]: bool
```

A constant declaration is just a specific form of a variable declaration. It contains a list of one or more initialized variables separated by commas:

```
const initialized_var_definition, initialized_var_definition, ...
```

Some examples of constant declarations are

```
const N: int := 100, twoN: int := 2*N
const PI: real := 3.141592654
const PASS: char := 'C'
const error_msg: string[17] := "boom: fatal error"
const gears[7]: int:= (12, 13, 14, 15, 17, 19, 21)
```

The declaration of `gears` uses an array constructor, described in Section 2.4, to specify the values of the array.

The declaration of an initialized variable or constant can sometimes be simplified. The compiler infers the type of the variable or constant to be the type of the initialization expression. For example, the declarations of variables `front` and `rear` given earlier can be simplified as follows:

```
var front := 0, rear := 0
```

Also, all of the above constant declarations can be simplified as follows:

```
const N := 100, twoN := 2*N
const PI := 3.141592654
const PASS := 'C'
const error_msg := "boom: fatal error"
const gears := (12, 13, 14, 15, 17, 19, 21)
```

Here, `error_msg`'s size (17) is inferred. Also the number of elements in `gears` (7) is inferred from the type of the array constructor (`[7] int`).

A constant declaration must give a type (1) when the initial value can belong to two or more distinct types or (2) when the desired type differs from the type of the initial value. The former case occurs for pointer, capability, and file types, which share the literals `null` and `noop`. Similarly, a variable or constant that is intended to be a real must be initialized with a real literal, not an integer literal. For example, the following two declarations are *not* equivalent:

```
var radius: real := 32
var radius := 32
```

The first declares a real variable; the integer literal 32 is converted to a real (see Section 2.12). The second declares an integer variable, since its type is inferred from the integer literal. To avoid problems stemming from such type inference, we always initialize all real variables with real literals. For example, we would write the first declaration as

```
var radius: real := 32.0
```

If this declaration were ever shortened by omitting its type, the literal would dictate that its type would still be real.

Care should also be taken in omitting type information in string variable declarations. For example, the following declarations are *not* equivalent:

```
var line: string[80] := ""
var line := ""
```

In the second declaration, the maximum length of line is determined by the size of the initialization expression, i.e., 0. In this case line can hold only the empty string.

Unlike the declaration of an initialized variable or constant, the declaration of an uninitialized variable must always specify the variable's type. In this case a list of identifiers can be declared to have the same type. The initial value of an uninitialized variable is undefined.

Two predefined functions are defined on variable and constant arrays. The function lb returns the value of the lower bound of its argument. The function ub returns the upper bound. For a multi-dimensional array, these functions by default return the bounds of the first dimension. Bounds for the other dimensions can be obtained by specifying the desired dimension as a second argument; that argument must be an integer literal. To illustrate, consider the declaration:

```
var a[10]: int, q['a':'z',-2:4]: real
```

The following are some values of lb and ub for these arrays:

expression	value	expression	value
lb(a)	1	lb(q,1)	'a'
ub(a)	10	lb(q,2)	-2
lb(q)	'a'	ub(q,2)	4
ub(q)	'z'	ub(a,1)	10

Note how the type of the value returned by these functions is the type of the specified bound.

2.6 References and Dereferences

A variable's name is used to refer either to the value of the variable or to the storage location associated with the variable. Which meaning is intended depends on the context in which the reference occurs. When the name of a variable appears as part of an expression, the variable is dereferenced to obtain its value. When the name of a variable appears on the left-hand side of an assignment, the address of the storage associated with variable is used. A reference to a variable that is an array, record, union, or string can contain more than the variable's name to specify just a piece of the entire variable. The above discussion also applies to a constant, except it can appear only as part of an expression, i.e., not on the left-hand side of an assignment. The rest of this section addresses how to reference and dereference pieces of arrays, records, unions, and strings, as well as how to use pointers.

Subscripting and Slicing

Array variables or constants can be subscripted and sliced. The general form is a list of one or more bounds—but no more than the number of dimensions in the array—separated by commas:

> [*bound*, *bound*, ...]

Each bound can specify either a subscript or a slice. A subscript is just an expression, such as

> *expr*

This specifies exactly one element in the associated range of the array. (However, as seen below, that element might be an entire sub-array.) In contrast, a slice can specify multiple, contiguous elements. A slice has one of four forms:

> *expr* : *expr* or *expr* : *   or * : *expr* or *

The values of the two expressions in the first form determine the elements, and therefore the size, of the slice. Each of the next two forms of a slice contains one expression and one *, which is taken to be either the lower or upper bound of the range from which the slice is taken. The final form of a slice uses a single * to specify all elements in the range. (The * can also be used in the declaration of a formal array parameter to indicate that its size depends on the size of the actual parameter; see Section 4.1 for details.)

The simplest case is when all bounds are subscripts, i.e., none are slices. To illustrate, suppose we have two arrays declared as follows:

```
var a[1:10], b[1:5,1:4]: int
```

Then `a[3]` is the third element of `a`, `b[2,3]` is the third element of the second row of `b`, and `b[2]` is the entire second row of `b`.

The opposite case is when all bounds are slices. The dimensionality of the result is the same as that of the original array. For example, the slice `a[i:j]` is a vector containing

```
a[i], a[i+1], ..., a[j]
```

A slice may have zero elements but not a negative number of elements. Thus, `j-i+1` must be at least zero in the above example. The slice `a[*:j]` is the same as `a[1:j]`, and the slice `a[*]` is the same as `a[1:10]`. The slice `b[1:2,4:5]` is a two-dimensional array specifying the "upper-right corner" of `b`. The slice `b[2:4]` is a two-dimensional array with three rows and four columns; its elements are the second, third, and fourth rows of `b`. The slices `b[*]` and `b[*,*]` are each the same as array `b`. Note that subscripting and slicing differ in the dimensionality of their results. For example, `b[2]` is a one-dimensional array whereas `b[2:2]` is a two-dimensional array.

Between the above extreme cases falls the general case, in which some bounds are subscripts and some are slices. The dimensionality of the result is the number of slices, where a bound of `*` is assumed for any unspecified bound. For example, the following specifies the second row of `b`:

```
b[2,*]
```

It is a one-dimensional array of four elements. Similarly, the slice

```
b[*,3]
```

is a one-dimensional array with the five elements in column three of `b`. The slice `b[3,2:4]` is a one-dimensional array with three elements—namely, `b[3,2]`, `b[3,3]`, and `b[3,4]`. As a final example, if `m` is a three-dimensional array, then `m[3,2:4]` is a two-dimensional array.

Multiple subscript and slice specifications can appear consecutively, as in `b[2][3]` and `b[*][3]`. If all such specifications contain only subscripts, then the overall effect is equivalent to a single specification with multiple subscripts; e.g., `b[2][3]` is interchangeable with `b[2,3]`. (Recall that the first form, which places each subscript in its own pair of brackets, is also allowed in array declarations; see Section 2.5.) However, if any of the consecutive specifications contains a slice, the effects are *not* equivalent. For example, b[*,3], as seen above, is the third column of b, whereas b[*][3] is the third row of b (recall that b[*] is the same as b).

As further examples of subscripts and slices, the following expressions are equivalent; each indicates the fourth element of a:

```
a[4]    a[1:*][4]    a[2:*][3]
```

The following six expressions are also equivalent:

```
b[2,2:3]    b[2][2:3]    b[2,*][2:3]    b[2:2][1][2:3]
b[2:2][1:*][1][2:3]    b[1:*][2][2:3]
```

Each indicates the one-dimensional array consisting of the second and third elements in the second row of b.

The use of slices has a few restrictions. Assignments can be made to a single slice of an array, unless it is either sliced again or subscripted after being sliced. A slice cannot appear as an operand of the swap operator (see Section 2.9). An array of strings cannot be assigned to a slice of another array of strings if their maximum lengths differ. Finally, slices cannot be passed as reference parameters (see Chapter 4).

Array subscripts and slices must have the same type as that of the corresponding range in the declaration of the variable. They must also have values within the declared range of values. The subscripts of a slice have the same type, T, as the dimension that is being sliced; the lower bound of a slice is the value in type T that corresponds to 1, i.e., the result of the conversion $T(1)$ (Section 2.12 describes conversion functions). As an example, suppose we are given the following declarations:

```
type foo = enum(f1, f2, f3, f4, f5, f6)
var c[f1:f6]: int
```

Slices of c will have subscripts of type foo and values beginning with f1. For example, c[f3:f5] is a one-dimensional array containing three elements; it has subscripts f1, f2, and f3. Thus c[f3:f5][f2] is the same as c[f4].

Specifying Record and Union Fields

The value of a field in a record variable can be obtained by following the name of the variable by a dot (.) and the name of the desired field. For example, suppose x is declared as

```
var x: rec( name: string[10]; grade: int )
```

The fields of variable x are then referenced as x.name and x.grade.

As with records, the value of a field in a union variable can be obtained by
following the name of the variable by a dot (.) and the name of the field. It is
up to the programmer to keep track of which field of a union represents the
current value of the union. To illustrate, consider the following declaration:

```
var uper: union( name: string[10]; id: int )
```

The value of uper is given by uper.name or uper.id. The programmer can
keep track of which value is current with another variable, as in

```
var uper_which: enum( NAME, ID )
```

When uper is changed, the programmer should also change uper_which;
e.g., if 89765 is assigned to uper.id, then the programmer should assign ID
to uper_which. The value of uper_which will typically be used in if
statements to distinguish between the ways to interpret the value in uper.

Using Pointers

With pointer variables, the value of the object to which the variable points
can be obtained by following the name of the variable by a hat (^). Suppose
we have the following pointer variable declarations:

```
var p: ptr int
var pp: ptr ptr int
var prec: ptr rec(i1,i2: int)
```

Some examples of pointer dereferencing are:

```
p^      # the integer to which p points
pp^     # the integer pointer to which pp points
pp^^    # the integer to which pp^ points
prec^   # the record to which prec points
```

It is illegal to dereference a pointer whose value is null, i.e., a pointer that
does not point to any object. In the above example, then, we have assumed
that p, pp, pp^, and prec are not null.

The unary address-of operator, @, is used to obtain the address of a
variable or constant, which then can be assigned to a pointer variable. For
example, if i is an integer variable, its address is @i, which can be assigned
to p declared above. Pointers to constants are allowed; however, care must be
taken in the use of such a pointer to avoid modifying the constant's value. It
is an error to dereference a pointer if its value is the address of a variable or
constant whose scope has ended. (See Section 2.13 for scope rules.)

Specifying Substrings

A substring of a string variable consists of the characters in zero or more consecutive positions, which are numbered starting with 1. A substring is referenced by following a string variable's name with

> [*expr*]   or   [*expr* : *expr*]

The first form references an individual position; the result is of type character. In the second, more general form, the index of the first expression must be at least 1, and the index of the second expression must be no more than the current length of the string; the result is of type string and its length is the number of characters in the substring. For example, the following reference parts of string variable s:

```
s[3]    s[2:4]    s[i:j-1]
```

A substring is legal only if all the referenced positions fall within the current string. Thus s[3] is legal only if s's current length is at least 3; s[2:4] is legal only if s's current length is at least 4. The current length of a string variable cannot, therefore, be changed by assigning to a piece of the string beyond its current length; the only way to change the current length is by assignment (or input) to the entire string variable.

Specifying More Complex References and Dereferences

The above ways to reference parts of user-defined variables and to dereference pointers can be combined as necessary for more complicated user-defined variables. For example, suppose we have the following declarations:

```
type point = rec(x, y: real)
type primary_color = enum(red, blue, yellow)
type rectangle = rec(upleft, botright: point;
                     color: primary_color;
                     label: string[20] )
var display[1:N]: rectangle
var prect: ptr rectangle
```

Then sample references include the following:

```
display[3].color         # the color of the
                         # third displayed rectangle
display[3].label[1:4]    # the first four characters
                         # of the label of display[3]
```

```
display[3].upleft.x        # the x coordinate of the
                           # upleft point of display[3]
prect^.upleft.x            # the x coordinate of the
                           # upleft point of rectangle
                           # to which prect points
```

Note that in the last reference, prect^ is a record, so its upleft field is referenced using a dot.

2.7 Dynamic Storage Allocation

Two predefined functions provide dynamic storage allocation and deallocation:

new(*type*)   and   free(*expr*)

Function new returns a pointer to a new instance of storage for a variable whose type is specified by the type argument. If sufficient storage is not available to satisfy new's request, the program aborts. Procedure free releases the storage of an object allocated by new pointed to by the expression, which must evaluate to a pointer type. A freed object must not be referenced after it has been freed. The function free has no effect if its argument is null.

Dynamically allocated objects are referenced using pointers in the same ways as other objects are referenced using pointers. For example, suppose we have the following declarations:

type point = rec(x, y: real);   var a: ptr point

Further suppose that a's value has been set to new(point). Then a^ is the entire record to which a points, and a^.x and a^.y are its two fields.

2.8 Expressions

We have already seen in this chapter how expressions can be formed from literals and operators (e.g., 1+2), and from array and record constructors. More generally, operands in expressions can be literals, references to constants and variables, constructed values, and invocations of predefined and user-defined functions. We have also encountered many of the predefined functions in this chapter; we will discuss the others as they are needed. All predefined functions are summarized in Appendix C.

An expression—what we have been calling an *expr*—has one of two general forms:

> *operand_list*   or   (*expr*)

An operand list consists of one or more operands separated by binary operators, as follows:

> *operand binary_operator operand binary_operator* ...

The binary operators are those that we have already seen (e.g., + and <=) and the assignment and swapping operators described in the next section. Operands are the ones we have already seen—literals, references, etc.—or expressions preceded by unary operators, as in:

> *unary_operator expr*

The unary operators are those previously mentioned, such as not and -, and the preincrement and predecrement operators described in the next section. (There are also unary postincrement and postdecrement operators, which follow an expression.)

Expressions compute values. They are evaluated in a way that is consistent with operator precedence and associativity, and with the presence of parentheses. Suppose we have the following declarations:

```
type person = rec( name: string[10]; grade: int )
var k: person := person("karl", 92)
var per: ptr person := @k
var groups := (10, 20, 30, 40)
var x := 4, y:= 5, z := 6
var p: ptr int := @x
```

Then examples of expressions and their values include the following:

expression	*value*
k.name	"karl"
-length(k.name)	-4
k.grade-10	82
"hi" || " there"	"hi there"
perˆ.grade/groups[4]	2
(x+y)*z	54
pˆ * groups[2]	80

2.9 Assignment and Swapping Operators

An assignment operator evaluates an expression and assigns its value to a variable. The form of an assignment is

> *variable* := *expr*

Assignment is defined for all kinds of variables: simple variables, arrays, array slices, entire records, record fields, and so on. The type of the expression and the type of the variable must be compatible (e.g., identical), as described in Section 2.11.

As examples, consider the following declarations:

```
var i := 0, j, k: int, sum := 0
var h := 10.2, w := 4.8, area: real
```

Then the following are legal assignments:

```
sum := sum + i; area := h*w
i := i+1; j := i*89; k := i*89
```

Assignment is an operator. It associates right-to-left and has precedence lower than the other operators. Thus the assignments to j and k above can be written using a multiple assignment:

```
j := k := i*89
```

Evaluation of the assignment first calculates i*89 and then assigns that value to k and to j. The above separate assignments to i, j, and k can also be written as

```
j := k := (i := i+1) * 89
```

The assignment to i must be parenthesized to obtain the desired precedence; otherwise, the value i+89 would assigned to i, j, and k.

Augmented assignment operators can sometimes simplify the writing of expressions. Their form is

> *variable augmented_assignment_operator expr*

The augmented assignment operators are

```
**:=     *:=      /:=      %:=      +:=      -:=
&:=      >>:=     <<:=     |:=      ||:=
```

Their meanings are derived from their base operator. For example, +:= means to add the value of the expression to the variable. Thus the following two lines are equivalent:

```
sum +:= i;  i +:= 1
sum := sum + i;  i := i+1
```

The address of the variable in an augmented assignment is computed just once. Hence execution of the following two assignments (independently) might yield different results if evaluation of f has side effects:

```
a[f(x)]  *:= 10
a[f(x)]  := a[f(x)]  * 10
```

In particular, f is evaluated once in the first assignment but twice in the second.

Another group of convenient assignment operators are the increment and decrement operators. Their forms are

variable ++   *variable* --   ++ *variable*   -- *variable*

These operators are known as postincrement, postdecrement, preincrement, and predecrement, respectively. They may be used with ordered types, reals, and pointers.

An increment or decrement of an ordered type assigns the next or previous value of that type, if there is one; an increment or decrement of a real adds one or subtracts one. The value of the expression depends on whether the increment or decrement operator is a prefix or postfix operator. For postfix operators, the variable is incremented or decremented *after* its value is used. For prefix operators, the variable is incremented or decremented *before* its value is used. As with augmented assignments, the address of the variable is evaluated only once.

Assume i, j, and k are integer variables. The following are equivalent:

```
++i        # preincrement
i++        # postincrement
i +:= 1    # augmented assignment
i := i+1   # conventional assignment
```

Next consider these three lines of assignments:

```
i := i+1;  j := i*89;  k := i*89
j := k := ++i * 89     # equivalent to first
j := k := i++ * 89     # not equivalent
```

The second is just a more concise form of the first. The third, however, is not equivalent since it uses the unincremented value of i. The result of assigning to a given variable more than once in an expression is undefined, as in the following:

```
i := i++   # i's value is undefined after execution
```

An increment or decrement of a pointer causes it to point to the successor or predecessor in memory of its current target. For example, a pointer to an array can be used to step through the array. Variables of type ptr any may not be incremented or decremented because the size of the target is not known. With pointer variables, the increment and decrement operators must be used with care so they always point to an object of the appropriate type.

The swap operator exchanges the values of two variables, which must have the same type. Its form is

> *variable* :=: *variable*

For example, the values of variables j and k can be interchanged by

```
j :=: k
```

The value of the entire expression is the value of its right-hand variable. Consider the following expression:

```
i := j :=: k
```

It interchanges the values of the variables j and k, and then assigns the original value of k to i. Like the augmented assignment operators, the swap operator determines the addresses of its variables just once.

2.10 Basic Input/Output

Values can also be assigned to variables by reading them from input. Values of expressions can be written to output. The simplest forms of input and output use the predefined read and write routines.

The basic form of an invocation of the read function contains a list of one or more variables separated by commas:

```
read( variable, variable, ... )
```

This normally assigns one value from the standard input file to each variable in the given list. Values in the input must be separated by white space.

Reading into a string variable, however, consumes an entire line of input, assuming the string is long enough. Read returns the number of values successfully read; the predefined constant EOF is returned if the end-of-file is reached before any values are found.

The basic form of an invocation of the write routine contains a list of zero or more expressions separated by commas:

```
write( expr, expr, ... )
```

The write routine evaluates each expression and outputs its value to the standard output file. It writes one blank between successive output values and a newline after the last output value. Thus a write with no expressions outputs only a newline.

As a simple example, assume the standard input file contains a sequence of integers separated by white space. Then the following code reads the input and writes every value on a separate line of the standard output file:

```
var value: int
do read(value) != EOF -> write(value) od
```

The loop terminates when the end of the input file is reached.

Another output routine is writes, which is like write except no blank or newline characters are implicitly written. We use this routine for printing a prompt on the same line on which the response is to be typed, as in:

```
writes("enter the number of grades: "); read(num)
```

We also use writes when output from more than one place in a program is to be kept on the same line, e.g., for values output from within a loop.

These descriptions should be sufficient for the reader to understand most of the programs in this book. The complete description of these routines and brief descriptions of other input/output routines appear in Chapter 6; see Appendix C for further details.

2.11 Type Equivalence

SR is a strongly typed language: every object has a type that is (mostly) determinable at compile time, and only objects of equivalent types can be assigned to one another. This section outlines the rules that determine whether two objects are type equivalent.

Type equivalence in SR is based on *structural equivalence*. An object can be assigned to another object provided they have the same structure. Two objects have the same structure if they have the same number of dimensions and the same number of elements in each dimension, and if corresponding pairs of basic elements have the same type. As a simple example, consider the following code:

```
var a, b: int, c: char
a := b
a := c     # illegal
```

The first assignment is legal. However, the second is illegal since its two sides have different types. (The one, important exception to this rule is that integers can be assigned to reals; they are implicitly converted, as described in the next section.)

Two records have the same structure if they have the same number of fields and each corresponding field has the same structure, independent of field names. Consider the following declarations:

```
type r1 = rec( a: int; b: real )
type r2 = r1
type r3 = rec( c: int; d: real )
type r4 = rec( c: real; d: int )
var v1: r1, v2: r2, v3: r3, v4: r4, v5: r1
var v6: rec( e: int; f: real )
var v7: rec( g, h: int; i: real )
```

Types r1, r2, and r3 are equivalent to each other and to the type of variable v6. Thus variables v1, v2, v3, v5, and v6 can be assigned to one another. However, type r4—and hence the type of v4—is not equivalent to any of the other types, nor is the type of variable v7.

Two enumeration types are structurally equivalent if they define the same number of literals. The names of the enumeration types and their literals are irrelevant. Consider the following type declarations:

```
type primary_color = enum(red, blue, yellow)
type machine_name = enum(ivy, holly, thyme)
type books = enum(dictionary, thesaurus)
```

The first two types are equivalent to one another, but not to the third. This means, for example, that the comparisons blue = holly and red = thyme are permitted (and evaluate to true and false, respectively). However, the comparison blue = thesaurus is not permitted.

Signatures provide the basis for checking whether two objects have the same structure. Every expression and variable (including formal parameters) has a signature. The signature of an object represents its basic type, its dimensionality, and the number of elements it contains.

The signature of an expression is built from the signatures of each operand according to the effects of different operators. For example, a comparison of two integer expressions (more precisely, expressions with integer signatures) has a boolean signature. Type conversion functions, described in the next section, are used to convert a value with one signature into a value with another signature.

The signature of a composite object contains a list of the signatures of its components. In forming record and union signatures, field names are ignored; only the type structure is encoded. Instances of * in array slices are replaced by the appropriate upper or lower bound, as discussed in Section 2.6; then the total number of elements is calculated.

To illustrate signatures, consider the declarations:

```
var a, b[1:10], c['a':'j'], g[1:5,1:2]: int
var d: string[10]; const f := 2.71828
type r1 = rec( a: int; b: real )
var v1: r1, v2: rec( c: int; d: real )
var p: ptr int, q: ptr r1
```

Using these declarations, the following table shows some variables and expressions that have identical signatures:

Signature	*Expressions*
int	a b[2] 23 a+b[2] v2.c p^ q^.a
real	f v1.b 7.81 q^.b
char	'x' lb(c) d[4]
string[10]	d "distribute" d[6:10]||d[1:5]
[10] int	b c c[*] (1, [9] 0)
[4] int	b[3:6] c['b':'e']
[5,2] int	g ([5] (0, 1))
[2,2] int	g[2:3] (g[2], g[3])
ptr int	p @b[2] @q^.a
rec(int; real)	v1 v2 r1(3,.8) q^

Arrays b and c have the same signature since they have the same number of elements of the same type, even though the types of their dimensions differ.

An expression can be assigned to a target variable provided they have compatible signatures. Scalars can be assigned to scalars of the same type, and arrays can be assigned to arrays of the same dimensionality, size for each dimension, and element type.

In addition, a string expression can be assigned to a string variable if the variable's maximum length is sufficient. Moreover, an array of string expressions can be assigned to an array of strings, again providing that the maximum length of the elements of the array is sufficient for each string expression.

Suppose we have the declarations given earlier in this section. Then the following assignments are signature compatible:

```
a := 23; a := b[2]; c['b'] := a+b[2]
b := c; b := (1, [9] 0); b[2:*] := ([9] 0)
g := ([5] (0, 1)); b[2:3] := g[2]
p := @b[2]; a := p^; v1 := r1(3,.8)
d := "abcdefgh"; d := d[*:6]; d := d[3:4]
d := string('a'); d := string(([10] 'a'))
```

However, the following assignments are *not* signature compatible:

```
# **** illegal assignments ****
a := 'a'; c['b':'e'] := a+b[2]
a := b[2:2]; a := b[2:3]; g[2] := g[3:3]
g := c; g := ([10] 0); b[2:3] := g[2:2]
v1 := f; b := ([9] 0); p := b[2]; v1 := 3
d := 'a'; d := ([10] 'a')
d := "abcdefghijklmnop"; d := ([10] "a")
```

The last assignment is illegal because the constructor produces an array of 10 strings, each of length one, and an array cannot be assigned to a simple string variable.

The signature compatibility of some assignments can be determined only when the program executes. For example, consider

```
b[2:a] := c['b':'e']
```

Whether it is legal depends on the value of a. If a is 5, then the two slices have the same size, so the assignment is legal. Note that the type part of a signature can always be determined when the program is compiled, but the size part sometimes needs to be checked when the program executes.

Additional rules for calculating signatures and determining whether they are compatible apply for formal parameters to operations, for capabilities, and for resources. These rules are similar to those described above and are discussed in Chapters 4 and 5.

2.12 Type Conversions

A value with one signature can sometimes be converted into a value with another signature. Such type conversion occurs in one of two ways: *implicitly* or *explicitly.* The only implicit type conversion in SR is the conversion of integers to reals. All other type conversions must be performed explicitly by means of type conversion functions.

Implicit Conversion: Integer to Real

The conversion of integers to reals occurs implicitly within expressions. For example, the following code is legal:

```
var r: real, i: int
r := 3; r := i * 2.34; r := i / 3
```

In the first assignment, the integer value 3 is converted to a real when it is assigned to r. In the second, i's value is converted to its real equivalent before the multiplication occurs. In the third, the *integer* result of the division is converted to a real when it is assigned to r. Note that the effect of this assignment is generally different from the following:

```
r := i / 3.0
```

Here i is converted to a real before the division, thus the value assigned to r will include any fractional part of the real result.

Care should be taken when using the predefined functions, because some allow either integer or real arguments, but others allow only real arguments, in which case the integer argument is converted to a real. The abs predefined function is an example of the former. It returns a real or integer value depending on the types of its arguments. An example of the latter kind of predefined function is sqrt. It returns the (real-valued) square root of its real argument.

The implicit conversion of integers to reals applies only to simple values, not to arrays or records. For example, consider the following declarations:

```
var a[10]: real, b[10]: int
var c: rec(x,y: real), d: rec(x,y: int)
var e: rec(x,y: real), f: rec(x: real; y: int)
```

Then each of the following assignments is *illegal*:

```
a := b;   c := d;   e := f
```

Although integers are implicitly converted to reals, reals are *not* implicitly converted to integers. Thus the following assignment is *illegal*:

```
i := r / 3.0
```

The desired conversion must be accomplished using one of the conversion functions defined below.

Explicit Conversion Functions

Predefined functions provide the means to convert value from one type to another. The functions operate on the five basic types—boolean, integer, real, character, and string—and three user-defined types—enumeration, pointer, and arrays of characters. Except in a few cases, any value of one of these types can be converted into a value of another of these types. The exceptions result in errors. The conversion functions reflect what the programmer tends to expect. They can therefore save the programmer from writing code, for example, to convert strings to integers. Some conversions, while allowed, make little sense, e.g., boolean to pointer. However, they are provided for reasons of consistency. Here we just present an overview of the conversion functions, leaving the details to Appendix C.

A predefined function is defined for and named after each basic type. The type of the return value of each function is the same as its name; the actual return value depends on the type and value of its argument. For example, `int(x)` returns an integer value that depends on `x`'s type and value. This function is partially defined as follows: If `x` is a real, its integer part is returned. For example, `int(-12.87)` is `-12`. If `x` is a string or an array of characters, then `x` must have the form of an integer literal, possibly preceded by a + or -; leading or trailing white space is ignored. Thus `int(" -34 ")` is `-34`. The definitions of the remaining predefined functions of this kind (`bool`, `char`, `real`, and `string`) are similar in spirit.

In addition to the predefined functions listed above, a predefined function is defined for and named after each user-defined alias of a record, pointer, or enumeration type or of any other convertible type. The return value of each function is the same as its name. For example, if type `primary_color` is defined to be `enum(red,blue,yellow)`, then `primary_color(1)` is `blue`. Similarly, if type `age` is defined to be `int`, then `age(" -34 ")` is `-34`.

2.13 Blocks, Scope Rules, and Naming

A block contains declarations and statements. Blocks in SR include globals, resources, and procs, as well as the syntactic construct *block*. The first three kinds of blocks will be described in Chapters 4 and 5. The final kind is used, for example, as the body of if and do statements. It consists of zero or more components separated by semicolons (or newlines):

> *block_component; block_component; ...*

Each block component is either a declaration or a statement. Note that a block may be empty; this is sometimes useful when developing a program.

All objects are visible from the point of their declaration to the end of the block in which they are declared. Declarations may therefore contain expressions that reference previously declared objects. Thus, as a block is executed, declarations are at least conceptually evaluated as they are encountered. Consider, for example, the declarations

```
const N := 10, TwoN := 2*N
```

Here the initialization of TwoN uses the value of N. Also, the values of constants and the sizes of arrays can vary between executions of a block. Consider, for example,

```
# outer block
var n: int
if ... ->
   # inner block
   const Z := n+1; var a[1:n]: int
```

Each time the inner block is entered, the expression n+1 is evaluated and assigned to Z; then the number of elements in a is set to n's current value, and appropriate space for a is allocated.

Declarations and statements within blocks may be intermixed. This permits, for example, code such as:

```
var n: int
writes("enter the number of numbers: "); read(n)
var a[1:n]: int
```

Here the number of elements in array a is the value read for variable n.

Objects declared in outer blocks are visible in a nested block until an object with the same identifier is declared in the nested block (if one is). It is valid in a nested block to reference an object declared in an outer block, and then to declare a new object of the same name, as in:

```
# outer block
const N := 8
if ... ->
   # inner block
   const X := N*8
      ... # outer N is used up through here
   var N := 10   # this N used in rest of inner block
   N := N*3
```

Here N is declared in both the outer and inner blocks. The inner block references N to initialize X and then declares its own N. In general, however, we consider such use to be bad programming practice because the meaning of such an object—N in this case—depends on where in the block it is used.

Most blocks appear implicitly, e.g., as bodies of procs or if statements. Blocks can also be declared explicitly using a begin statement, which has the following form:

```
begin block end
```

Begin statements are used to limit the scope of temporary variables. For example, consider the following:

```
var a, b: int
  ... # a and b visible here
begin
  var c[1:1000]: real
    ... # a, b, and c visible here
end
  ... # a and b visible here
begin
  var c, d[1:2048]: char
    ... # a, b, c, and d visible here
end
  ... # a and b visible here
```

As noted, the scope of a variable declared in an inner block ends at the end of that block. Begin statements can reduce "name-space pollution" by limiting the scope of objects to where they are needed. They can also reduce the storage required by a program. In the above example, an implementation can use the same storage space for the variables in the two inner blocks since their scopes are disjoint.

Identifiers declared in the same block must generally be unique. However, field names in records are required to be unique only with respect to others in the same record definition. Similarly, parameter (and result) identifiers in resource and operation declarations are required to be unique only with respect to each other (see Chapters 4 and 5).

Enumeration literals, unlike identifiers, cannot be redeclared in nested blocks; each such literal must belong to exactly one enumeration type. Furthermore, enumeration literals cannot be hidden by declaring other objects of the same name. Thus the following variable declaration is illegal:

```
type primary_color = enum(red, blue, yellow)
var blue: int    # **** illegal declaration ****
```

Exercises

2.1 Explain why evaluation of `xor` cannot be short-circuit.

2.2 Is `-3` a literal or an expression? Explain.

2.3 Is `4` an integer literal, a real literal, or both? Explain. Also explain why `x+4` is a real expression if `x` is a real variable.

2.4 Give the values of the following expressions:

```
length("01\23456")
length("ab\2cdef")
```

2.5 Is it possible to write a string literal whose first two characters are `"01"`, whose third character is `"\2"`, and whose remaining characters are `"3456"`? Explain.

2.6 Is the expression `x+++y` legal? If so, what is its meaning?

2.7 Is the expression `x+++++y` legal? If so, what is its meaning?

2.8 Complete the following table for all the different machine architectures to which you have access:

a	b	a%b	a mod b
1	3		
-1	3		
-2	3		
1	-3		
2	-3		

2.9 Is the expression `a < b < c` legal? Explain.

2.10 Most real numbers cannot be represented exactly in the binary encodings used on digital computers. This can sometimes lead to unexpected results. Furthermore, when a real is output by `write`, the printed value is not exactly the one that was stored within the machine. Try running the following program on your machine:

```
resource e()
   var a := 1.0
   a := a + .1; a := a + .1
   write(a, 1.2, a = 1.2)
end
```

Explain the output from the program.

2.11 For each of the following variable declarations, give an equivalent declaration that uses an inferred type, or explain why that is not possible.

```
var s: string[10] := "abcdef"
var r: real := 10
var c: char := 'a'
```

2.12   Give two examples of values for s and t such that s is less than t but int(s) is greater than int(t).

2.13   Consider the following code:

```
var t: rec(t1, t2: int)
t.t1 := 1; t.t2 := 2
```

It declares the variable t to be of type "anonymous" record, and then assigns values to t's fields.

(a) Is it possible to initialize a variable, as part of its declaration, whose type is an "anonymous" record? If so, show how to simplify the above code. If not, explain why not.

(b) Is it possible to build an "anonymous" record constructor? If so, show how to simplify the above code. If not, explain why not.

2.14   Several predefined functions have return values that depend on the type of their arguments. List the predefined functions described in this chapter that have that property, and list those that do not.

2.15   Explain why the following code is incorrect:

```
var x[10]: int := ([2] ([5] 1))
```

2.16   Suppose that m is declared as

```
var m[4,5,6]: int
```

(a) Specify m[1,2,3] in three other ways.

(b) Give the signature for each of the following:

```
m[1,2,3]    m[1]    m[1,2]    m[1:1]
m[1,2:2]    m[1,*,3]
```

2.17   Consider the following code fragment:

```
var y[11:15,1:4]: int
x := y[12:14][3:3][1]
```

What signature must x have? Suppose the declaration of y is changed to the following:

```
var y['f':'j',1:4]: int
```

Rewrite the assignment to account for the new declaration. What signature must x now have?

2.18   Show how to declare a record type that can be used in building a binary tree. Assume each node has a single integer field and pointers to its left and right children, if present. Also show how to declare a root pointer, and give code to build a tree containing a few nodes.

2.19 Consider the following declarations:

```
type primary_color = enum(red, blue, yellow)
type machine_name = enum(ivy, holly, thyme)
type books = enum(dictionary, thesaurus)
```

Determine which of the following expressions are legal, and give the values of the legal expressions:

```
dictionary = ivy          thyme = blue
machine_name(ivy)         machine_name(thesaurus)
int(dictionary) = ivy     int(dictionary) = int(ivy)
int(thyme) = int(blue)    int(thyme = blue)
```

2.20 Consider the following expression:

```
a := (b := 2) + (c := 3)
```

Is the expression still legal if the parentheses are removed? If so, does it have the same value? If not, explain why not.

2.21 Is the following a legal program?

```
resource main()
  var a, b: int
  (a := 2) + (b := 3)
  write(a, b)
end
```

Explain. If it is legal, give its output.

2.22 Explain why the following is illegal:

```
a :=: b :=: c
```

2.23 Consider the following program fragment from Section 2.13:

```
var a, b: int; ...
begin
  var c[1:1000]: real; ...
end
   ...
begin
  var c, d[1:2048]: char; ...
end
```

Suppose an integer variable requires four bytes of storage, a real variable requires eight bytes of storage, and a character variable requires one byte. Assume that arrays require only space to store their elements (i.e., there is no additional overhead). Finally, assume that variables can start at any address regardless of their type (i.e., there are no alignment constraints).

What is the minimal amount of storage required by the above program fragment? Explain.

2.24   Consider the declarations of mutually recursive record types from Section 2.4:

```
type r1 = rec(a: char; p2: ptr r2)
type r2 = rec(b: real; p1: ptr r1)
```

What happens if r2 is a type declared in an outer block and is visible in the current block?

## CHAPTER 3

Sequential Control

In this chapter we introduce the SR statements that can alter the flow of control in sequential programs. We begin by examining the two simplest control statements, skip and stop. We then examine the alternative (if) statement. Finally, we describe the repetitive (do and for-all) statements and the related exit and next statements. Two additional sequential control statements, one for invoking a procedure and one for returning control from a procedure, are described in Chapter 4. Statements that alter the flow of control in concurrent programs are described in Part II.

3.1 Skip Statement

The skip statement has no effect and terminates immediately. Its form is simply

```
skip
```

It is SR's "empty" statement and is typically used in guarded commands (see Section 3.3) to indicate that there is no action to take when the associated guard is true.

Since a block may be entirely empty, `skip` is not actually necessary. However, we provide it to accommodate those programmers who prefer using an explicit statement to indicate that there is nothing to do.

3.2 Stop Statement

The stop statement terminates execution of an entire program (after flushing any buffered output). It has one of two forms:

> ```
> stop   or   stop(expr)
> ```

If *expr* is present, its integer value is returned as the exit status to the command that started program execution; the default exit status is zero. The UNIX convention is that a zero exit status indicates successful completion and a nonzero status, typically 1, indicates failure. (If the exit status is nonzero, final code in the main resource is not executed; see Chapter 5 for details.)

3.3 If Statement

The if statement is SR's only alternative statement. It combines aspects of the if and case statements found in other languages. An if statement contains a list of one or more guarded commands separated by boxes:

> ```
> if guarded_command [] guarded_command [] ... fi
> ```

Each guarded command consists of a boolean expression—the "guard"—and a block containing declarations and statements:

> *expr* -> *block*

The guarded command list can optionally be followed by an else command, which has the form

> ```
> [] else -> block
> ```

An if statement is executed by evaluating each guard at most once, until one evaluates to true or all evaluate to false; the order in which the guards are evaluated is non-deterministic. If some guard evaluates to true, the corresponding block is executed; when that block terminates, the if statement terminates. If no guard evaluates to true and the else command is present, its block is executed; otherwise the if statement terminates immediately without executing any block.

We view `else` as an abbreviation for the negation of the disjunction of the guards (however, the guards are not reevaluated). Note that an if statement ending with "`[] else -> skip`" is equivalent to the same statement without the else command since `skip` is essentially an empty block.

As a simple example, the following if statement sets x to its absolute value:

```
if x < 0 -> x := -x    fi
```

It is equivalent to

```
x := abs(x)
```

which employs the abs predefined function. As another simple example, the following sets minimum to the smaller of the two values x and y:

```
if x <= y -> minimum := x
[] y <= x -> minimum := y
fi
```

Here, if x and y have the same value, either of the assignment statements is executed. Which assignment statement is executed is not known, and in this case it does not matter (as the programmer should ensure in similar cases).

The previous example can also be written using an else command:

```
if x <= y -> minimum := x
[] else -> minimum := y
fi
```

The net effect is the same as above, but this statement is slightly different when x and y have the same value. In particular, minimum is assigned x because all the guards are evaluated to determine if one is true *before* the else clause is considered. Of course, computing the minimum could be written more concisely using the min predefined function:

```
minimum := min(x,y)
```

Consider a solution to the problem of converting a lowercase ASCII character to its uppercase equivalent:

```
# if ch is a lower case ASCII letter,
# convert it to upper case
if ch >= 'a' and ch <= 'z' ->
    ch := char(int(ch)-32)
fi
```

The if statement above determines if the given character, ch, is a lowercase character. If so, the assignment statement converts ch to its uppercase equivalent. The conversion uses the fact that the integer value of a lowercase ASCII character is 32 greater than that of the corresponding uppercase ASCII character; for example, the integer equivalents of 'a' and 'A' are 97 and 65, respectively. Since SR does not allow arithmetic on characters, the above expression first uses the int predefined function to convert the character to its equivalent integer value, then subtracts 32 to change the case, and finally uses the char predefined function to convert the result back to a character.

SR's if statement is based on one proposed by Dijkstra [1976]. It differs, however, in two ways. First, if no guard evaluates to true in Dijkstra's if statement, the entire program aborts. In SR the program continues execution with the statement following the if statement. Second, SR's if statement provides an else command. We find that these differences make SR's if statement easier to use than Dijkstra's.

As noted above, guards are evaluated in a non-deterministic order. Thus the programmer should not assume that guards are evaluated in some particular order. For example, assume a is an array declared as a[1:10], and consider the following:

```
if i < 1 or i > 10 -> write("i is out of range")
[] a[i] = x -> write("found")
fi
```

Execution of this if statement might begin by evaluating the second guard, a[i] = x. This will cause the program to abort if i is out of range.

The above if statement can be corrected in two ways. The first way is to include the negation of the first guard as a predicate in the second guard:

```
if i < 1 or i > 10 -> write("i is out of range")
[] not (i < 1 or i > 10) and a[i] = x ->
      write("found")
fi
```

Since evaluation of and is short-circuit, a[i] is evaluated only if i is in range. The second way to correct the erroneous program is to use nested if statements as follows:

```
if i < 1 or i > 10 -> write("i is out of range")
[] else -> if a[i] = x -> write("found")   fi
fi
```

Again a[i] is evaluated only if i is in range.

It should be clear that SR's if statement is different from the if statements found in languages such as Pascal, C, or Modula-2. In Modula-2, for instance, the previous example can be written as follows:

```
(**** this code is written in Modula-2, not SR ****)
IF (i < 1) or (i > 10) THEN
    WriteString("i is out of range"); WriteLn
ELSIF a[i] = x THEN
    WriteString("found"); WriteLn
END
```

In Modula-2 the second guard is evaluated only if the first guard evaluates to false.

One final point about SR's if statement regards side effects in the evaluation of guards. When an if statement has just one guarded command, and possibly an else command, the single guard is guaranteed to be evaluated; hence the side effect will occur (unless evaluation is short-circuited). We find such if statements useful when checking input for errors. For example, the following checks that a file name was specified on the command line:

```
if getarg(1, fname) = EOF ->
    write(stderr, "usage: a.out filename"); stop (1)
fi
```

If it was, the file name is assigned to `fname` by `getarg`; if not, the program stops executing and returns an exit status of 1. Similarly, the following if statement ensures that data was given to the program:

```
if read(j) = EOF ->
    write(stderr, "Error: need input data"); stop (1)
fi
```

If so, the data is assigned to `j` by `read`; if not, again the program stops.

Now consider the case where an if statement has more than one guarded command, and one or more of the guards can have a side effect. When such a statement is executed, the programmer cannot know which of the guards have actually been evaluated and consequently which, if any, of the side effects have occurred. To illustrate this point, suppose two procedures `f` and `g` return boolean values and both have the side effect of modifying their arguments. Then evaluation of the following will alter x or y or both:

```
if f(x) -> ...
[] g(y) -> ...
fi
```

Because of this non-determinism, we strongly discourage the use of side effects in guards of if statements that have more than one guarded command.

3.4 Do Statement

The do statement is used for indefinite iteration. Like the if statement, it contains a list of one or more guarded commands separated by boxes:

> do *guarded_command* [] *guarded_command* [] ... od

The guarded command list can optionally be followed by an else command.

The meaning of the do statement is also similar to that of the if statement. On each iteration, the guards are evaluated until one evaluates to true or all evaluate to false; the order in which the guards are evaluated is non-deterministic. If some guard is true, the block in the corresponding command is executed, and then execution of the do statement is repeated. A do statement terminates when all its guards are false or a stop, exit, or return statement is executed. (The exit statement is described in Section 3.6; the return statement is described in Chapter 4.)

As in the if statement, the optional else command is selected if none of the guards is true. Thus a do statement containing an else command will terminate only if a stop, exit, or return statement is executed within the loop—or if a stop statement is executed in a procedure called from within the body of the do statement.

As an example, the following do statement skips over blanks in string `str`:

```
pos := 1
do pos <= length(str) & str[pos] = ' ' -> pos++ od
```

It sets `pos` to the position of the leftmost nonblank character or to `length(str)+1` if the string is all blank.

As another example, consider the problem of computing the greatest common divisor (GCD) of positive integers `x` and `y`. Our solution to this problem employs two facts about GCD. First, for positive integers a and b, $GCD(a, a)$ is a. Second, if a is greater than b, then $GCD(a, b)$ is the same as $GCD(a - b, b)$. We use the second fact to reduce the given values until they are equal, at which point the first fact says both values are the desired GCD.

```
X := x;   Y := y
do X < Y -> Y := Y-X
[] Y < X -> X := X-Y
od
gcd := X
```

This do statement employs two guarded commands; the first reduces Y, the second reduces X. Assuming x and y are positive, the do statement terminates when X and Y are equal, at which point both have the desired value.

The above two-arm do statement could be replaced by a single-arm do statement and an if statement:

```
do X != Y ->
   if X < Y -> Y := Y-X
   [] Y < X -> X := X-Y
   fi
od
```

This loop is essentially what one would program in a language like Pascal or C. The multi-arm solution is more concise, however, which is why we prefer it. The above example also shows how to translate a multi-arm do statement into a single-arm one, at least in this case. (Exercise 3.2 explores the general case.)

3.5 For-All Statement

The for-all statement is used for definite iteration. It is a very convenient abbreviation for a commonly occurring form of the do statement (see Exercise 3.5). The for-all statement contains a list of one or more quantifiers separated by commas and a block of declarations and statements:

> fa *quantifier, quantifier, ... -> block* af

Each quantifier introduces a new bound variable and gives an initial value for that variable, an iteration direction, a final value, an optional step size, and an optional part called a such-that clause. We first describe the basic form and then describe the optional parts.

To specify that a bound variable is to take on all values in a range, in increasing order, a quantifier is written as

> *variable* := *initial_expr* to *final_expr*

Decreasing values for the bound variable are specified by

> *variable* := *initial_expr* downto *final_expr*

Each bound variable is an implicitly declared new variable. Its type is that of the initial expression; the type of the final expression must be compatible. The scope of a bound variable is the enclosing for-all statement. A bound variable can be used within the for-all statement from the point of its definition (the end of the initial expression) to the end of the statement. For example, a bound variable in one quantifier can be used in an expression in a subsequent quantifier in the same for-all statement.

In general, the block within a for-all statement is executed for each combination of values of the bound variables, and then the for-all statement terminates. (Like a do statement, a for-all statement terminates earlier if a stop, exit, or return statement is executed.) In for-all statements with multiple quantifiers, the rightmost bound variable varies the most rapidly, then the next to rightmost, and so on. Initial and final expressions are evaluated as needed (exact details are discussed at the end of this section).

Three simple examples of the basic for-all statement should make its meaning clearer. The following outputs the numbers 1 though 10 in order:

```
fa i := 1 to 10 -> write(i) af
```

The type of i is determined to be int. Similarly, the following for-all statement outputs the letters A through Z in order:

```
fa i := 'A' to 'Z' -> write(i) af
```

Here, though, the type of i is determined to be char. Finally, consider the following statement:

```
fa i := 1 to 3, j := i-1 downto 0 -> write(i,j) af
```

In this case the value of j, the second bound variable, depends on i, and j iterates in decreasing order. Thus the statement outputs the following:

```
1 0
2 1
2 0
3 2
3 1
3 0
```

In each of the above examples, the bound variable iterates across all values in the specified range. This corresponds to a default step size of one value on each iteration. To specify a different step size, one can append a by clause to a quantifier:

```
by step_expr
```

If the type of the bound variable is other than real, then *step_expr* must be an integer-valued expression that specifies how many values to skip on each iteration. For example, the first for-all statement below prints the odd numbers between 1 and 20, and the second prints every third letter between A and Z (Y is the last letter printed):

```
fa i := 1 to 20 by 2 -> write(i) af
fa c := 'A' to 'Z' by 3 -> write(c) af
```

If the direction in a quantifier is `to`, then the step size should be positive; if the direction is `downto`, then the step size should be negative. For example, if the step size were –2 in the first for-all statement above, the loop would not terminate since the value of `i` never becomes larger than 20.

A by clause can also be used with a bound variable whose type is real. In this case, *step_expr* must produce a real or an integer, which will be cast to a real. However, because most real numbers cannot be represented exactly on binary machines, one should take great care when using real-valued step sizes. For example, on the Sun SPARC architecture, the last value printed by the following loop is 1.90000:

```
fa r := 1.0 to 2.0 by 0.1 -> write(r) af
```

This occurs because the double-precision floating-point representation of 0.1 is slightly larger than the true value. In contrast, the last value printed by the following loop is in fact 2.00000:

```
fa r := 1.0 to 2.0 by 0.2 -> write(r) af
```

This occurs because the double-precision floating-point representation of 0.2 is slightly smaller than the true value. To guard against potential problems, the value of the final expression should be slightly larger than the true value (or smaller with `downto`) Alternatively, one could determine how many iterations are desired, use an integer bound variable, and multiply the bound variable by a real scale factor in the body of the loop to compute the corresponding real value.

The other optional component of a quantifier is a such-that clause, which appears at the end (after the by clause, if that is present). A such-that clause has the following form:

```
st expr
```

Here, *expr* is a boolean expression. When a quantifier contains a such-that clause, the bound variable takes on only those values for which *expr* evaluates to true. All values in the specified range of the bound variable are enumerated, but a value is not used if *expr* evaluates to false.

Many problems can be elegantly solved using such-that clauses. For example, the following code fragment sets cnt to the number of zeros in the array v:

```
# count the number of zeros in array v
cnt := 0
fa i := lb(v) to ub(v) st v[i] = 0 -> cnt++ af
```

The such-that clause ensures that cnt is incremented only if $v[i] = 0$. The above code fragment has the same effect as

```
# count the number of zeros in array v
cnt := 0
fa i := lb(v) to ub(v) ->
   if v[i] = 0 -> cnt++ fi
af
```

We prefer the former because of its conciseness.

Sorting an array can also be specified concisely using a for-all statement. For example, the following sorts array a into non-decreasing order:

```
# sort array a
fa i := lb(a) to pred(ub(a)),
    j := succ(i) to ub(a) st a[i] > a[j] ->
        a[i] :=: a[j]
af
```

The body of the loop uses the swap statement to swap the values of a[i] and a[j]. The such-that clause ensures that the body is executed only if a[i] and a[j] are out of order. In the example, we have used the predefined functions pred and succ to make the code a bit more general than it would be if we had used the expressions ub(a)-1 and i+1. In particular, the above code works if the type of a's subscript is any ordered type, such as char, for which subtraction and addition are not defined.

The problem of transposing a matrix illustrates another interesting use of a for-all statement. A concise solution is

```
# transpose matrix m[1:N,1:N]
fa i := 1 to N, j := i+1 to N -> m[i,j] :=: m[j,i] af
```

Again, the range of j depends on i, and the swap statement is used to interchange elements.

For-all statements can, of course, be nested. The previous example can be written (less concisely) as follows:

```
# transpose matrix m[1:N,1:N]
fa i := 1 to N ->
    fa j := i+1 to N -> m[i,j] :=: m[j,i] af
af
```

As another example of nested for-all statements, consider a solution to the problem of multiplying two matrices:

```
# set c[1:L,1:N] to a[1:L,1:M] * b[1:M,1:N]
fa row := 1 to L, col := 1 to N ->
    var sum := 0
    fa k := 1 to M -> sum +:= a[row,k] * b[k,col] af
    c[row,col] := sum
af
```

Here the body of the outer `fa` contains statements that need to be executed before and after the inner `fa`. (Exercise 3.7 explores how the above fragment can be rewritten without using nested `fa`'s.)

As described earlier, the expressions specifying the bounds in a quantifier are evaluated as needed. In particular, the initial expression is evaluated just once; the final expression is evaluated once to determine if the loop should be executed initially and again after each iteration of the loop. Expressions in a quantifier are permitted to have side effects; also, bound variables and the value of the final expression are permitted to be modified in the body of a for-all statement (see Exercises 3.9 and 3.10). However, we consider these to be bad programming practices.

3.6 Exit and Next Statements

The exit statement is used to force early termination of the smallest enclosing iterative statement. Its form is

```
exit
```

The next statement is used to force return to the loop control of the smallest enclosing iterative statement. Its form is

```
next
```

Within a do statement, execution of `next` causes the do statement's guards to be reevaluated. Within a for-all statement, execution of `next` causes the next combination of bound variable values to be assigned; if no values remain, the for-all statement terminates.

Exit and next statements may appear only within loop bodies (or within the concurrent invocation statement described in Chapter 7). Because exit and next statements transfer control, they typically appear as the last statement in the body of a for-all statement that has a such-that clause or as the last statement within an if statement nested within a loop. In the latter case, the if statement is also forced to terminate when the exit or next statement is executed.

Consider again the example in Section 3.4 that uses a do statement to skip over blanks in a string. An equivalent program fragment using a for-all statement and an exit statement is

```
pos := length(str)+1
fa i := 1 to length(str) st str[i] != ' ' ->
    pos := i; exit
af
```

The initialization of pos ensures that it is set correctly if str is all blank.

Another typical use for an exit statement arises in handling input. For example, this code fragment uses exit to break out of the loop:

```
do true ->
    writes("enter a number > 0 (or = 0 when done): ")
    read(x)
    if x = 0 -> exit
    [] x < 0 -> write("number must be >= 0")
    [] x > 0 ->
        var fact := 1
        fa i := 2 to x -> fact *:= i af
        write(x, "factorial is", fact)
    fi
od
```

This example can also be written using both exit and next statements:

```
do true ->
    writes("enter a number > 0 (or = 0 when done): ")
    read(x)
    if x = 0 -> exit
    [] x < 0 -> write("number must be >= 0"); next
    fi
    var fact := 1
    fa i := 1 to x -> fact *:= i af
    write(x, "factorial is", fact)
od
```

In this case, the body of the third arm of the previous if statement has been moved outside the if statement, and the next statement is used to skip over that code when x is negative.

Finally, consider the problem of searching a two dimensional array for the first position of a zero element. We assume the array has such an element and that searching is to proceed first across row 1, then row 2, and so on. This problem can be solved as follows:

```
# find first position of a zero in a[1:N,1:N]
fa row := 1 to N, col := 1 to N st a[row,col] = 0 ->
    rowpos := row; colpos := col
    exit
af
write(rowpos,colpos)
```

Again, the such-that clause leads to a compact solution since it avoids the need for an if statement in the body of the for-all statement.

The previous example brings up two potential programming pitfalls. As shown above, values of bound variables that are needed outside a for-all statement must be saved in other variables. This is necessary because the scope of a bound variable ends at the end of the for-all statement in which it is declared. One potentially nasty program bug can arise in conjunction with this scope rule. In particular, a programmer who forgets that the bound variables are new variables might try to solve the above problem as follows:

```
# **** incorrect code ****
var row, col: int
 . . .
# find first position of a zero in a[1:N,1:N]
fa row := 1 to N, col := 1 to N st a[row,col] = 0 ->
    exit
af
write(row,col)
```

This is a legal program fragment because row and col are declared in the outer scope. However, it will most likely not output the correct results. To prevent such problems, we recommend naming bound variables differently from other variables in the current scope.

The second pitfall can arise if a for-all statement with two quantifiers is rewritten as a nested for-all statement. For example, consider rewriting the correct code as follows:

```
# **** incorrect code ****
# find first position of a zero in a[1:N,1:N]
fa row := 1 to N ->
    fa col := 1 to N st a[row,col] = 0 ->
        rowpos := row; colpos := col
        exit
    af
af
write(rowpos,colpos)
```

The problem here is that the exit statement causes just the inner loop to be
exited. We leave it to the reader to figure out how to exit both nested loops
(see Exercise 3.12).

Exercises

3.1   (a) Describe the execution of the following if statement when nw and nr are
both zero:

```
if nw=0 -> write("A")
[] nw=0 and nr=0 -> write("B")
[] else -> write("C")
fi
```

(b) Describe the differences in execution of the if statement in (a) and the
following if statement:

```
if nw=0 and nr!=0 -> write("A")
[] nw=0 and nr=0 -> write("B")
[] else -> write("C")
fi
```

3.2   Show how to translate a multi-arm do statement into an equivalent single-arm
one. First assume the guards have no side effects. Then explain whether or not
that assumption is necessary for your translation to work. If it is, then devise a
more general translation that works even if side effects can occur.

3.3   Show the output from

```
fa i := 1 to 10 st i mod 2 = 1,
    j := i-1 downto 0 st j/2 != i  ->
        write(i,j)
af
```

3.4   Rewrite the quantifier in the following for-all statement so it uses a by clause
instead of a such-that clause:

```
fa i := 1 to 10 st i mod 2 = 1 -> ... af
```

3.5   Consider the following code fragment:

```
fa i := 1 to N st i != 5, j := i+1 to N -> block af
```

Write an equivalent code fragment without using `fa`. Assume that *block* does not contain an `exit` or a `next`. Explain whether or not that assumption is necessary for your fragment to work.

3.6   Rewrite the array sorting program fragment from Section 3.5 so that it does not use a such-that clause, multiple quantifiers, or a swap statement.

3.7   Rewrite the solution to the matrix multiplication problem from Section 3.5 without using nested for-all statements. (Hint: Use an extra for-all statement to initialize the result matrix to zero.)

3.8   Write a program fragment to determine the leftmost position of the smallest element in array `a[1:N]`, where `N>1`.

3.9   Explain why the following two code fragments are in general not equivalent:

```
# fragment 1
++count
fa i := 1 to count -> ... af

# fragment 2
fa i := 1 to ++count -> ... af
```

3.10   Let `s` be a string variable whose current length is at least 1 and at most half of its declared maximum length. To append `length(s)` asterisks to `s`, we can use

```
s ||:= string( ([length(s)] '*') )
```

Explain why the following is *not* equivalent:

```
# **** incorrect code ****
fa i := 1 to length(s) -> s := s || "*" af
```

Correct the above so that it is equivalent to the original assignment.

3.11   Without using either exit or next statements, write a program fragment that is equivalent to the following:

(a) the input-handling loops in Section 3.6

(b) the two-dimensional array search in Section 3.6

3.12   Show how to break out of both loops in a nested for-all statement.

3.13   Execute and explain the output from the following program:

```
resource foo()
  var count := 4
  do not count < 4 -> write("a", count); count-- od
  count := 4
  do not (count < 4) -> write("b", count); count-- od
end
```

## CHAPTER 4

Procedures

This chapter examines how procedures are declared and invoked. We shall see that the mechanism for defining a procedure is really an abbreviation that involves two more general mechanisms: an operation declaration and a proc. While the procedure abbreviation is sufficient in many cases, using the more general combination yields additional flexibility for both sequential and concurrent programming. This chapter also introduces operation capabilities, which serve as pointers to operations, and optypes, which specify the parameters and return value of an operation. The general mechanisms introduced in this chapter—i.e., operation declarations, procs, operation capabilities, and optypes—are also used in concurrent programming; Part II describes their forms and uses in that context.

4.1 Procedure Declaration

A procedure defines a body of code that can be invoked from other code. It can take parameters and return a value. A procedure declaration takes one of two forms, depending on whether it returns a value. A procedure that does not return a value has the form

```
procedure procedure_id ( formal_list )
   block
end
```

A procedure that returns a value—i.e., a function—is declared similarly; the only difference is that the name and type of the return value must also be specified by appending a returns clause to the procedure heading:

```
procedure procedure_id ( formal_list )
     returns variable_name : type
  block
end
```

In either case the procedure name can optionally appear after the keyword `end`.

A procedure's formal list consists of zero or more formal parameter specifications separated by semicolons:

parameter_specification; parameter_specification; ...

A parameter specification defines one or more parameters of the same type. The specification consists of a list of one or more variable names, which are separated by commas, and a type:

variable_name, variable_name, ... : type

To specify how parameters are passed, the list of variable names can also be preceded by either `var`, `val`, `res`, or `ref`; the meanings of these parameter-passing methods are described below.

The variable names in a formal list and the return variable (after `returns`) have almost the same form described in Section 2.5:

variable_id or *variable_id dimensions*

One additional form of dimension is allowed, however. The sizes of array and string parameters (but not results) may depend on the arguments of an invocation. This is denoted by the use of * for a range bound or for the string size.

A procedure is executed when it is called, as described in the next section. A procedure terminates when it executes its last statement or when it executes a return statement (see Section 4.3).

A simple example should make the above description more concrete. Consider the following program for computing factorials of integers:

```
resource main()
  procedure factorial(x: int)
      var fact := 1
      fa i := 2 to x -> fact *:= i af
      write(x, "factorial is", fact)
  end
```

```
                # find factorial for each positive number input
                var x: int
                do true ->
                    writes("enter a number > 0 ")
                    writes("(or = 0 when done): ")
                    read(x)
                    if x = 0 -> exit
                    [] x < 0 -> write("number must be >= 0")
                    [] x > 0 -> call factorial(x)
                    fi
            od
        end
```

Procedure `factorial` has a single integer parameter, x, and no return value. It is invoked by a call statement, which is described in more detail in the next section. On each iteration of the above loop for which $x > 0$, the value of x is passed to `factorial`. The body of the procedure is then executed anew. In particular, a new copy of local variable `fact` is created and initialized to 1 each time `factorial` is called. When `factorial` terminates, control is returned to just after the call statement, and the do loop is then repeated.

A procedure must be declared before it is used. More precisely, the procedure heading, but not necessarily the entire body of the procedure, must appear before the procedure is invoked. Thus, a procedure can invoke itself recursively. Procedure declarations cannot be nested.

Parameters are passed to procedures by copying or by address; the return value is passed by copying. Value parameters (`val`) are copied in, result parameters (`res`) and the return value are copied out, and variable parameters (`var`) are copied both in and out. On the other hand, reference parameters (`ref`) are passed by address. The default parameter kind is `val`; this default was used for parameter x in the `factorial` procedure above.

Passing a parameter by copy-in/copy-out (i.e., `var`) often has the same effect as passing it by reference. However, passing by reference is more efficient for large data structures such as arrays because passing just the address of an array takes less time and space than does copying all the elements of an array. However, reference parameters should not be passed between virtual machines (address spaces) since the value of a reference parameter, which is a memory address, cannot be used safely.

As mentioned, the sizes of array and string parameters may depend on the arguments of an invocation. This is denoted by the use of $*$ for one of the range bounds or for the string size. When the operation is invoked, the implicit value of $*$ becomes whatever is required to match the corresponding attribute of the actual parameter. This value can be determined by means of the predefined functions `lb`, `ub`, and `length`. For example, consider the following partial program, which declares a procedure for sorting an array of

integers, declares three arrays, and then invokes the sort procedure three
times:

```
resource main()
  procedure sort(var a[1:*]: int)
      fa i := lb(a) to ub(a)-1,
          j := i+1 to ub(a) st a[i] > a[j] ->
              a[i] :=: a[j]
      af
  end

  var x[1:20], y[2:30], z['a':'z']: int
  # initialize x, y, and z
    ...
  call sort(x)
  call sort(y)
  call sort(z)
end
```

The formal parameter of `sort`, `a`, is preceded by `var` so that changes made to
it by `sort` are copied back to the invoker. (A reference parameter could also
be used in this example.) The bounds of `a` are integers. The lower bound is
always 1, but the upper bound depends on the size of the actual parameter
passed by each invocation, as shown in the following table:

Invocation	ub(a)
sort(x)	20
sort(y)	29
sort(z)	26

The type of `a`'s bounds is always integer, although the bounds of the arrays
passed to `sort` need not be; e.g., `z`'s bounds are characters. This is
permissible since, as described in Section 2.11, the type of an array is
determined by the number of elements in the array and by its base type but
not by its dimension type.

We now give an example of a formal string parameter whose size depends
on the actual parameter. Consider a procedure that centers a string within a
field 20 characters wide by prepending and appending dots as needed. (We
use dots instead of blanks as our "padding" character so they can be seen in
the output.) For example, the following table shows some sample input and
the resulting output:

Input	Centered output
now	. . . . .now. . . . .
is the	. . . . . . .is the. . . . . . .
time for	. . . . . .time for. . . . . .
all good men	. . . .all good men. . . .

An odd number of dots is split so that the extra one is placed on the right side of the original string. The following program reads in a string, centers it in a field 20 characters wide, and outputs the result:

```
resource main()
  procedure center(var s: string[*])
      var fill := maxlength(s) - length(s)
      var front := fill/2
      s := string( ([front] '.') ) ||
          s || string( ([fill-front] '.') )
  end

  # read in a string; center it; repeat.
  var str: string[20]
  do read(str) != EOF ->
      call center(str); write(str)
  od
end
```

Procedure center uses * to declare its formal string parameter, s, so it can accept argument strings of any size. (The above code, however, only passes strings of size 20 to center.) Parameter s is declared as a var parameter so that changes made to it get reflected back to the corresponding actual parameter. The code in center uses the predefined function maxlength to determine the maximum number of characters that s can hold. The value of maxlength applied to a string parameter whose size is * is the size of the actual parameter; in the above code, maxlength always returns 20 since center is always passed str. The code in center also uses the predefined function length to determine the current number of characters stored in parameter s. The difference between maxlength and length is the number of dots that are needed to center s. The rest of center's code puts roughly half those dots on the left of the original string and the rest on the right.

Although the sizes of array and string parameters may depend on the arguments of an invocation, the result variable may not; i.e., it may not use *. Instead one should use a var or res parameter.

4.2 Procedure Invocation

As shown in the previous section, a procedure is invoked by call statements. The general form of a call statement is

```
call operation ( expr_list )
```

The `call` keyword can be omitted, giving a slightly shorter form:

```
operation ( expr_list )
```

The operation field is the name of a procedure. (This field can also be an operation name, which is declared in an operation declaration, or a capability variable; these topics are discussed later in this chapter and in Chapter 5.) The expression list consists of zero or more expressions separated by commas:

```
expr, expr, ...
```

Even if the expression list is empty, the parentheses are required in a call statement (see Exercise 4.1).

A call statement is executed by first evaluating the argument expressions; these must agree in both number and type with the corresponding formal parameters. The arguments are assigned to the formal parameters of the procedure, and the procedure body is then executed. A call statement terminates when the called procedure has terminated and the results (if any) have been returned. Then execution continues in the caller immediately after the point from which it called the procedure.

A procedure that returns a value can also be invoked from within an expression. This kind of invocation has the same form as a call statement without the `call` keyword. The semantics is also nearly the same as for a call statement. The one additional requirement is that the type of the procedure's return value must be valid at the point of the invocation in the expression. To illustrate, consider a procedure, `sigma`, that computes the sum of the first n integers:

```
procedure sigma(n: int) returns sum: int
    sum := 0
    fa i := 1 to n -> sum +:= i   af
end
```

This procedure might be invoked as follows:

```
var x, y: int
x := 10 + sigma(y)
```

Here, `sigma`'s type is `int`, which is valid as an operand of `+`. The value returned from `sigma` is added to `10`, and that sum is assigned to `x`.

A procedure that returns a value, while generally invoked as part of an expression, can also be invoked in a call statement. In such a case, the return value from the procedure is discarded. This can sometimes be useful when the procedure has a side effect. For example, suppose we have written a procedure `pop` that returns the value currently on the top of a stack and has the side effect of popping that value from the stack. If we want to pop the top element from the stack but do not want to examine it, then we can execute `call pop()` or simply `pop()`.

4.3 Return Statement

A return statement transfers control to the end of the enclosing procedure; it causes the procedure and the invocation it is servicing to terminate. The form of the return statement is simply

```
return
```

As mentioned in Chapter 3, executing a return statement also terminates any enclosing if, do, and for-all statements. Because a return statement transfers control and any statement following it would be unreachable, it should appear only as the last statement in a block. If a procedure returns a value, the return variable should be assigned to before a return statement is executed; otherwise the return value is undefined.

As an example, consider the following procedure:

```
# return true if x is on list pointed at by head
# type node is rec(value: int; ...; nxt: ptr node)
procedure search(x: int) returns found: bool
    var p: ptr node
    p := head
    do p != null ->
        if p^.value = x -> found := true; return fi
        p := p^.nxt
    od
    found := false
end
```

If value `x` is on the list, return variable `found` is set to `true` and then a return statement is executed. The above procedure body can be rewritten so that it does not use a return statement (see Exercise 4.2), but in general to do so can result in cumbersome code.

4.4 Operation and Proc Declarations

A procedure declaration is really an abbreviation for an operation declaration
and a proc. A procedure is sufficient in simple cases. However, the requirement that a procedure be declared before it is used is a limitation—it
constrains the order in which procedures appear within a resource, and, more
importantly, it does not allow for mutually recursive procedures. To support
data abstraction, it is also necessary to be able to split a procedure exported
from a resource or global into its specification part (operation declaration)
and its implementation part (proc). Finally, operations and procs are at the
heart of SR's concurrent programming mechanisms, as we shall see in Part
II. This section describes these two fundamental mechanisms.

An operation declaration gives one or more operation definitions separated
by commas:

> op *operation_definition* , *operation_definition* , ...

Each operation definition declares the name of an operation, the types of its
parameters and how they are passed, and the type of its return value. (SR
also provides arrays of operations, which are used with receive and input
statements, as described in Part II.) An operation definition is much like a
procedure heading, i.e., the part of the procedure that declares parameters
and the return value. It has one of two forms:

> *operation_id operation_specification*
> *operation_id operation_specification operation_restriction*

An operation specification gives parameters and an optional return value
much in the same way that a procedure declaration does. The form of an
operation specification depends on whether there is a return value, as follows:

> (*parameter_specification_list*)
> (*parameter_specification_list*) returns *variable_name* : *type*

A parameter specification list has the same form as a procedure's parameter
list (see Section 4.1).

An operation restriction indicates how the operation can be invoked. The
four different operation restrictions are

> {call}   {send}   {call, send}   {send, call}

The operation resulting from a procedure declaration has the call restriction.
The send restriction is used in concurrent programming (see Sections 7.1 and
9.3). The default restriction is {call, send}, i.e., no restriction.

The following are three examples of operation declarations:

```
op insert(item: person)
op differ(s1, s2: string[*]) returns place: int
op left(i: int) returns lft: int
```

These operations could also appear in the same operation declaration:

```
op insert(item: person),
   differ(s1, s2: string[*]) returns place: int,
   left(i: int) returns lft: int
```

Parameter and return names are required in a procedure declaration since they are needed in the procedure body. However, they are optional in an operation declaration since they must be supplied later in the implementation of the operation (see below). For example, `left` above could be declared as

```
op left(int) returns int
```

Because a parameter's name documents its role, we will always include it. In any event, the parameter-passing mode must be given unless it is `val`.

An operation declaration can also employ an operation type (optype) to specify the parameterization, as described in the next section.

Each operation is implemented by one proc.* The operation declaration must appear before the proc is declared and before the operation is invoked. A proc declaration has one of two forms, depending on whether the corresponding operation was declared with a return value. A proc implementing an operation without a return value has the form

> `proc` *operation_id* (*formal_id_list*)
>   *block*
> `end`

A proc implementing an operation with a return value has the form

> `proc` *operation_id* (*formal_id_list*) `returns` *result_id*
>   *block*
> `end`

As for procedures the name of the proc can also appear immediately after the

---

*The term "proc" is a pun. It is an abbreviation of the words procedure and process. These terms are themselves abbreviations for special uses of procs, as described at the start of this section and in Section 7.1, respectively.

end keyword. The formal identifier list is a list of zero or more identifiers separated by commas:

id, *id*, ...

A proc is similar in form to a procedure. However, its declaration specifies only the identifiers that are to be used in the proc's body to reference the formal parameters and to construct the return value. These identifiers will often be the same as the corresponding identifiers in the op declaration, but they need not be. The type of each identifier is determined by the type of the corresponding parameter specification in the operation's declaration. Therefore, the number of formal identifiers must equal the number of formal parameters in the corresponding operation declaration. Like procedures, procs cannot be nested.

As examples the following procs implement the insert, differ, and left operations declared above:

```
# Insert item into info array; stop if out of room.
proc insert(item)
  if count >= N ->
    write(stderr,"insert: no room"); stop(1)
  fi
  info[++count] := item
end


# Determine first place strings s1 and s2 differ.
# Return 0 if the strings are the same.
proc differ(s1, s2) returns first_place
  var i := 1, len := min(length(s1), length(s2))
  do i <= len & s1[i] = s2[i] -> i++ od
  if i > len & length(s1) = length(s2) ->
      first_place := 0
  [] else ->
      first_place := i
  fi
end differ


# Compute left neighbor of philosopher i.
proc left(i) returns lft
  lft := (i-2) mod 5 + 1
end
```

Note how the procs specify only parameter identifiers, not their types or parameter passing methods. Also note how a proc can use identifiers different from those that appeared in the corresponding operation declaration. For example, the return value from `differ` is referenced within the proc as `first_place`, but in the operation declaration it is named `place`.

As another example, consider the partial sorting program from Section 4.1. There `sort` was declared as a procedure and placed before call statements that invoked it. Suppose instead that we want to place the code for `sort` after it is invoked. To do this we can split the `sort` procedure into its two underlying parts: an operation declaration and a proc that implements that operation. The partial program then becomes

```
resource main()
   op sort(var a[1:*]: int)

   var x[1:20], y[2:30], z['a':'z']: int
   # initialize x, y, and z
      ...
   call sort(x)
   call sort(y)
   call sort(z)

   proc sort(a)
        fa i := lb(a) to ub(a)-1,
            j := i+1 to ub(a) st a[i] > a[j] ->
                a[i] :=: a[j]
        af
   end
end
```

As a final example, we develop a simple expression evaluator. In particular, we want to write a program to evaluate expressions described by the grammatical rules

expr	::=	term { + term }
term	::=	factor { * factor }
factor	::=	number | (expr)

Here we enclose items in braces to indicate they may be repeated zero or more times, and we use | to indicate choice. Our tokens are +, *, (,), and numbers, which are just strings of digits. The above rules recognize, for example, the following expressions:

33 (33) 2*8+7 2+8*7*6 22*(8+3)

The rules also impose the normal precedence of * over +, and they allow parentheses for grouping.

The following program repeatedly reads in a string giving such an expression, uses recursive descent parsing to evaluate the expression, and then outputs its value. The program uses three procs to perform the evaluation, one corresponding to each rule. The procs are mutually recursive. For example, on input "(33)", expr calls `term`, `term` calls `factor`, `factor` calls `expr`, and so on. We therefore must use operation declarations and procs instead of procedures. (At least one of these procs could be written as a procedure; see Exercise 4.3.) Note that the program is not very robust since it does not check its input for errors.

```
# Evaluate simple arithmetic expressions;
# assume no white space or mistakes in input.
resource evaluator()
  op expr() returns ans: int
  op term() returns ans: int
  op factor() returns ans: int
  var s: string[100] # string to evaluate
  var pos: int   # position in s to evaluate

  # read and evaluate expressions until end of input
  do true ->
      writes("enter expression: ")
      if read(s) = EOF -> write(); exit fi
      s := s || "$"   # append sentinel to s
      pos := 1
      write(expr())
  od

  proc expr() returns ans
    ans := term()
    do s[pos] = '+' ->
        pos++
        ans +:= term()
    od
  end

  proc term() returns ans
    ans := factor()
    do s[pos] = '*' ->
        pos++
        ans *:= factor()
    od
  end
```

```
      proc factor() returns ans
        if s[pos] = '(' ->
            pos++
            ans := expr()
            pos++   # skip over ')'
        [] else ->   # convert substring to integer
            ans := 0
            do '0' <= s[pos] & s[pos] <= '9' ->
                ans := 10*ans + int(s[pos]) - int('0')
                pos++
            od
        fi
      end
    end evaluator
```

4.5 Operation Types

An operation type (optype) declaration introduces a new identifier that is a synonym for the specified type of operation. Operation types can be used in operation and capability declarations. They are to operations what type declarations are to variables: They declare patterns that will be used more than once. The form of an optype declaration is

> optype *optype_id* = *operation_specification operation_restriction*

The operation specification and optional operation restriction have the forms and meanings described in Section 4.4. The = may be omitted if desired.

A simple example of an optype declaration is

> optype intfun = (n: int) returns sum: int

The pattern, intfun, consists of a single integer parameter and an integer return value. The declaration can also be written as either of the following:

> optype intfun(n: int) returns sum: int
> optype intfun(int) returns int

These have more the appearance of an operation declaration.

Operation declarations can use optypes instead of explicitly giving operation specifications. This form of operation declaration is

> op *operation_id*, *operation_id*, ... : *optype_id*

There must at least one operation identifier. The : may be omitted if desired. An example of an operation declaration that uses the intfun optype is

```
op fact: intfun
```

It declares fact to be an operation whose specification is given by intfun; i.e., fact has a single integer parameter and an integer return value. The operation fact must then be implemented by a proc, such as

```
proc fact(n) returns prod
     prod := 1
     fa i := 2 to n -> prod *:= i af
end
```

We use optypes for the abstraction they provide in specifying related parameter specifications. (They also help avoid repetitious typing.) For example, the operations expr, term, and factor in the expression evaluator example at the end of the previous section can be declared using an optype that expresses their common parameterization and return value:

```
optype etftype = () returns ans: int
op expr: etftype
op term: etftype
op factor: etftype
```

These declarations can be written even more concisely as follows:

```
optype etftype () returns int
op expr, term, factor: etftype
```

4.6 Operation Capabilities

An operation capability is a pointer to an operation. Such pointers can be assigned to variables, passed as parameters, and used in invocation statements; invoking a capability has the effect of invoking the operation to which it points. A variable or parameter is defined to be an operation capability by declaring its type in one of the following three ways:

```
cap operation_specification
cap operation_id
cap optype_id
```

In each case the capability is defined to have the specified parameterization.

In the first case, it is that given in the operation specification; in the second and third cases, it is that given by the named operation or optype.

An operation capability can be bound to any user-defined operation having the same parameterization. When parameterization is compared, only the signatures of formals and return values matter; formal and return identifiers are ignored. (If there are operations restrictions, they must also match.) Capabilities can also be compared using the = and != relational operators; however, the other relational operators (e.g., <) are not allowed for capabilities since no ordering is defined among them.

Some simple examples will illustrate the declaration and use of operation capabilities. Suppose we have the following declarations:

```
op d(x: int)
op e(var x: int)
optype s = (x: int)
op f(x: real) returns y: real
op g(a: real) returns b: real
```

Then the following declares three capability variables:

```
var x: cap d
var y: cap f
var z: cap s
```

Some of the ways these variables can be used are

```
x := d      # x now points to operation d
x(387)      # invoke operation d with argument 387

if ... -> y := f    # make y point to one of f or g
[] else -> y := g
fi
write(y(4.351))     # invoke what y points to

z := x

if y = f -> ...   fi  # capabilities can be compared
```

However, the following statements are illegal for the reasons indicated:

```
x := e      # e's parameter is a var; x's is a val
d := e      # d is an operation; cannot assign to it
z(3,45)     # z requires a single parameter
```

Note how the name of an operation in effect acts as a capability constant. It cannot be assigned to, but its value can be used to invoke an operation, assigned to capability variables, and compared with other capabilities.

As a more realistic example, consider the follow procedure, which approximates the area under a curve (function) by means of the trapezoidal rule. The procedure has four parameters. The first three specify the end points and number of intervals to use. The fourth is a capability for the function that defines the curve.

```
optype realfun = (x: real) returns fx: real {call}
# return area under the curve f(x) for a <= x <= b
# using trapezoidal rule with n intervals
procedure trapezoidal(a, b: real; n: int;
          f: cap realfun ) returns area: real
    var x := a
    var h := (b-a)/n
    area := (f(a)+f(b))/2
    fa i := 1 to n-1 ->
        x +:= h; area +:= f(x)
    af
    area *:= h
end
```

This procedure might be used as follows:

```
procedure fun1(x: real) returns fx: real
    fx := x*x + 2*x +4
end
procedure fun2(x: real) returns fx: real
    fx := sin(2*x)
end
# output area under some curves
write(trapezoidal(0.0,1.0,200,fun1))
write(trapezoidal(0.0,3.1415927/2,1000,fun2))
```

The first invocation of trapezoidal will find the area under fun1 between 0 and 1 using 200 intervals. The second will find the area under fun2 between 0 and 3.1415927/2 (i.e., ending at $\pi/2$) using 1000 intervals.

Capability variables can also take on two special values: null and noop. Invocation of a capability variable whose value is null causes a run-time error. In general, invocation of a capability variable whose value is noop has no effect. However, arguments in the invocation are evaluated so any side effects they have will occur. Also, if the invocation appears in an expression, the return value is undefined.

As an example of the use of `noop`, suppose we are writing a terminal-independent program that has a screen repaint command. We want the user to be able to invoke the repaint command by simply executing

```
repaintcap()
```

For terminals with screens, we would set `repaintcap` to the name of the procedure that will actually repaint the screen. For a paper terminal, however, invocations of the repaint command should be ignored, so `repaintcap` would be set to `noop`. The advantage of using `noop` is that it simplifies code by eliminating testing for special cases, which might depend on information that is not readily available where it is required.

We shall see later that `null` is useful if we want to make sure that a capability variable has a value. Operation capabilities are also useful in multiple-resource programs. In fact, another form of capabilities—resource capabilities—are essential in such programs. We cover these topics in Chapter 5.

Exercises

4.1 The invocation of a parameterless procedure, say `foo`, can be written as `foo()`. The line containing just `foo` is also legal, but its meaning is different. (The same applies to capabilities for parameterless operations.) Explain.

4.2 Rewrite the search procedure in Section 4.3 so that it does not use a `return` statement.

4.3 Consider the expression evaluation program in Section 4.4. At least one of `expr`, `term`, or `factor` can be written as a procedure. Rewrite the declarations using procedures wherever possible. Explain your answer.

4.4 Suppose we are writing an array-sorting program. For large arrays we want to use quicksort, but for small arrays we want to use selection sort. An outline for the program follows:

```
resource main()

    procedure selectsort(var a[1:*]: int)
        # selection sort code
    end

    procedure quicksort(var a[1:*]: int)
        # quicksort code
    end

    var n: int; read(n)
    var x[1:n]: int
    # read values into x
    const threshold := ... # some value
```

```
            if n <= threshold -> call selectsort(x)
            [] else -> call quicksort(x)
            fi
            # print results
        end
```

Rewrite this program to use a capability variable to invoke the appropriate sorting routine. In particular, there should be only one call statement.

## CHAPTER 5

Resources and Globals

The programs we have written so far, except for some in Chapter 1, have consisted of just a single resource. In this chapter we show how to write programs that consist of more than one resource. In general, an SR program consists of a collection of resources and globals. Resources and globals both have modular structures, but they are created and used differently. A resource defines a *template* from which resource instances can be created dynamically; resource instances can also be destroyed. A global is essentially a single, unparameterized, automatically created instance of a resource.

A resource can be viewed as an abstract data type in that it consists of a *specification* part, which specifies the interface of the resource, and a *body* part, which contains the code that implements the abstract object.

A global is a collection of objects shared by resources and other globals in the same address space (virtual machine). Globals have several different forms that reflect their different usages. In its simplest usage, a global contains declarations of types, constants, and variables that are used throughout a program. In this case a global contains only a specification part. In its more complicated usage, a global also contains operations and associated code to provide a library. In this case a global has both a specification part and a body containing code. In all cases the form of a global is quite similar to that of a resource.

As mentioned above, resources and globals have a number of similarities. In fact resources could be used in place of globals in some cases. However, as we shall see, two key differences exist that demonstrate the utility of globals. First, globals allow variables to be shared among all resource instances; resources allow variables to be shared only by procs within each resource instance. Second, procs declared in the spec of a global can be referenced outside the global directly via the global's name; such procs declared in the spec of a resource must be referenced outside the resource indirectly through a resource capability for the resource instance. These differences affect how one writes programs and their performance.

The reader familiar with Modula-2 (see, e.g., [Wirth 1982]) will note some similarities between Modula-2's modules and SR's resources. Both provide the notion of separating specification and implementation, and both employ an import mechanism. The key difference is that SR resources are dynamic, whereas Modula-2's modules are static. That is, the number of resource instances in an SR program can grow or shrink during its execution, whereas the number of modules in a Modula-2 program is determined when the program is compiled. SR globals are similar to Modula-2's modules in that both are static, although an SR program can contain multiple instances of a global in different virtual machines (see Chapter 12).

5.1 Resource Specifications and Bodies

Each resource is composed of two parts: the *spec*, which specifies the interface of the resource, and the *body*, which contains the code that implements the resource. The general form of a resource is

>   resource *resource_name*
>   *imports*
>   *constant*, *type*, or *operation declarations*
>   body *resource_name* (*parameters*)
>   *imports*
>   *declarations*, *statements*, *procs*
>   *final code*
>   end *resource_name*

The parameters and all the parts in the spec and body are optional, as is the resource name following end.

The objects declared in a resource spec are implicitly exported and hence are visible to other resources. Import clauses are used to acquire access to objects exported by other components. The spec for a resource also gives the parameterization for instances of that resource; these parameters must be passed by value. A resource spec may not contain variable declarations or statements, and arrays of operations or semaphores (see Part II) must have constant sizes.

A resource body gives the implementation of a resource. The body contains procs, which implement actions, and declarations, which introduce objects shared by all components inside the body. A body can optionally include initial code and/or final code. The initial code, which consists of the executable statements in the body, is executed when the resource is created; the final code, which is a block of code enclosed within `final` and `end`, is executed when the resource is destroyed. (See Section 5.7 for further details about initial and final code.) Although objects declared in a resource's spec are visible both inside and outside the resource, objects declared in a resource's body are visible only in the body.

Body components can be declared in any order. For example, declarations and procs may be intermixed. (This is consistent with the intermixing of declarations and statements within blocks that we have already seen.) This is useful for grouping together variables and procs that use them. Resource bodies and blocks can also contain import clauses.

As an example, the following code defines a stack resource:

```
resource Stack
   type result = enum(OK, OVERFLOW, UNDERFLOW)
   op push(item: int) returns r: result
   op pop(res item: int) returns r: result
body Stack(size: int)
   var store[1:size]: int, top: int := 0
   proc push(item) returns r
      if top < size -> store[++top] := item; r := OK
      [] top = size -> r := OVERFLOW
      fi
   end
   proc pop(item) returns r
      if top > 0 -> item := store[top--]; r := OK
      [] top = 0 -> r := UNDERFLOW
      fi
   end
end Stack
```

The spec of `Stack` declares two operations, `push` and `pop`, and type `result`; these are visible outside the resource. The spec also declares the resource parameter `size`. The body of `Stack` contains the declarations of variables used in implementing the stack abstraction and procs that implement the two operations. Note how the number of elements in `store` depends on the resource parameter `size`. As we shall see later in this chapter, values are assigned to resource parameters when resource instances are created.

5.2 A Simpler Form of Resource

If a resource does not export any objects—i.e., there are no declarations in its spec—then a simpler form of resource declaration can be used. In particular, the keyword `body` and the second instance of the resource identifier may be omitted. For example, consider the following resource:

```
resource foo
body foo(x, y: int)
  # some code
end foo
```

It can be written equivalently, and more concisely, as

```
resource foo(x, y: int)
  # some code
end foo
```

Such a resource still has a spec, but it consists simply of the resource identifier and parameters, in this case `foo`, `x`, and `y`.

5.3 Separate Resource Spec and Body

The spec and body for a resource can be separated. The separated parts can appear in the same source file or in separate source files. In either case a body must be compiled after its spec, and it should be recompiled whenever its spec changes. (Appendix D describes the **srm** tool, which generates UNIX Makefiles that will ensure that source files are compiled in the necessary order.)

The `Stack` resource seen earlier can be rewritten with a separate spec and body. Its new spec becomes

```
resource Stack
  type result = enum(OK, OVERFLOW, UNDERFLOW)
  op push(item: int) returns r: result
  op pop(res item: int) returns r: result
body Stack(size: int) separate
```

The only change is the keyword `separate` placed at the end of the spec. The body of `Stack` must now be identified as being part of `Stack`. That is done by placing the `body` keyword and the name `Stack` at the beginning of the code in the body. Thus `Stack`'s new body looks like

```
body Stack
  # same declaration and procs as before
end Stack
```

5.4 Imports

When one resource wants to use another, it must import the other resource. An import clause specifies one or more resource or global names separated by commas:

```
import name, name, ...
```

It may appear anywhere a declaration may appear, e.g., in the spec of a resource or in code within a block. An import clause gives access to the objects in the named resources or globals. In keeping with the scope rules of SR, those objects are visible from the point of the import clause to the end of the importing block.

To illustrate, consider the following outline of a resource, which imports the `Stack` resource given above:

```
resource Stack_User()
   import Stack
   var x: Stack.result
   ...
end
```

It declares a variable, x, whose type is declared in the spec of `Stack`. Specifically, the *qualified name* `Stack.result` means the name `result` declared in the spec of `Stack`.

The use of qualified names allows imported objects to have the same names as local objects or as objects being imported from other resources. However, if the name of an imported object is unique in the importing scope—and it does not conflict with the name of a predefined function—then the name need not be qualified with the resource name. In the above example, assuming that we did not declare the name `result` later in `Stack_User`, we could write the declaration of x simply as

```
var x: result
```

5.5 Creating and Destroying Resource Instances

As mentioned earlier, instances of resources can be created during program execution. Since several instances of a given resource can be active at the same time, we need some means to distinguish between the different instances; this is provided by resource capabilities.

A create expression is used to create an instance of a resource. Its form is

```
create resource_name ( arguments )
```

Execution of `create` returns a *resource capability*, which acts as a pointer to an instance of the named resource. This capability is subsequently used to invoke operations in the resource instance or to destroy the instance. Most often a create expression appears in an assignment:

```
res_cap_var := create resource_name ( arguments )
```

In this case *res_cap_var* must have type `cap` *resource_name* (or a compatible type).

Execution of a create expression causes a new instance of the named resource to be created, its parameters to be assigned values from the specified arguments, and its initial code to be executed. The create expression terminates, and returns a resource capability, when the initial code in the new instance completes.

The following code creates and uses two instances of `Stack`:

```
resource Stack_User()
   import Stack
   var x: Stack.result
   var s1, s2: cap Stack
   var y: int
   s1 := create Stack(10); s2 := create Stack(20)
      . . .
   s1.push(4); s1.push(37); s2.push(98)
   if (x := s1.pop(y)) != OK -> ... fi
   if (x := s2.pop(y)) != OK -> ... fi
      . . .
end
```

The first instance of the `Stack` resource, `s1`, is created with 10 elements; the second, `s2`, with 20. The operations and parameter declared in `Stack`'s spec and the variables declared in `Stack`'s body are instance specific. That is, each instance of `Stack` has its own copies of the operations `push` and `pop`, its own value of `size`, and its own copy of `top` and `store`. The operations are referenced outside `Stack` via capability variables, e.g., `s1.push` (within `Stack` the operations can be referenced directly). In contrast, constants and types declared in a spec are associated with the resource, not with each instance. Thus, as seen earlier, `result` is associated with the resource `Stack`. It is therefore referenced as `Stack.result` (or simply `result` if the name is unique, as described at the end of the previous section).

Execution of a program begins with implicit creation of one instance of the program's main resource. That resource's initial code is executed (see Section 5.7); it can in turn create other resources. The main resource is a resource that is not imported by any other resource in that program; it is specified when the program is linked (see Appendix D for details). In a program consisting of the `Stack` and `Stack_User` resources, the main resource is `Stack_User`.

The `destroy` statement destroys a resource instance. Its form is

> `destroy` *expr*

The type of the expression must be a capability for a resource; typically the expression will simply be a resource capability variable. When a resource instance is destroyed, its optional final code is executed. Execution of destroy terminates when that code completes. Execution of destroy causes a run-time error if the resource instance has already been destroyed.

When an SR program terminates—because either all processes in the entire program have terminated or a stop statement was executed (with an exit status of zero)—the initially created instance of the main resource is implicitly destroyed. Hence, any final code in that resource will be executed. It can in turn destroy other instances of resources.

5.6 Resource Capability Variables

Resource capability variables are returned by create expressions and used within destroy statements. They can also be used in a number of other ways. If their signatures match, they can be assigned to or compared with one another. The signature of a resource is determined by the operations it declares in its spec. Two resources are signature-compatible if they declare the same number of signature compatible operations (see Chapter 4) in the same order. For example, `Stack` and the following resource are signature-compatible:

```
resource St
  type status = enum(NORMAL, OVER, UNDER)
  op add(item: int) returns r: status
  op drop(res item: int) returns r : status
body St() separate
```

The names of the operations are different, and resource `St` does not have a resource parameter whereas `Stack` does. However, neither of these is relevant in determining a resource's signature. All that matters are the number of operations, the order in which they are declared, and the types of their parameters and return values. Thus the following code fragment is legal:

```
var s1, s2: cap Stack, s3: cap St
  ...
s1 := create Stack(10)
s3 := s1    # just copy s1
```

As a result of the second assignment, s3 points to the same instance of Stack as s1. This means that the following actually invokes the push operation of the instance of Stack pointed to by s1:

```
s3.add(5)
```

Neither Stack nor St is signature compatible with

```
resource S
  type status = enum(NORMAL, OVER, UNDER)
  op add(item: int) returns r : status
  op drop(res item: int) returns r: status
  op query(item: int) returns b: bool
body S() separate
```

This is because S has an extra operation, query.

Resource capability variables can also be used in assignments to or from operation capabilities. Continuing the previous example, assume s1 points to an instance of Stack and consider the following:

```
var c: cap (item: int) returns r: Stack.result
c := s1.push
```

Invocations of c are now invocations of s1.push. Continuing on, consider

```
s2.push := s1.push
```

This makes invocations of s2.push the same as s1.push. That is, an invocation of s2.push now pushes an item onto the stack whose resource capability was originally assigned to s1. (This kind of assignment is probably not a good idea in this example, but it is sometimes handy.) On the other hand, s2.pop is not affected by the assignment to s2.push; hence an invocation of s2.pop still applies to the stack whose resource capability was originally assigned to s2.

Resource capability variables can also be assigned the special values null and noop. Invocation of an operation in a resource capability whose value is null causes a run-time error; if its value is noop, the invocation has no effect. Similarly, execution of destroy causes a run-time error if the resource capability has the value null; it has no effect if the resource capability has the value noop. A capability with value noop is useful for representing unwritten "stubs" when developing programs.

One predefined function, myresource(), deals with resource capabilities. It returns a capability for the resource in which it is executed. As indicated, it takes no arguments.

5.7 Initial and Final Code

Recall that initial code is executed when a resource is created. Similarly, final code is executed when a resource is destroyed.

Initial code appears as "top-level" code within a resource; that is, initial code is at the same level as procs and resource variables. It may be interspersed with these. The way in which initial code is executed is like any other block of code: from top to bottom, subject, of course, to control statements and procedure calls. Initial code may also contain blocks; these blocks can, for example, hide local variables used to initialize global variables.

Final code appears as a single block of code. It is introduced by the keyword final and terminated by the keyword end. It may appear anywhere within the resource body, but it is usually placed at the bottom. Final code is used to clean up right before the resource instance disappears. For example, a resource instance that has dynamically allocated a linked list structure should, as part of its final code, free that structure.

The following resource outline illustrates initial and final code, demonstrating the points discussed above:

```
resource foo()
  const N := 10; var a[N]: int
  fa i := 1 to 10 -> a[i] := i af
  procedure ... end
  const S := 20
  var b[S,S]: int
  begin    # code to initialize b
    var c := 0
    fa i := 1 to S, j := 1 to S ->
      b[i,j] := c++
    af
  end
  procedure ... end
  final ... end
end
```

The initial code first initializes a and then initializes b. It uses a begin block in initializing b to restrict the scope of the variable c to that block. When an instance of `foo` is created, the initialization of a and b completes before the create expression terminates. Declarations are, in effect, executed as they are encountered. This allows statements and declarations to be intermixed, as they are above, and allows sizes of arrays to depend on computed values, as seen in Section 2.13. (However, it can also interact oddly with final code; see "Cautions and Pitfalls" in Appendix D.)

5.8 Extending Resources and Abstract Resources

One resource can also extend another resource. An extend clause can appear in the spec of a resource. It contains one or more resource names separated by commas:

```
extend resource_name, resource_name, ...
```

The effect is to bring in all declarations from the extended resources, including import and extend clauses, just as if they were being declared in the resource containing the `extend`. Thus, extend is like textual inclusion. Extending a resource also implicitly imports that resource.

If a resource extends more than one resource, the extended resources are inherited in the order they are named in the extend clause(s). The effect of extend is cumulative: A resource inherits the objects declared in resources it extends, as well as in resources they extend, and so on.

As an example, consider writing a stack resource that also provides an operation that returns the number of items currently on the stack. This can be done by extending the stack resource seen earlier:

```
resource NewStack
  extend Stack
  op count() returns r: int
body NewStack(size: int) separate
```

The spec of `NewStack`, in effect, declares one type and three operations: `result`, `push`, and `pop` (from `Stack`) and `count` (declared here). The body of `NewStack` must provide code that implements all three operations; code from `Stack` is *not* in any sense automatically included in the body of `NewStack`. (SR supports only declaration inheritance, not also the code inheritance that is provided by some object-oriented languages.)

It is sometimes convenient to write a resource spec that will never have a body. Such a spec might be extended by one or more other resources. This kind of spec is called an *abstract* resource. Its form is much like a regular resource but without a body:

```
resource resource_name
   imports
   constant, type, or operation declarations
end resource_name
```

As an example, the original `Stack` resource (see Section 5.1) could be written using the following abstract resource:

```
resource Abstract_Stack
   type result = enum(OK, OVERFLOW, UNDERFLOW)
   op push(item: int) returns r: result
   op pop(res item: int) returns r: result
end Abstract_Stack
```

Then `Stack` would be rewritten as

```
resource Stack
   extend Abstract_Stack
body Stack(size: int)
   # body as in Section 5.1
end Stack
```

5.9 Mutually Importing Resources

Two resource specs can import each other. The import of a resource spec is processed when first encountered. Subsequent imports of the same resource specs, including recursive imports, are ignored. This "subsequent import" rule prevents infinite recursion. However, declarations preceding the mutual import statements have already been processed when the rule takes effect, so they are available to both resources.

One resource can reference an object in a second resource's spec anytime after importing the second resource. Moreover, the second resource can reference declarations in the first resource's spec as long as the declaration appears before the clause that imports the second resource.

As an example, the following two resources are legal:

```
resource A
  const u := 100
  import B
  const v := B.x+10
  op foo(c: cap B)
end

resource B
  const x := 200
  import A
  const y := A.u+20
end
```

The value of A.v is 210 and the value of B.y is 120. Note how the parameter in operation foo, declared in resource A, is a capability for resource B. On the other hand, the above resources would not be legal if A were changed to

```
resource A
  const u := 100
  import B
  const v := B.y+10   # changed from x to y; illegal
end
```

The problem in this case is one of circularity: v depends on y, which in turn depends on u. The safe, simple rule is, one spec should not depend on anything in another spec that appears after the clause that imports it.

Another way to determine whether mutually importing resources are legal is to consider how each resource expands when their imports are replaced by the specs of the imported resources. The expanded resources should have no forward references. For example, in the three example resources above, import B would be replaced by B's two constant declarations, and import A would be replaced by A's two constant declarations. In doing the replacements, qualified names would be introduced as needed.

5.10 The Simple Form of Globals

The simplest form of global is used to declare constants, types, and variables that will be shared by resources or other globals. In this case a global consists of a spec alone:

```
global global_name
    imports
    declarations
end
```

As shown, a global can contain an import clause, which has the same form we saw for resources. As with resources, objects declared in the spec part of a global are visible to components that import it.

As an example, the following global declares two constants, TAB and CR:

```
global Characters
    const TAB := '\t'   # Horizontal Tab
    const CR  := '\r'   # Carriage Return
end
```

As a second example, the following global declares three types:

```
global Node
    type node = rec(value: char; link: ptr node)
    type head = ptr node
    type tail = ptr node
end
```

Finally, the following global declares a constant and a shared variable:

```
global Matrix
    const N := 20
    var m[N,N]: int := ([N] ([N] 0))
end
```

These three globals might be used in a resource as follows:

```
resource foo()
    import Characters, Node, Matrix
    var x: Node.node
    ...
    if x.value = Characters.TAB -> ... fi
    ...
    Matrix.m[3,4] :=: Matrix.m[4,3]
    ...
end
```

Note that `node`, `TAB`, and `m` are referenced in `foo` using their qualified names. If those names are unique and do not conflict with the names of predefined functions, the simpler, unqualified names could be used instead.

5.11 The General Form of Globals

Like resources, globals can also have bodies. This form of global is used when the initialization of variables declared in the spec is more complicated than can be specified in the spec. A body can also be used to implement shared operations. For example, a shared procedure is implemented by putting its operation declaration in the spec of a global and putting its proc declaration in the body of the global. (A procedure declaration cannot appear in a spec because it contains code.)

As with resources, the spec and body of a global can be combined, or they can be compiled separately. The combined form is

```
global global_name
    imports
    declarations
body global_name
    imports
    declarations, statements, procs
    final code
end global_name
```

All names declared in the spec are exported; those in the body are private. When the spec and body are compiled separately, the form of the spec is

```
global global_name
    imports
    declarations
body global_name separate
```

And the form of the body is as follows:

```
body global_name
    imports
    declarations, statements, procs
    final code
end global_name
```

The body of a global *must* be compiled before the global is imported by a resource or another global. (This requirement makes it possible to generate efficient code.) The items in the spec and body can appear in any order; the above orders indicate only what a programmer would commonly use.

At most one instance of a global will be created per virtual machine. (All our programs in Part I execute within a single virtual machine; Part II—Chapter 12 in particular—shows how to execute a program on multiple virtual machines.) An instance of a given global is (implicitly) created when the first import of that global is encountered during execution. This first import may appear within the specification of a resource, in which case the global is created during the creation of the first instance of that resource. Because one global can import another, recursive creation may be required.

Creation of a global entails executing the initial code in its body, if any is present. Because globals are created at the point of import, variables exported by globals exist and are initialized (if done so by the global's declaration or initial code) before they are used by code in the importer. For example, code after the import can use variables declared in the global. It also can invoke a procedure in the global that uses variables declared at the global's top level.

If a global contains final code, that code is executed if the global is destroyed. This permits possible cleanup, e.g., of libraries, and is analogous to final code in resources. Globals imported directly or indirectly by the main resource are destroyed when the program terminates (unless a stop statement is executed with a nonzero exit status). Globals are also destroyed if the address space containing the global is destroyed (see Chapter 12). If global A imports global B, then A is finalized before B in case the final code in A uses objects in B.

As an example of a global with a body, consider the following:

```
global Diagonal
  const N := 20
  var a[N,N]: real := ([N] ([N] 0.0))
body Diagonal
  fa i := 1 to N -> a[i,i] := i af
end Diagonal
```

The spec uses an array constructor to initialize all elements of matrix a to zero. The body then sets the diagonal elements to a different value. (This specific initialization of a can be specified in a single array constructor, but not nearly as concisely.)

As another example, consider the following outline of a global:

```
global Screen
  op refresh(), move_to(x,y: int)
  op up(), down(), left(), right()
  op write(x: string[*])
body Screen
  proc refresh()
    ...
  end
  proc move_to(x,y)
    ...
  end
  var where_x := 0, where_y := 0
  # initially, clear the screen, and
  # move the cursor to the home position
  refresh(); move_to(where_x,where_y)
  # declarations of procs for
  # up(), down(), left(), right(), write()
end Screen
```

This global provides a library of operations for screen management. All objects declared inside the body of Screen, such as where_x and where_y, are private to Screen. The only objects visible to Screen's importers are those declared in Screen's spec.

A global such as Screen could be written as a resource. However, this would require (1) creating an instance of the resource and (2) passing a capability for that instance to every resource that wishes to invokes its operations. This leads to cumbersome, less efficient programs. In contrast, the objects exported by a global can be used simply by importing the global. Also, a global can export shared variables, which a resource cannot (since an instance might be in an address space different from that of a resource that uses it).

Exercises

5.1 Give the body of NewStack (Section 5.8).

5.2 Show how NewStack (Section 5.8) could be written to extend Abstract_Stack.

5.3 Consider the declarations of A and B in Section 5.9. Would it be legal if the declaration of u appeared after import B? Explain.

5.4 Show the expansions (as described in Section 5.9) of the two declarations of resource A. Identify the forward reference in the expansion of the second declaration of A.

5.5   (a) Consider the following program:

```
resource foo()
  write("hello world")
end

global g
  import foo
body g
  create foo()
  final
    write("goodbye world")
  end
end

resource main()
  import g
end
```

Trace the order in which components are created and destroyed, and explain the output of the program.

(b) Explain the output of the program if main is changed to

```
resource main()
  import g
  final
    write("main is dead")
  end
end
```

(c) Suppose foo and g in the program in (a) are changed to

```
resource foo()
  write("hello world")
  final
    write("foo is dead")
  end
end

global g
  import foo
body g
  var fc := create foo()
  final
    destroy fc
    write("goodbye world")
  end
end
```

What will the output of the program be now? What if the destroy statement in g is moved to follow the write statement?

5.6   Resources can be used in place of globals, although they are not as convenient in that role. Demonstrate this by rewriting the globals `Diagonal` and `Screen` (see Section 5.11) as resources. Assume that the code using the two globals appears in several resources. Show how code using the globals would be written and contrast that with how code using the new resources would be written.

## CHAPTER 6

Input/Output and External Operations

The previous chapters, as well as those in Part II, describe language mechanisms that are assumed to exist in any implementation of SR. In addition, each implementation must provide some means for communicating with input/output devices. It is also useful to be able to include routines written in other programming languages as part of SR programs.

This chapter describes mechanisms in our current, UNIX-based implementation for communicating with input/output devices, accessing command-line arguments, and invoking operations written in other programming languages. Input/output is supported by a collection of mechanisms that provide access to the underlying UNIX file system. Similarly, access to command-line arguments is supported by mechanisms that reflect the structure of the underlying UNIX interface. Functions written in C (or another language having a compatible calling sequence) can be declared in SR code as *external operations* and can be invoked directly.

This chapter introduces the notion of a file in SR; functions for simple, formatted, and character I/O; functions for accessing command-line arguments; and the use of external operations. This chapter also gives examples showing how the input/output and other mechanisms can be used; later chapters use these mechanisms in their examples as well. Appendix C contains further details on the predefined functions described in this chapter.

6.1 Files and File Access

Input/output in the UNIX implementation of SR is supported by an additional data type, `file`, and several operations on this type. A variable of type `file` contains a descriptor for a UNIX file; it can be thought of as being a capability for the associated file. There are five predefined file literals, all of which are reserved words. Three of the literals are used to access the corresponding UNIX file:

stdin	the standard input device (usually the keyboard)
stdout	the standard output device (usually the display)
stderr	the standard error device (usually the display)

The UNIX process executing an SR program inherits stdin, stdout, and stderr from the command that starts execution of an SR program.

The other file literals are null and noop. Attempting to access a file whose descriptor has value null results in an error. Attempting to read from a file whose descriptor has value noop returns an immediate end of file indication; other operations on such a descriptor have no effect.

In addition to the basic type file, there are two predefined enumeration types:

```
type accessmode = enum(READ, WRITE, READWRITE)
type seektype = enum(ABSOLUTE, RELATIVE, EXTEND)
```

These types define enumeration literals used as arguments to the open and seek operations. Finally, there is one predefined integer constant:

```
const EOF := -1
```

As described below, EOF is sometimes the return value on file access operations.

Files are created or opened by the predefined function open. Files are flushed, closed, and removed by the predefined functions flush, close, and remove, respectively.

The following program fragment illustrates the use of open:

```
var f: file
f := open("foo", READ)
if f = null ->
  write("Error:  cannot open data file"); stop (1)
fi
```

It attempts to open the file foo for read access, getting back the result in the file variable f. If the open is unsuccessful—e.g., because the file foo does not exist in the directory in which the program is executed—the program fragment prints an error message and stops immediately.

6.2 Input/Output Operations

Open files are accessed using several predefined functions: read and write provide a simple I/O facility; printf and scanf provide a formatted I/O facility; get and put provide I/O on streams of characters; seek and where support random access to disk files.

Simple I/O

The functions read, write, and writes are the easiest to use. We described them in Section 2.10 and used them throughout the preceding chapters.

The general form of these functions is slightly more complicated than what we described earlier. In particular, the first argument of each function can specify the file to which the function applies; if omitted, stdin is used for the read function, and stdout is used for the write functions. For example, the following two invocations are equivalent:

```
read(stdin, x)
read(x)
```

Similarly, the following are equivalent:

```
write(stdout, x)
write(x)
```

Suppose that we want to initialize an $n \times n$ adjacency matrix m by reading pairs of values from a file. Suppose further that we have already opened the file and assigned the result of open to file variable f, as shown in the previous section. The following program fragment shows how to read from the file associated with f:

```
var m[n,n] := ([n] ([n] 0))  # adjacency matrix
do true ->
  var i, j, r: int
  r := read(f, i, j)
  if r = EOF -> exit
  [] r = 0 or r = 1 ->
      write(stderr, "bad or missing data"); stop (1)
  fi
  if i<1 or i>n or j<1 or j>n ->
    write(stderr, "coordinates out of range"); stop (1)
  fi
  m[i,j] := m[j,i] := 1
od
```

This program fragment uses a single `read` to read each coordinate pair. It checks `read`'s return value to ensure that the data is valid and to determine when to exit the loop. It also uses the file constant `stderr` to direct its error messages to the standard error file instead of the standard output file (i.e., `stdout`) as would be the default if no file were specified in the invocations of `write`.

Formatted I/O

The I/O functions `printf` and `scanf` provide more control over the format of output and input. They are similar to their namesakes in the C language. The variants `sprintf` and `sscanf` are similar to `printf` and `scanf`, except that output is placed in, or input comes from, a string rather than a file.

The general form of an invocation of `printf` is

```
printf(f, fmt, x1, x2, ...)
```

The arguments `x1`, `x2`, `...` are expressions whose values are output to file `f` according to the format string `fmt`. As with other output functions, `f` can be omitted, in which case `stdout` is used. The format string, `fmt`, is given in a form very close to that in C (see Appendix C for differences). For example, the conversion character `%d` is used for outputting integers, and `%b` is used for outputting booleans.

As a simple example, the output of

```
printf("a[%d] is %d\n", i, a[i])
```

might be

```
a[14] is -234
```

Here the output is to `stdout` and includes a newline, as specified by the `\n` in the format string.

As a slightly more complicated example, the following program fragment outputs the adjacency matrix `m` from the previous section in a tabular format:

```
fa i := 1 to n ->
  fa j := 1 to n -> printf( "%4d", m[i,j]) af
  printf("\n")
af
```

The inner loop prints the `i`-th row, each element in a field four characters wide. The final `printf` prints a newline; alternatively, `write()` would have had the same effect. Using `printf` instead of `write` allows control over spacing in the output. In this example, it ensures that the output is neatly aligned even if the numbers have different numbers of digits. One possible output from the program fragment is

```
1   0   1   1
0   1   0   1
1   0   1   0
1   1   0   1
```

The other formatted I/O functions—scanf, sprintf, and sscanf—are similar to printf in their arguments. The difference is that the first argument to sprintf and sscanf must be a string. To demonstrate, consider the following program fragment:

```
if sscanf(s,"%2d%3d",a,b) != 2 ->
   write(stderr,"bad format"); stop (1)
fi
```

It uses sscanf to break a string into two integer variables. If s is "12345", for example, it would assign 12 to a and 345 to b. The value returned by sscanf (and scanf) is the number of conversions that were successful. The arguments to the scanning functions are variables, not pointers to variables as they would be in a C program. Note that the type conversion function int could also be used to perform the above conversions, as follows:

```
a := int(s[1:2])
b := int(s[3:5])
```

However, should either conversion fail, the program fragment would abort immediately within the call to int without control being returned as it is when the scanning functions are used.

Character I/O

The character I/O functions, get and put, treat the input and output as being streams of characters, without interpretation.

The get function has the following specification:

```
get(f: file; res str: string[*]) returns int
```

It reads characters from file f, or stdin if f is omitted, and stores them in str. If the input file contains at least maxlength(str) characters, that many are read. Otherwise all remaining characters are read. If at least one character is read, get returns the number of characters that were read and sets the length of `str` to that value. If end-of-file is encountered immediately, no characters are read and `get` returns `EOF`.

The `put` function is parameterized similarly to `get`, but it does not modify its argument or return a value. It has the following specification:

```
put(f: file; str: string[*])
```

It writes `length(str)` characters from `str` to file `f`, or to `stdout` if `f` is omitted.

The argument to `get` can also be a character array, in which case the entire array is filled (unless `EOF` is encountered). Similarly, the argument to `put` can also be an array of characters, in which case the entire array is written.

To illustrate, suppose the standard input contains

```
ab
cde
```

(that is, two lines of characters, with no preceding or trailing blanks). Consider the execution of the following program fragment on that data:

```
var s, t: string[4]
get(s); get(t)
```

It sets s to `"ab\nc"` and t to `"de\n"`. Note how `get` treats the (invisible) newline character \n just like the other characters.

Random Access

The `seek` and `where` functions are used to randomly access data within files. They both take a file argument, which must be open. A read/write pointer is associated with each file. It records the offset within the file of where the next I/O operation will apply; initially it is at the beginning of the file and has value 0. Invoking `seek` moves the read/write pointer; `where` just returns the current value of that pointer.

The `seek` function has the following specification:

```
seek(f: file; t: seektype; offset: int)
     returns pos: int
```

The effect of invoking `seek` depends on the seek type t, as follows:

t	*Effect on read/write pointer*
ABSOLUTE	set to offset
RELATIVE	incremented by offset
EXTEND	set to the end of the file plus offset

The return value is the new value of the read/write pointer. When t is RELATIVE or EXTEND, the value of offset can be negative as long as the resulting position is within the file.

The where function has the following specification:

```
where(f: file) returns pos: int
```

It returns the current position of the read/write pointer in file f.

The following program fragment illustrates the seek function:

```
var f: file, e: int
f := open("foo", READWRITE)
e := seek(f, EXTEND, 0)     # find length of file
fa i := 0 to e by 2 ->
  seek(f, ABSOLUTE, i); put(f,"*")
af
close(f)
```

The first seek determines the number of characters in the file. The loop then writes * over every other character in the file, starting with the first one.

6.3 Command-Line Arguments

Two predefined functions—numargs and getarg—provide access to the arguments of the UNIX command that invoked execution of an SR program. These can be used, for example, to parameterize a program.

The function numargs returns the number of user-supplied arguments, not counting the command name, on the command line. The function getarg reads the command-line argument specified positionally by its first parameter into its second (result) parameter; it also returns an integer value. The type of getarg's second parameter can be int, bool, char, real, string, array of char, pointer, or enum (although literals are not recognized). The format of the command arguments is the same as for the read function. The getarg function returns a positive number if successful and a nonpositive number if not; see Appendix C for details.

The following program fragment gives two simple examples showing how
getarg can be used:

```
# get file name into pn and start node into sn
var pn: string[40]
if getarg(1, pn) = EOF ->
  write(stderr, "usage: a.out datafile [startnode]")
  stop (1)
fi
var sn := 1     # default value
getarg(2, sn)   # if unsuccessful, sn is unchanged
```

The first use of getarg attempts to read a file name (i.e., a string) from the
command line into pn. If no command-line argument is present, the program
fragment outputs an error message and halts. The second use of getarg
attempts to read an integer from the command line into sn. If the second
command-line argument is not present or it is not an integer, sn's value of 1
is not modified and program execution just continues.

6.4 External Operations

External operations provide access to operations that are implemented in
languages other than SR. We have found external operations particularly
useful to gain access to routines in mathematical, windowing, and system
libraries. The current SR implementation supports external operations for
functions compatible with the C calling sequence.

An external operation is declared just as a regular operation, except the
keyword op is replaced by the keyword external. External operations can
be declared only at the resource or global level, not within a proc. An external operation is invoked just as a regular operation and can return a value.

The rules for converting parameters and return values between SR and C
are implementation dependent. The current implementation supports
passing most SR types as parameters. For example, an SR enum parameter
is converted to or from a C int. As another example, an SR string is
converted to or from a null-terminated C string, i.e., a pointer to a character.
Appendix C defines such conversions in detail.

The following program fragment shows how to use an external operation
to obtain the name of the host on which the program fragment is executing:

```
external gethostname(res s: string[*]; namelen: int)
  ...
var hname: string[31]
gethostname(hname, maxlength(hname))
```

It declares the UNIX system call `gethostname` as an external operation and then invokes that operation. The C string returned by the system call is automatically converted to an SR string and then assigned to `hname`.

When an SR program uses external operations, the SR linker **srl** automatically searches the standard C library to find an implementation of the operation. The programmer can also supply to **srl** the names of object files produced from C code and can specify other libraries to search. See Appendix C for details on externals and Appendix D for information on **srl.**

Exercises

6.1 Is `put(s)` always the same as `writes(s)`? Explain.

6.2 Rewrite the seek program fragment in Section 6.2 so it does not use an ABSOLUTE seek, only EXTEND and RELATIVE seeks.

6.3 Develop an SR program that calls, as an external operation, a C routine `cindex(s,c)`, which returns the index of character `c` in string `s` or zero if `c` does not appear in `s`. Hint: Use the C library routine `index` (described in UNIX man page `string(3)`) in writing `cindex`.

6.4 Write a program that has same effect as the UNIX `tee` command. Namely, the program should copy the standard input file to the standard output file and to any other files specified on the command line.

## PART II

Concurrent Aspects

This part of the text introduces SR's mechanisms for concurrent programming. SR is rich in the functionality it provides: dynamic process creation, semaphores, message passing, remote procedure call, and rendezvous. All are additional variations on ways to invoke and service operations.

In Chapter 4 we introduced operation declarations and procs. An operation declaration defines a communication interface; a proc defines how invocations of that operation are to be serviced. We also saw in Chapter 4 that a procedure in SR is merely an abbreviation for an operation declaration for the procedure heading plus a proc for the procedure body. A procedure is invoked by a call statement or function invocation.

Operations, procs, and calls are three of the bases for SR's concurrent programming mechanisms. To these we add send invocations and input statements.

SR allows construction of distributed programs in which resources can be placed on two or more machines in a network. Hence the caller of a proc might be in a resource on one machine, and the proc itself might be in a resource on another machine. In this case the call of a proc is termed a *remote procedure call*.

When a proc is called, the caller waits until the proc returns. SR also provides the send statement, which can be used to *fork* a new instance of a proc. Whereas a call is synchronous—the caller waits—a send is asynchronous—the sender continues. In particular, if one process invokes a proc by sending to the corresponding operation, a new process is created to execute the body of the proc, and then the sender and new process execute concurrently. SR also provides process declarations, which are the concurrent programming analog of procedure declarations. A process declaration is an abbreviation for an operation declaration, a proc, and a send invocation of that operation.

Processes in a concurrent program need to be able to communicate and synchronize. In SR, processes in the same resource can share variables and operations declared in that resource. Processes in the same address space can also share variables and operations exported by globals. Processes can also communicate by means of the input statement, which services one or more operations. A process executing an input statement delays until one of these operations is invoked, services an invocation, optionally returns results, and then continues. An invocation can either be synchronous (call) or asynchronous (send). A call produces a two-way communication plus synchronization—a *rendezvous*—between the caller and the process executing an input statement.* A send produces a one-way communication—i.e., *asynchronous message passing*.

To summarize, the bases for SR's concurrent programming mechanisms are operations and different ways to invoke and service them. Operations can be invoked synchronously (call) or asynchronously (send), and they can be serviced by a proc or by input statements (in). This yields the following four combinations:

Invocation	Service	Effect
call	proc	procedure call (possibly remote)
call	in	rendezvous
send	proc	dynamic process creation
send	in	asynchronous message passing

These combinations are illustrated by the four diagrams in Figure II.1. The squiggly lines in the diagrams indicate when a process is executing; the arrows indicate when an explicit invocation message or implicit reply message is sent.

One virtue of SR's approach is that it supports abstraction of interfaces. In particular, SR allows the declaration of an operation to be separated from the code that services it. This allows resource and global specifications to be written and used without concern for how an operation is serviced.

Another attribute of SR is that it provides abbreviations for common uses of the above interaction possibilities. We have already seen the procedure declaration and have mentioned the process declaration, which abbreviates a common pattern of creating background processes. The receive statement abbreviates a common use of an input statement to receive a message. Semaphore declarations and V and P statements abbreviate operations and send and receive statements that are used merely to exchange synchronization signals. In addition to these abbreviations, SR provides three

---

*For readers familiar with Ada, the input statement combines and generalizes aspects of Ada's **accept** and **select** statements.

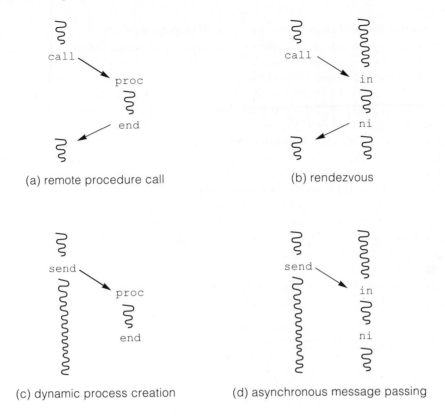

(a) remote procedure call   (b) rendezvous

(c) dynamic process creation   (d) asynchronous message passing

Figure II.1. Process interaction mechanisms in SR.

additional kinds of statements that also deal with operations: concurrent invocation, forward, and reply.

SR also allows the programmer to control the large-scale issues associated with concurrent programming. For constructing distributed programs, SR provides what is called a *virtual machine*—a named address space in which resource instances can be created and globals can be shared. An SR program consists of one or more virtual machines. Virtual machines, like resources, are created dynamically; each can be placed on a different physical machine. Communication between parts of a program located on different virtual machines is handled transparently.

Processes in a distributed program need to be able to communicate, and in many applications communication paths vary dynamically. This is supported in SR by operation and resource capabilities, which were introduced in Chapters 4 and 5. An operation capability is a pointer to a specific operation;

a resource capability is a pointer to all the operations exported by a resource. These can be passed as parameters and hence included in messages.

As in Part I, we describe the concurrent aspects of SR in a bottom-up manner, from simpler mechanisms to more powerful ones. This also follows the historical order in which the various concurrent programming mechanisms that appear in SR were first developed. While reading these chapters, keep in mind that all the process interaction mechanisms are based on invoking and servicing operations. Chapter 7 describes process creation and execution. Chapter 8 discusses how semaphores are declared and used. Chapter 9 introduces the mechanisms for asynchronous message passing. Chapter 10 describes remote procedure call, and Chapter 11 describes rendezvous. Chapter 12 presents the notion of a virtual machine as an address space and shows how to create and use virtual machines. Finally, Chapter 13 describes three ways to solve the classic dining philosophers problem; the solutions illustrate several combinations of uses of the mechanisms presented in the other chapters in this part.

Further discussion of most of these concurrent programming mechanisms, in a more general context, appears in the textbook by Andrews [1991].

## CHAPTER 7

Concurrent Execution

Processes are at the heart of concurrent programming. They represent independent threads of control, each of which executes sequential code. The programs in Part I contain just a single thread of control and hence were sequential programs; those in Part II contain multiple threads of control.

This chapter describes the SR mechanisms for creating processes, all of which are based on operations. We first describe process declarations, which provide a simple way to create single processes and families (arrays) of processes. Process declarations are actually an abbreviation for SR's more general process-creation mechanism: sending to an operation that is implemented by a proc. The concurrent invocation statement provides a third way to create processes. The final section describes process scheduling and priorities.

7.1 Process Declarations

We have already seen that the body of a resource or global can contain procs and procedures. It can also contain processes. The following is the simplest form of a process:

```
process process_id
    block
end
```

The process name can optionally appear after the keyword end. A process declaration can also contain a list of one or more quantifiers to specify

multiple instances of the same process. Such a family (array) of processes
has the form

```
process process_id ( quantifier, quantifier, ... )
    block
end
```

Quantifiers have the same form as in the for-all statement (see Chapter 3).

Processes in a resource or global are created when the resource or global is
created. In particular, processes are created as their declarations are
encountered in executing the resource's or global's initial code. (The initial
code continues as soon as a process is created; it does not wait for the process
to terminate.) For process declarations that contain quantifiers, one instance
of the process is created for each combination of values of the bound
variables. Each instance of the process has access to the associated values of
the bound variables; these are implicitly passed arguments to the instance.

As a simple example, consider the following resource:

```
resource foo()
    var x := 0
    process p1
        x +:= 3
    end
    var a[10]: int
    fa i := 1 to 10 -> a[i] := i af
    process p2
        x +:= 4
    end
end
```

This resource contains two processes, p1 and p2. When foo is created, first x
is initialized, then p1 is created, then a is initialized, and finally p2 is
created. The processes execute at the same time, at least conceptually.
Above, each process unsafely accesses resource variable x. Resource variables are not automatically protected from concurrent access; mutual exclusion
must be programmed explicitly, e.g., using semaphores (see Chapter 8).

The order in which processes execute is non-deterministic. Thus in the
above example, the order in which processes p1 and p2 execute their
assignments is not known. Similarly, suppose that the first of the following
calls of the write function is added to p1 and that the second is added to p2:

```
write("in p1", x)   # added to process p1
write("in p2", x)   # added to process p2
```

The order in which the writes are executed is also non-deterministic. Moreover, the output from one write might be interleaved with the output from the other. Synchronization can be used to control the output in such cases.

As another example of process declarations, consider the following:

```
resource mult()
  const N := 20
  var a[N,N], b[N,N], c[N,N]: real
  # read in some initial values for a and b
  ...
  # multiply a and b in parallel; place result in c
  process multiply(i := 1 to N, j := 1 to N)
      var inner_prod := 0.0
      fa k := 1 to N ->
          inner_prod +:= a[i,k]*b[k,j]
      af
      c[i,j] := inner_prod
  end
  final
    # output values from c
  end
end
```

It employs an N × N array-like family of processes to perform matrix multiplication. Each process computes one element in the result matrix. When mult is created, first code is executed to initialize a and b, and then N*N instances of multiply are created. Each instance of multiply can determine its own "identity" through i and j; these are different in each instance. Since instances of multiply only read values from a and b and write disjoint parts of c, these variables can safely be accessed concurrently. The final code in mult is executed when all processes complete execution. It just outputs values from c.

A program with multiple processes terminates when all processes have terminated, a deadlock has occurred, or a stop statement is executed. Any final code in the main resource is then executed, and globals imported by the main resource are destroyed (unless a stop statement is executed with a non-zero exit status).

7.2 The Unabbreviated Form of Processes

The process abbreviation given in the previous section is handy when the number of instances to create is known in advance and when processes are to be created at the same time a resource instance or global is created. In some cases, though, processes need to be created as a program executes, say in response to input or to actions occurring in other parts of the program. To understand the general mechanism for creating processes, it is first useful to examine the constituent pieces of the process abbreviation.

A process declaration is really an abbreviation for an operation declaration, a proc, and a send invocation. The difference between a send invocation and a call invocation is that a send is asynchronous (i.e., non-blocking) whereas a call is synchronous (i.e., blocking). That is, a send does not wait for the invoked proc to return any results; it terminates immediately after passing the arguments to the proc. A new process is created to execute the proc; it executes in parallel with the process that executed send.

Resource `foo` in Section 7.1 can be written equivalently, without employing process declarations, as follows:

```
resource foo()
   var x := 0
   op p1() {send}
   send p1()         # fork p1
   proc p1()
        x +:= 3
   end
   var a[10]: int
   fa i := 1 to 10 -> a[i] := i af
   op p2() {send}
   send p2()         # fork p2
   proc p2()
        x +:= 4
   end
end
```

The changes are that `p1` and `p2` are now declared as operations, and their code is now written as procs. Also, `foo`'s initial code now contains explicit sends to create an instance of each process.

The declarations of operations `p1` and `p2` above include what is called an *operation restriction*. In particular, `p1` is declared as

```
op p1() {send}
```

This specifies that `p1` may be invoked only by a send statement. An operation declaration may include an operation restriction if the programmer wishes to specify—and have enforced—the ways in which the operation may be invoked. Two operation restrictions are

```
{call}   and   {send}
```

An operation that results from a process declaration has the send restriction. An operation that results from a procedure declaration has the call restriction; hence procedures may be invoked only by call statements. If an operation declaration does not specify an operation restriction, the operation may be invoked by both `call` and `send`. This can also be specified explicitly as follows:

```
{call, send}   or   {send, call}
```

Resource `mult` given in Section 7.1 can also be rewritten without the process abbreviation. The changed part is as follows:

```
# multiply a and b in parallel
# place result in matrix c
op multiply(i,j: int) {send}
fa i := 1 to N, j := 1 to N ->
    send multiply(i,j)
af
proc multiply(i,j)
    # body unchanged
end
```

The `multiply` process is replaced by an operation and a proc. The operation has two parameters and a send restriction. The for-all statement in the initial code creates an instance of the proc for each pair of values of the bound variables. Clearly, it is simpler to use the process abbreviation whenever possible!

As another example of how processes can be created dynamically, consider the following resource:

```
resource compressor
  op compress(filename: string[*])
body compressor()
  proc compress(filename)
      # open file filename, compress its contents,
      # and then close it.
  end
end
```

It declares an operation, `compress`, in its spec. An instance of the resource can be created by executing

```
var c: cap compressor
c := create compressor()
```

Subsequently, the `compress` operation may be invoked from outside the resource, as follows:

```
send c.compress("data1")
send c.compress("data2")
```

Each invocation of `compress` causes a new process to be created within `compressor`. The invoker does not wait for that process to terminate before it continues executing. A process declaration could not be used in cases like this because the invocation that causes processes to be created occurs outside the resource.

Since a process declaration is actually an abbreviation for an operation declaration and a proc, additional instances of the proc may be created dynamically by explicit send invocations. For example, suppose the programmer initially wants two instances of a process `foo`. This could be specified by a process declaration:

```
process foo(id := 1 to 2)
  # body of foo
end
```

Later, an additional instance of `foo` could be created by, for example, executing

```
send foo(17)
```

The value of `id` in the new instance will be 17.

7.3 Concurrent Invocation

The concurrent invocation statement provides another mechanism for creating processes dynamically. It consists of one or more concurrent commands separated by // delimiters:

> co *concurrent_command* // *concurrent_command* // ... oc

Each concurrent command consists of an invocation and optionally a block of postprocessing code. It thus has two forms:

> *invocation*   or   *invocation* -> *block*

The invocation part of a concurrent command is a call invocation, send invocation, or a simple assignment that calls a user-defined function. (SR does not provide a general cobegin statement in which concurrent commands can be arbitrary statement lists. Such a statement is difficult to implement because each statement list would need to be able to access the stack of the enclosing proc.)

A concurrent command can be preceded by an optional quantifier enclosed in parentheses to specify a collection of invocations, one for each combination of values of the bound variables. The scope of such a bound variable extends to the end of the concurrent command.

The next subsection describes the meaning and gives examples of concurrent invocation statements without postprocessing code. The subsection following that describes and illustrates postprocessing code.

Concurrent Invocation Without Postprocessing Code

As a simple example, consider the following concurrent invocation statement:

```
co p(3) // q() // a := r(x,y) oc
```

It consists of three invocations: one each of p, q, and r. The final invocation assigns the value that r returns to a.

Execution of a concurrent invocation statement first starts all invocations in parallel. A concurrent invocation statement with no postprocessing code terminates when all its invocations have completed. The above co therefore terminates when all three of its invocations have terminated.

As a more complete example, the following resource uses processes to compute the partial sums of integers from 1 up to the value of command-line argument n. The program initializes sum[1:n] so that sum[i] is equal to i. When the do loop terminates, each sum[i] is the sum of the integers from 1 to i. The program uses what is called a parallel prefix algorithm: Start with distance d equal to 1. Then add sum[i-d] to sum[i] in parallel (for all i greater than d), double d, and repeat until d is at least n. To avoid interference between the processes, an extra array, old, is used for temporary storage of a copy of sum.

```
resource partial_sums()
  var d := 1, n: int; getarg(1,n)
  var sum[n], old[n]: int

  procedure save(i: int)
      old[i] := sum[i]
  end
  procedure update(i: int)
      if i > d -> sum[i] +:= old[i-d] fi
  end
```

```
# initialize sum
fa i := 1 to n -> sum[i] := i af

# for all i, set sum[i] to 1 + ... + i
do d < n ->
    co (i := 1 to n) save(i) oc
    co (i := 1 to n) update(i) oc
    d +:= d     # double the distance
od

# print results
fa i := 1 to n -> write(i, sum[i]) af
end
```

Each iteration of the do loop uses two concurrent invocation statements. Each of these uses a quantifier to create n processes. The first group of processes executes save to copy old values of sum into old. The second group executes update to calculate new values for sum. Each of the concurrent invocation statements uses the bound variable i as an argument in its invocations. This is permitted since the scope of the quantifier variable extends through the concurrent command.

As another example, the following program implements a parallel version of the familiar quicksort algorithm:

```
resource quick()
  op sort(var a[1:*]: int)
  var n: int; getarg(1,n)
  var a[1:n]: int
  # read in data to be sorted; code not shown
  write("input:"); fa i := 1 to n -> write(a[i]) af
  sort(a)
  write("sorted:"); fa i := 1 to n -> write(a[i]) af

  proc sort(a)
    if ub(a) <= 1 -> return fi
    var pivot := a[1], lx := 2, rx := ub(a)
    do lx <= rx ->
        if a[lx] <= pivot -> lx++
        [] a[lx] > pivot -> a[lx] :=: a[rx]; rx--
        fi
    od
    a[rx] :=: a[1]
    co sort(a[1:rx-1]) // sort(a[lx:ub(a)]) oc
  end
end quick
```

The `sort` proc first partitions argument array `a` into two parts, `a[2:lx-1]` and `a[rx+1:ub(a)]`, based on the value of pivot element `a[1]`. It then swaps the pivot with the rightmost value in the left partition. Finally, `sort` uses a concurrent invocation statement to recursively sort each of the partitions in parallel.

Concurrent Invocation With Postprocessing Code

Execution of a concurrent invocation statement that has postprocessing code is slightly more complicated than one that does not have such code. Again, all invocations are first started in parallel. Then, as each invocation terminates, the corresponding postprocessing block is executed, if there is one. Postprocessing blocks are executed one at a time; they are *not* executed concurrently and thus can change variables without requiring mutual exclusion. Execution of `co` terminates when all postprocessing blocks have terminated or when some postprocessing block executes an exit statement.

As an example, consider the following program fragment:

```
cnt := 0
co (i := 1 to n st a[i] != 0) p(i) ->
    cnt++; write(cnt, i)
oc
```

It uses a quantifier to invoke `p` once for each value of `i` such that `a[i]` is non-zero. The postprocessing block counts the number of such invocations as they complete and outputs their indices. The use of the bound variable `i` in the postprocessing block is legal since the scope of the quantifier variables extends to the end of postprocessing block. Since the postprocessing blocks are executed one at a time, the update of `cnt` need not be protected by a critical section and the output will not be interleaved.

As another example, consider the following:

```
# read one copy of a replicated file,
# recording which response was received first
co (i := 1 to 4) fd[i].read(arguments) ->
    which_one := i; exit
oc
```

It uses a quantifier to initiate four invocations. When any of the invocations terminates, the postprocessing code records, in `which_one`, the index of that invocation and then exits without waiting for the other invocations to complete.

If a postprocessing block exits before all invocations have terminated, the outstanding invocations are not canceled; they will still be serviced, but the invoker will not wait for them to complete nor get back results. Thus the `co` in the above example waits for just one of the four invocations it initiates to complete. The other three will presumably complete sometime, but the invoker is in no way affected by their completion; indeed, the invoker may no longer exist.

A postprocessing block in a concurrent invocation statement can also contain a next statement. As in a for-all statement, execution of `next` within a postprocessing block causes execution of that postprocessing block to terminate; the enclosing `co` then delays until another invocation terminates, or the `co` terminates if all invocations have terminated.

7.4 Process Scheduling and Priorities

Processes in an SR program execute concurrently, at least conceptually. Consequently, statements that access shared variables may need to be protected by critical sections to insure they execute with mutual exclusion. This can be implemented using semaphores (see Chapter 8) or the input statement (see Chapter 11).

An SR program begins execution with one process that executes the top-level statements in the main resource. This process has priority zero. A process can set its priority to another integer value by calling the predefined function `setpriority`; it can determine its priority by calling `mypriority` (see Appendix C for details). When one process creates another, the new process inherits the priority of its creator. Thus, if no process in a program calls `setpriority`, all processes execute at the same priority, i.e., zero.

At all times, each processor executes one of the highest priority unblocked processes. Processes of equal priority are executed in round-robin order. If a process calls `setpriority` and lowers its priority, it will relinquish its processor to a higher-priority process, if there is one.

Exercises

7.1 Could the final code in the `mult` resource in Section 7.1 be written instead as part of `mult`'s initial code? Explain.

7.2 In the matrix multiplication code in Section 7.2, suppose the `send` in the for-all loop were replaced by `call`. Would the program still work as intended? Explain.

7.3 Write a concurrent invocation statement that polls N voters for yes or no votes and terminates when at least `N/2` responses have been received. Assume N is even.

7.4 Repeat the previous exercise, but terminate the concurrent invocation statement when a majority of identical responses have been received. Again assume N is even.

7.5   In the resource `partial_sums` in Section 7.3, consider replacing the two concurrent invocation statements by the single statement:

```
co (i := 1 to n) save(i) -> update(i) oc
```

Would the program still be correct? Explain. Conjecture as to whether it would run faster or slower than before.

7.6   In the resource `partial_sums` in Section 7.3, consider replacing the two concurrent invocation statements by the single statement:

```
co (i := 1 to n) save_and_update(i) oc
```

The proc `save_and_update` combines the actions of the two procs `save` and `update`. Would the program still be correct? Explain. Conjecture as to whether it would run faster or slower than before.

7.7   Trace the execution of the quicksort program in the `quick` resource (see Section 7.3) on input "3 4 2 5 0 1". How many processes are created? What is passed to and returned by each instance of `quick`?

7.8   Consider rewriting the concurrent invocation statement that uses `cnt` (see Section 7.3) with the for-all statement:

```
fa i := 1 to n st a[i] != 0 ->
    p(i); cnt++; write(cnt, i)
af
```

What differences, if any, are there between the executions of these two statements? Explain.

7.9   What differences, if any, are there between the executions of the following two statements?

```
co (i := 1 to n) send q(i) oc
fa i := 1 to n -> send q(i) af
```

Assume q is serviced by a proc.

7.10 What differences, if any, are there between the executions of the following two statements?

```
co (i := 1 to n) send q(i) -> write(i) oc
fa i := 1 to n -> send q(i); write(i) af
```

Assume q is serviced by a proc.

7.11 The eight-queens problem is concerned with placing eight queens on a chess board in such a way that none can attack another. One queen can attack another if they are in the same row or column or are on the same diagonal.

Write a parallel program to generate all 92 solutions to the eight-queens problem. (Hint: Use a recursive procedure to try queen placements and a second procedure to check whether a given placement is acceptable.)

7.12   The quadrature problem is to approximate the area under a curve, i.e., to approximate the integral of a function. Given is a continuous, non-negative function $f(x)$ and two endpoints l and r. The problem is to compute the area of the region bounded by $f(x)$, the x axis, and the vertical lines through l and r. The typical way to solve the problem is to subdivide the regions into a number of smaller ones, use something like a trapezoid to approximate the area of each smaller region, and then sum the areas of the smaller regions.

Write a recursive function that implements a parallel, adaptive solution to the quadrature problem. The function should have four arguments: two points a and b and two function values $f(a)$ and $f(b)$. It first computes the midpoint between a and b, then computes three areas: from a to m, m to b, and a to b. If the sum of the smaller two areas is within EPSILON of the larger, the function returns the area. Otherwise it recursively and in parallel computes the areas of the smaller regions. Assume EPSILON is a global value.

7.13   Gaussian elimination with partial pivoting is a method for reducing real matrix $m[1{:}n, 1{:}n]$ to upper-triangular form. It involves iterating across the columns of m and zeroing out the elements in the column below the diagonal element $m[d, d]$. This is done by performing the following three steps for each column. First, select a pivot element, which is the element in column d having the largest absolute value. Second, swap row d and the row containing the pivot element. Finally, for each row r below the new diagonal row, subtract a multiple of row d from row r. The multiple to use for row r is $m[r, d]/m[d, d]$; subtracting this multiple of row d has the effect of setting $m[r, d]$ to zero.

Write a program that implements the above algorithm. Use parallelism whenever possible. Assume every divisor is non-zero; i.e., assume the matrix is non-singular.

## CHAPTER 8

Semaphores

Semaphores are a low-level but efficient synchronization mechanism. They are used in SR programs to synchronize the activities of processes. For example, they can be used to implement mutually exclusive access to shared data.

A semaphore is a non-negative integer that is accessed by means of two special operations, P and V.* If s is a semaphore, V(s) increments the value of s, and P(s) delays its caller until s is positive and then decrements s. A V is used to signal the occurrence of an event, and a P is used to delay until an event has occurred.

This chapter describes how semaphores are declared and shows how they can be used. As mentioned in the introduction to Part II, SR's semaphores are actually an abbreviation of a particular form of message passing. Section 9.3 discusses this concept in detail.

8.1 Semaphore Declarations and Operations

A semaphore declaration contains a list of one or more semaphore definitions separated by commas:

> sem *sem_definition*, *sem_definition*, ...

Each semaphore definition specifies either a single semaphore or an array of

---

*Semaphores were invented by Dijkstra [1968a], who is Dutch. The operations P and V are mnemonics for the Dutch words *passeren* and *vrygeven*, which mean "to pass" and "to release," respectively.

semaphores and optionally gives the initial value(s) of the semaphore(s). A
semaphore definition has the following general form:

sem_id dimensions := *expr*

The dimensions and initialization clause are both optional. Dimensions are
specified as they are for other arrays (see Section 2.4). The value(s) of the
initialization expression must be non-negative since semaphores are non-
negative. The default initial value of each semaphore is zero.

The two standard semaphore operations, P and V, have the general forms

P (*sem_id subscripts*)
V (*sem_id subscripts*)

Subscripts are omitted for simple semaphores. For an array of semaphores,
the subscripts specify a specific element of the array; e.g., a V on the second
element of s[1:10] is written V(s[2]).

To illustrate one use of semaphores, consider the following instance of the
standard critical section problem. Suppose N processes share a resource
variable, e.g., a counter. Access to the counter is to be restricted to one
process at a time to ensure that it is updated atomically. An outline of an SR
solution follows:

```
resource CS()
  const N := 20    # number of processes
  var x := 0       # shared variable
  sem mutex := 1   # mutual exclusion for x
  process p(i := 1 to N)
    # non-critical section
      ...
    # critical section
    P(mutex)  # enter critical section
    x := x+1
    V(mutex)  # exit critical section
    # non-critical section
      ...
  end
end
```

The mutex semaphore is initialized to 1 so that only a single process at a time
can modify x.

Processes wait on semaphores in first-come, first-served order based on
the order in which they execute P operations. Thus waiting processes are
treated fairly: A process waiting on a semaphore will eventually be able to

proceed after it executes a P, assuming a sufficient number of Vs are executed on that semaphore.

As mentioned, SR supports arrays of semaphores. They are often used in managing collections of computing resources (e.g., printers or memory blocks) or in controlling families of processes. Typically one semaphore is associated with each computing resource or each process. For example, suppose that N processes are to enter their critical sections in circular order according to their process identities, i.e., first process 1, then process 2, and so on up to process N, with the cycle then repeating. This can be expressed as follows:

```
resource CS_Ordered()
  const N := 20  # number of processes
  sem mutex[N] := (1, [N-1] 0)
  process p(i := 1 to N)
    # non-critical section
    ...
    # critical section
    P(mutex[i])              # enter critical section
    ...                      # actual critical section
    V(mutex[(i mod N)+1])    # exit critical section
    # non-critical section
    ...
  end
end
```

The array of semaphores, mutex, has one element for each process p. It acts as a *split binary semaphore* [Andrews 1991]: At most one of the semaphores in the array is 1, the rest are 0. That corresponds to the desired property that only one process at a time can be in its critical section. The element of mutex that is 1 indicates which process has permission to enter its critical section. As process i leaves its critical section, it passes permission to enter the critical section to the next process by signaling mutex[(i mod N)+1].

8.2 Barrier Synchronization

A barrier is a common synchronization tool used in parallel algorithms. It is used in iterative algorithms—such as some techniques for finding solutions to partial differential equations—that require all tasks to complete one iteration before they begin the next iteration. (A barrier might also be used to synchronize stages within an iteration.) This is called barrier synchronization since the end of each iteration represents a barrier at which all processes have to arrive before any are allowed to pass. (See [Andrews 1991] for further discussion and specific applications.)

One possible structure for a parallel iterative algorithm is to employ several worker processes and one coordinator process. The workers solve parts of a problem in parallel. They interact with the coordinator to ensure the necessary barrier synchronization. This kind of algorithm can be programmed as follows:

(8.2)
```
resource barrier()
   const N := 20  # number of processes
   sem done := 0, continue[N] := ([N] 0)
   # declaration of variables shared by workers
   process worker(i := 1 to N)
     do true ->
       # code to implement one iteration of task i
       V(done)
       P(continue[i])
     od
   end
   process coordinator
     do true ->
       fa w := 1 to N -> P(done) af
       fa w := 1 to N -> V(continue[w]) af
     od
   end
end
```

Each worker first performs some action; typically the action involves accessing part of an array determined by the process's subscript i. Then each worker executes a V and a P, in that order. The V signals the coordinator that the worker has finished its iteration; the P delays the worker until the coordinator informs it that all other workers have completed their iterations. The coordinator consists of two for-all loops. The first loop waits for each worker to signal that it is done. The second loop signals each worker that it can continue.

The above implementation of barrier synchronization employs an extra coordinator process and has execution time that is linear in the number of workers. It is more efficient to use a symmetric barrier with logarithmic execution time (see [Andrews 1991] and Exercise 8.6).

Semaphores can also be declared in the body or spec of a global. Within the body of a global, semaphores are used in the same way as within a resource's body—to provide synchronization for processes in the global's body. However, semaphores declared in the spec of a global are used slightly differently. In that role, they provide synchronization for processes executing inside or outside the global, possibly in many different resources. For example, if a global's spec declares shared variables, it might also declare a semaphore that processes would use to ensure exclusive access to the shared variables.

As an example, we can rewrite the code in the above `barrier` resource as follows to put the semaphores and coordinator process in a global. The spec of the global declares the semaphores; its body contains the coordinator process.

```
global barrier
   const N := 20  # number of processes
   sem continue[N] := ([N] 0)
   sem done := 0
body barrier
   process c
     do true ->
        fa w := 1 to N -> P(done) af
        fa w := 1 to N -> V(continue[w]) af
     od
   end
end
```

The main resource now contains just the worker processes:

```
resource workers()
   import barrier
   # declarations of variables shared by workers
   process worker(i := 1 to N)
     do true ->
        # code to implement one iteration of task i
        V(done)
        P(continue[i])
     od
   end
end
```

The advantage of using a global is that it separates the details of the coordinator process from the details of the workers. In fact, the workers could themselves be in different resources. The execution overhead of barrier synchronization is not affected by using a global.

Exercises

8.1   Consider the code in the `barrier` resource (see the start of Section 8.2). Can the array of semaphores, `continue[N]`, be replaced by a single semaphore? Explain.

8.2 Consider the code in the `barrier` resource (see the start of Section 8.2). Can the `done` semaphore be replaced by an array of N semaphores, with one element for each worker? Explain.

8.3 Eliminate the coordinator process from the code in the `barrier` resource (see the start of Section 8.2) by having the last worker that arrives at the barrier signal the other workers. Hint: Use a counter protected by a critical section.

8.4 In the global `barrier` (see the end of Section 8.2), why does the body contain a process? What would happen if the process code were written as initial code? Could the body of `barrier` be modified so that it did not use a process?

8.5 Rewrite the code in the global `barrier` and resource `workers` (see the end of Section 8.2) to hide all details about the implementation of the barrier in the body of the global. The global should export a single operation that the workers call when they arrive at the barrier. The semaphores are to be declared in the body of the global and hence are not to be used directly by the workers.

8.6 A *dissemination barrier* [Hensgen et al. 1988] is much more efficient than one implemented using a coordinator process. It consists of a series of stages in which each worker interacts with two others. Workers first interact with others that are distance 1 away, then distance 2 away, then distance 4 away, and so on. If there are n workers, the number of stages is the (ceiling of the) logarithm of n.

For example, suppose there are eight workers. In the first stage, worker 1 signals worker 2 then waits for worker 8, worker 2 signals worker 3 then waits for worker 1, and so on. In the second stage, worker 1 signals worker 3 then waits for worker 7, worker 2 signals worker 4 then waits for worker 8, and so on. In the third stage, worker 1 signals worker 5 and waits for worker 5, worker 2 signals worker 6 and waits for worker 6, and so on. At the end of the third stage, the workers can proceed past the barrier since each will know that all others have arrived.

Implement a dissemination barrier for 20 processes; use semaphores for synchronization. Compare its performance to either of the coordinator barriers in Section 8.2.

## CHAPTER 9

Asynchronous Message Passing

Asynchronous message passing is higher-level and more powerful than semaphores. As its name implies, it allows processes to communicate as well as synchronize by using operations to exchange messages.

Message passing in SR is accomplished by having processes send messages to and receive messages from operations. In this role, operations serve as queues that hold messages for receivers. The sender of a message continues immediately after the message has been sent. The receiver of a message delays until there is a message on the queue and then removes one. Thus the send statement is asynchronous (non-blocking) and the receive statement is synchronous (blocking).

This chapter first describes this new use of operations as message queues. We then show how the semaphore primitives described in the previous chapter are actually abbreviations for a specific form of asynchronous message passing. We also describe the use of data-containing semaphores, which are a generalization of standard semaphores. Finally, we describe how multiple processes can receive messages from the same operation and discuss the additional flexibility that provides.

SR's receive statement is actually just an abbreviation for a more general mechanism for receiving messages. That more general mechanism—the input statement—is discussed in Chapter 11.

9.1 Operations as Message Queues

As we saw in Chapters 4 and 7, operations can be implemented (serviced) by procs. In this case an operation definition specifies the proc's parameterization. Each invocation of the operation results in a new instance of the proc's code being executed to service the invocation. Specifically, a call invocation of a proc is like a procedure call (Chapter 4); a send invocation of a proc results in a new process being created (Chapter 7).

An alternative role of an operation is to define a message queue. In this role the operation has no corresponding proc. Instead, invocations of the operation (i.e., messages) are serviced by receive statements within one or more processes in the scope of the declaration of the operation. A receive statement removes an invocation from the message queue; the executing process delays if no invocation is present.

A send invocation of an operation serviced by receive statements causes the invocation to be appended to the message queue. The invoker continues immediately after the invocation has been sent. Note that this is consistent with send invocations to procs being asynchronous. Call invocations to operations serviced by receive statements are also allowed; this provides a synchronous form of message passing, which we discuss in Chapter 11.

A receive statement names an operation and gives a list of zero or more variables separated by commas. It has the following general form:

receive *op_id subscripts* (*variable*, *variable*, ...)

The subscripts are omitted for simple operations. They are used for arrays of operations and have the same form as used for subscripting other arrays. A receive statement specifies one variable for each parameter in the operation's definition; it must match the corresponding parameter's type.

As mentioned earlier, execution of receive removes an invocation from the message queue associated with the operation. The values of the arguments of that invocation are assigned to the variables in the receive statement. (These variables must already have been declared in the current scope.)

As an example, consider a three-process system. Each of two processes sends an ordered stream of messages to the third, which outputs the merge of the two streams. For simplicity, we assume that the messages contain just integers and that the end of each stream is indicated by a value greater than any possible value in the stream. Following is an outline of a solution:

```
resource stream_merge()
  const EOS := high(int)   # end of stream marker
  op stream1(x: int), stream2(x: int)
  process one
    . . .
    send stream1(y)
    . . .
    send stream1(EOS)
  end
```

```
      process two
         ...
        send stream2(y)
         ...
        send stream2(EOS)
      end
      process merge
        var v1, v2: int
        receive stream1(v1); receive stream2(v2)
        do v1 < EOS or v2 < EOS ->
          if v1 <= v2 -> write(v1); receive stream1(v1)
          [] v2 <= v1 -> write(v2); receive stream2(v2)
          fi
        od
        write(EOS)
      end
    end
```

This program uses two operations, `stream1` and `stream2`. The first process sends its numbers, including the end of stream marker `EOS`, to `stream1`, the second sends to `stream2`. The `merge` process first gets a number from each stream. It executes the body of the loop as long as one of the two numbers is not `EOS`. The if statement compares the two numbers, outputs the smaller, and receives the next number in the stream from which the smaller number came. If one stream "dries up" before the other, `v1` or `v2` will be `EOS`. Since `EOS` is larger than any other number in the stream, numbers from the non-dry stream will be consumed until it too is dry. The loop terminates when both streams have been entirely consumed.

9.2 Simple Client-Server Models

As further examples of asynchronous message passing, we now consider how to program several simple client-server models. A server is a process that repeatedly handles requests from client processes. For example, a disk server might read information from a disk; its clients might pass it requests for disk blocks and then wait for results.

We first consider the case of one client process and one server process. An outline of possible interactions between client and server is shown in resource `cs1` below. The processes share two operations: `request` and `results`. The client sends to the `request` operation and waits for results to be returned by receiving from the `results` operation; between the send and receive, the client can perform other work. The server waits for a request, performs the requested action, and sends the results back.

```
resource cs1()
  op request(...), results(...)
  process client
      ...
    send request(...)
    # possibly perform some other work
    receive results(...)
      ...
  end
  process server
    do true ->
      receive request(...)
      # handle request
      send results(...)
    od
  end
end
```

Unfortunately, the above code does not generalize directly if more than one client process is present. Specifically, one client can obtain the results intended for the other because the results operation would be shared by both of them. One way to generalize the code is to use an array of result operations, one for each client process. An outline of that kind of solution follows:

```
resource cs2()
  const N := 20   # number of client processes
  op request(id: int; ...), results[N](...)
  process client(i := 1 to N)
      ...
    send request(i, ...)
    # possibly perform some other work
    receive results[i](...)
      ...
  end
  process server
    do true ->
      receive request(id, ...)
      # handle request
      send results[id](...)
    od
  end
end
```

Here each client process passes its identity as part of its request message.
The identity is used by the server to send the results of a request back to the
client that initiated that request. Each client process receives from the one
element of the `results` operation that corresponds to its identity.

An obvious drawback of the code in resource `cs2` is that it requires the
number of clients to be known in advance. That requirement is not reasonable in many situations, such as when the server process is in a global
library. The `results` array in `cs2` provides a simple means to associate an
operation with each client process. Another way to achieve the same effect is
to declare an operation local to each client process:

```
resource cs3()
  optype results_type = (...)
  op request(results_cap: cap results_type; ...)
  const N := 20   # number of client processes
  process client(i := 1 to N)
    op results: results_type

      ...
    send request(results,...)
    # possibly perform some other work
    receive results(...)
      ...
  end
  process server
    do true ->
      var results_cap: cap results_type
      receive request(results_cap, ...)
      # handle request
      send results_cap(...)
    od
  end
end
```

Operation type `results_type` specifies the parameterization of result
messages. Each client declares a local operation, `results`, whose parameterization is given by `results_type`. It passes a capability for that operation
as the first parameter to `request`. The server receives that capability in
local variable `results_cap` and uses it to send back results to the operation
to which the capability points.

An important advantage of the above structure is that it permits any
client process to interact with the server. All the process needs is a results
operation to pass to the server. Clients can even be in different resources
than the server—even different virtual machines—as long as the `request`
operation is made visible by declaring it in the spec of the server resource.

Another variant of the client-server model is to have multiple servers. Consider the case where a new server is created for each client's request. The following outlines a solution:

```
resource cs4()
  optype results_type = (...)
  op request(results_cap: cap results_type; ...)
  const N := 20  # number of client processes
  process client(i := 1 to N)
    op results: results_type
    ...
    send request(results,...)
    # possibly perform some other work
    receive results(...)
    ...
  end
  proc request(results_cap, ...)
    # handle request
    send results_cap(...)
  end
end
```

The key difference between this code and that in resource cs3 is that the request operation is now serviced by a proc. Thus a new server process is created for each invocation of request. The parameterization of request is unchanged. Each server process uses the capability technique from cs3 to send results back to its client.

It is worth emphasizing that the only difference between resources cs3 and cs4 is the way the request operation is serviced. The client processes execute exactly the same code. This is significant since clients can invoke request without concerning themselves with how it is serviced—whether by a proc or by a receive statement.

9.3 Semaphores Revisited

SR's semaphores and P and V statements, as described in Chapter 8, are actually just abbreviations for operations and send and receive statements. Specifically, a semaphore is a parameterless operation (with the send restriction). A V on a semaphore corresponds to a send to the operation; a P corresponds to a receive on the operation. Initialization of the semaphore to *expr* corresponds to a for-all loop that sends to the operation *expr* times.

The mapping of semaphore primitives to their general unabbreviated forms is summarized in Table 9.1. A new variable, e, is introduced in the

Semaphore Primitive	*Corresponding Message Passing Primitive*
`sem s`	`op s() {send}`
`P(s)`	`receive s()`
`V(s)`	`send s()`
`sem s := ` *expr*	`op s() {send}; var e := ` *expr*
	`fa i := 1 to e -> send s() af`

Table 9.1. Correspondence between semaphores and message passing.

case where the semaphore declaration contains an initialization expression. Its use ensures that *expr* is evaluated just once.

To illustrate, recall the solution to the critical section problem given in resource `CS` in Section 8.1. It can be written equivalently using asynchronous message passing as follows:

```
resource CS()
   const N := 20        # number of processes
   op mutex() {send}  # mutual exclusion for x
   send mutex()        # initialize mutex
   var x := 0          # shared variable
   process p(i := 1 to N)
     # non-critical section
       ...
     # critical section
     receive mutex()  # enter critical section
     x := x+1
     send mutex()      # exit critical section
     # non-critical section
       ...
   end
end
```

The initialization of `mutex` consists of a single send, which places one message on `mutex`'s message queue. When a process attempts to enter its critical section, it attempts to remove an invocation from the message queue. If successful, it continues—`mutex`'s message queue remains empty until that process completes its critical section and sends an invocation to `mutex`. If a process is unsuccessful in its attempt to remove an invocation, it delays until such an invocation arrives and the process is the first process waiting for the invocation. (As with semaphores, processes access message queues in first-come, first-served order.) The message queue of `mutex` will contain at most one invocation; that corresponds to `mutex`'s value as a semaphore being at most one.

Using semaphores rather than the corresponding message passing primitives makes programs somewhat more concise and readable. However, in our implementation of SR, the two classes of mechanisms are equally efficient, and both are more efficient than general message passing. In particular, our implementation optimizes parameterless operations used as shown in Table 9.1 into the equivalent semaphore primitive.

9.4 Data-Containing Semaphores

A data-containing semaphore is conceptually a semaphore that contains data as well as a synchronization signal. It is, in essence, an unbounded buffer of messages that have been produced and not yet consumed. Such a semaphore is represented by an operation declared within a resource or a global. The data is passed as a parameter of the operation. Processes use send and receive statements to append data to or remove data from the operation's message queue; synchronization between processes accessing the queue is implicit through their use of send and receive statements.

A data-containing semaphore can be used, for example, to provide a pool of buffers shared by a group of processes. Consider the following code outline:

```
resource main()
  op pool(index: int)
  const B := 20          # number of buffers
  const N := 10          # number of processes
  var buffer[1:B]: T   # T is the buffer type
  fa i := 1 to B -> send pool(i) af
  process p(i := 1 to N)
    ...
    receive pool(x)     # request a buffer
    # use buffer[x]
    send pool(x)        # release the buffer
    ...
  end
end
```

Operation `pool` represents the buffer pool. The for-all loop in the initial code puts N invocations on `pool`'s message queue; each invocation contains the index of a free buffer. As shown in the above code, a process obtains a buffer by receiving the index of a free buffer from `pool`. When done with the buffer, a process returns it to the buffer pool by sending the index to `pool`. When used in this way, operation `pool` is a bounded buffer. In general, however, such an operation can contain an unbounded number of messages.

The advantage of using an operation's message queue to represent a buffer pool is that it saves the programmer from having to write code that explicitly implements a list of free buffers and code that synchronizes access to the list. The disadvantage is that such use of an operation queue is somewhat less efficient [Olsson 1990].

9.5 Shared Operations

Regular semaphores and data-containing semaphores are both examples of operations that are shared by more than one process. That is, more than one process can receive invocations from the operation's message queue. Shared operations are declared at the top level within a resource or global as opposed to being declared within processes as in resource `cs3` (see Section 9.2).

Shared operations are almost a necessity given that multiple instances of a process can service the same resource operation. The code in resource `CS` (see Section 9.3), for example, demonstrates this point: an invocation of `mutex` can be received by any instance of process `p`. The code in resource `cs2` (see Section 9.2) also contains a shared operation, `results`. By convention, however, each client process accesses only its own element of that operation array. Thus, *in effect*, the array elements are not shared in that code. In general, though, even array elements can be shared.

Another useful application of shared operations is for server work queues. In particular, a shared operation can be used to permit multiple servers to service the same work queue. Clients request service by invoking a shared operation. Server processes wait for invocations of the shared operation; which server actually receives and services a particular invocation is transparent to the clients. The shared operation may be declared at the top level of a resource or in a global. If the operation is declared in a resource, the server processes must be located within the same resource instance. If the operation is declared in a global `g`, the server processes may be located in `g` or in any resource or global that imports `g`.

As an example of using shared operations for a server work queue, consider the adaptive quadrature method for finding the area under a curve (i.e., a function). Given are a continuous, non-negative function `f(x)` and two values `l` and `r`, with `l < r`. The problem is to compute the area bounded by `f(x)`, the `x` axis, and the vertical lines through `l` and `r`. This corresponds to approximating the integral of `f(x)` from `l` to `r`. The following resource outlines a solution. It employs a shared operation, `bag`, which contains a bag of tasks. Each task represents a sub-interval over which the integral of `f` is to be approximated.

```
# Adaptive quadrature problem.
resource main()
  op bag(a, b, fofa, fofb: real)
  op result(area: real)
  var area: real := 0.0

  procedure f(x: real) returns fx: real
    ...
  end

  process administrator
    var l, r, part: real
    # initialize l and r to appropriate values
    send bag(l, r, f(l), f(r))
    do true ->
      receive result(part); area +:= part
    od
  end

  const N := 20   # number of worker processes
  process worker(i := 1 to N)
    var a, b, m, fofa, fofb, fofm: real
    var larea, rarea, tarea, diff: real
    do true ->
      receive bag(a, b, fofa, fofb)
      m := (a+b)/2; fofm := f(m)
      # compute larea, rarea, and tarea
      # using trapezoidal rule
      diff := tarea - (larea + rarea)
      if ... /* diff small enough */ ->
          send result(larea + rarea)
      [] ... /* diff too large */ ->
          send bag(a, m, fofa, fofm)
          send bag(m, b, fofm, fofb)
      fi
    od
  end

  final  # once program terminates, print results
    write("area is:", area)
  end
end
```

Initially, the administrator places in the bag one task corresponding to the entire problem to be solved. Multiple worker processes take tasks from the bag and service them, often generating two new tasks—corresponding to subproblems—that are put into the bag. Specifically, a worker takes a task—representing the interval [a, b]—from the bag, computes its midpoint m, and calculates three areas. The three areas are those of the three trapezoids defined by the points a, m, and b and the value of f at these three points. The worker then compares the area of the larger trapezoid with the sum of the areas of the two smaller ones. If these are sufficiently close, the sum of the areas of the smaller trapezoids is taken as an acceptable approximation of the area under f, and the worker sends it to the administrator using operation `result`. Otherwise, the worker adds to the bag the two subproblems of computing the area from a to m and from m to b.

After initializing the bag of tasks, the administrator repeatedly receives results, which are parts of the total area. It adds these to `area`. The computation terminates (in deadlock) when all message queues are empty and all processes are blocked; i.e., all tasks have been processed by workers, and all results have been received by the administrator. At this point the final code is executed. Variable `area` is declared as a resource variable, so it is accessible to both the administrator process and the final code.

An especially interesting aspect of the above algorithm is that it permits any number of worker processes! If there is only one, the algorithm is essentially an iterative, sequential algorithm. If there are more workers, subproblems can be solved in parallel. Thus the number of workers can be tuned to match the hardware on which the algorithm executes.

Another interesting aspect of the algorithm is that it uses final code to print the result. For this problem and many similar ones, it would be difficult for the processes themselves to determine when all tasks had been computed. Here the administrator would have to keep track of which parts of the area had been computed. (It is not sufficient for the administrator to wait for the bag to be empty because a worker may be about to put two new tasks in it.) Letting the SR implementation detect termination, and using final code to print the result, yields a much simpler algorithm.

Exercises

9.1   Rewrite the code in `stream_merge` (see Section 9.1) so `EOS` can be an arbitrary integer value that is not necessarily larger than the other values in the stream.

9.2   Rewrite the code in `stream_merge` (see Section 9.1) so it uses a family of two processes to represent the processes that produce the streams and an array of operations to represent the streams.

9.3   Generalize the previous exercise to have N processes producing streams.

9.4   Rewrite the code in resource `cs4` (see Section 9.2) so it uses arrays of result operations as in resource `cs2`.

9.5   What differences, if any, are there between the executions of the following two statements?

```
co (i := 1 to n) send q(i) oc
fa i := 1 to n -> send q(i) af
```

Assume q is serviced by receive statements executed by another process.

9.6   Recode the solution to the adaptive quadrature problem (see Section 9.5) so it uses a global for declaring `bag` and `result` and separate resources for the administrator and workers.

9.7   Recode the solution to the adaptive quadrature problem (see Section 9.5) without using final code. Hint: Have the administrator record what work has been finished and what remains to be done.

9.8   Copy the outline for the adaptive quadrature program (see Section 9.5) into a file. Fill in the details for a specific function `f` and for the body of the worker processes. Also change the number of workers, `N`, to a command-line argument.

Execute your program using different numbers of workers. How does the performance differ?

9.9   Write a program that implements the quicksort method of sorting using a shared bag of tasks. The tasks are slices of the data that need to be sorted. The administrator should put the initial data in the bag. A worker should remove a task, partition it into smaller tasks and put them back in the bag. If a task is small enough, say eight data elements, a worker should instead sort the data and send it to the administrator.

Execute your program using different input data and different numbers of workers. How does the performance differ?

9.10 Develop a distributed program to implement a compare/exchange sorting algorithm. Use `W` worker processes laid out in a line; each worker should communicate only with its one or two neighbors. If there are `N` items to sort, initially each worker should be given `N/W` items. Each worker should sort its items, exchange high and low elements with its neighbors, and repeat until all `N` items are sorted.

(a) Execute your program using different input data and different numbers of workers. How does the performance differ?

(b) Compare the performance of this program to your program for Exercise 9.9.

9.11 Develop a program to generate prime numbers using a shared bag of tasks. The tasks are odd numbers that should be checked for primality. The workers check different candidates. Each worker should have a local table of primes that it uses to check candidates. When a worker finds a new prime, it should send it to all the other workers.

Execute your program for different ranges of primes and different numbers of workers. How does the performance differ?

## CHAPTER 10

Remote Procedure Call

Remote procedure call (RPC) is another mechanism that is used in many applications. Two processes are involved: the process doing the call (the invoker or client) and the process created to service the call (the server). These processes are typically in different resources and might even be on different virtual or physical machines. The invoking process waits for results to be returned from the call. Thus remote procedure call is synchronous from the client's perspective.

Remote procedure call is accomplished in SR through yet another use of operations. To initiate a remote procedure call, the invoking process calls an operation. The operation is one that is serviced by a proc. A call invocation of a remote proc results in a process being created to service the invocation. A remote procedure call resembles a sequential procedure call both syntactically and semantically. The fact that the proc that services a call might be located on a different virtual or physical machine is transparent to the caller. (However, a remote procedure call takes longer than a local, sequential procedure call.)

This chapter first presents the SR mechanisms for remote procedure call. We then discuss the equivalence between remote procedure call primitives and send and receive primitives. We also describe three statements—return, reply, and forward—that can be used with remote procedure call to obtain additional flexibility. (The use of these statements with rendezvous is discussed in Chapter 11.)

10.1 Mechanisms for Remote Procedure Call

The mechanisms for remote procedure call are operation declarations, call invocations, and procs. Chapter 4 introduced these mechanisms and gave examples of how they are used; Chapter 7 discussed call invocations to procs from concurrent invocation statements. Recall, also, that a procedure is merely an abbreviation for an operation declaration and a proc that implements the operation.

In all cases the semantics of a call invocation to a proc is that a new process is created to execute the proc's code for the invocation. After initiating the call, the invoking process delays until the invoked process returns results to it. This semantics can often be implemented as a conventional procedure call (see below), but at least conceptually a new process is created to service each call.

This view of call invocations is useful since the invoked proc can be located in another resource, which might be located on another virtual or physical machine. (Chapter 12 describes virtual machines and how they are created and placed on physical machines.) This view also covers purely sequential procedure calls, such as those described in Part I. It is worth noting that process creation is considerably more costly than executing a standard sequential procedure call. Consequently the current SR implementation optimizes many call invocations of procs so they use a less expensive form of procedure call. See Appendix E for details.

To illustrate remote procedure call, recall the stack example in Chapter 5. Suppose we have a `Stack` resource identical to that in Section 5.1:

```
resource Stack
  type result = enum(OK, OVERFLOW, UNDERFLOW)
  op push(item: int) returns r: result
  op pop(res item: int) returns r: result
body Stack(size: int)
  var store[1:size]: int, top: int := 0
  proc push(item) returns r
    if top<size -> store[++top] := item; r := OK
    [] top=size -> r := OVERFLOW
    fi
  end
  proc pop(item) returns r
    if top>0 -> item := store[top--]; r := OK
    [] top=0 -> r := UNDERFLOW
    fi
  end
end Stack
```

Suppose we also have a `Stack_User` resource identical to that in Section 5.5:

```
resource Stack_User()
  import Stack
  var x: Stack.result
  var s1, s2: cap Stack
  var y: int
  s1 := create Stack(10); s2 := create Stack(20)
   ...
  s1.push(4); s1.push(37); s2.push(98)
  if (x := s1.pop(y)) != OK -> ... fi
  if (x := s2.pop(y)) != OK -> ... fi
   ...
end
```

As before, the invocations of `push` and `pop` from `Stack_User` are call invocations to operations serviced as procs in a different resource, `Stack`. As coded above, the instances of `Stack` created by `Stack_User` will be located on the same virtual machine as `Stack_User`. Hence the calls of `push` and `pop` will be local. However, the instances of `Stack` could be placed on one or two different virtual machines (see Chapter 12). In that case the calls would be remote. The syntax and semantics of the calls are the same; it is only the implementation, and consequently the performance, that is different.

As mentioned earlier, each call invocation of a proc results in a new process, at least conceptually. Suppose, for example, that `Stack_User` contains several processes, each of which invokes s1's and s2's `push` and `pop` operations. Each invocation of `push` and `pop` causes a new process to be created to execute the corresponding code. That can lead to more than one process manipulating the shared stack variables at the same time: Two processes, each executing on behalf of an invocation of `push`, can overflow the array, despite the explicit testing.

To avoid problems of accessing shared data, processes need to synchronize. In the `Stack` resource, a semaphore can be used to allow at most one process at a time to execute either `push` or `pop`. In the next chapter, we will see another way to solve this problem using a process and an input statement.

10.2   Equivalence to Send/Receive Pairs

A (remote) procedure call can be written equivalently as a send to a proc to create the process plus a receive to get back results when the process has completed. Consider, for example, the following simple code outline:

```
op p(val x: int; var y: int; res z: int)
process q
  var a, b, c: int
  . . .
  call p(a, b, c)
end
proc p(x, y, z)
  z := x+4; y -:= 10
end
```

The above code can be written equivalently as follows:

```
op p(x, y: int), r(y, z: int)
process q
  var a, b, c: int
  . . .
  send p(a, b)
  receive r(b, c)
end
proc p(x, y)
  var z: int
  z := x+4; y -:= 10
  send r(y, z)
end
```

The operation p has been replaced by a new version of p and a new results
operation, r. The call to the proc has been replaced by a send/receive pair.
The send passes the value and variable parameters to p; the receive gets the
variable and result parameters back from p.

   The above code works as long as only one process is invoking p. However,
if more than one process invokes p, each needs its own local results operation.
For this, we can use local operations and capabilities, as we did in resource
cs4 in Section 9.2. For example, suppose q is now a family of processes, each
of which invokes p:

```
op p(val x: int; var y: int; res z: int)
process q(i := 1 to ...)
  var a, b, c: int
  . . .
  call p(a, b, c)
end
proc p(x, y, z)
  z := x+4; y -:= 10
end
```

This code can be written equivalently as follows:

```
op p(x, y: int; rcap: cap(y, z: int))
process q(i := 1 to ...)
  var a, b, c: int
   ...
  op r(y, z: int)
  send p(a, b, r)
  receive r(b, c)
end
proc p(x, y, rcap)
  var z: int
  z := x+4; y -:= 10
  send rcap(y, z)
end
```

Here the operation p has been replaced by a new version; the third argument is a capability for an operation that is used to return the two results. Each invoking process now declares a local operation, r. Again the call to the proc has been replaced by a send/receive pair. A sending process passes the capability for its r to p; p sends results back to that operation.

The structure of the above code is very similar to what we saw earlier in the client-server code in resource cs4 (see Section 9.2). In fact, that code can be rewritten to use a call invocation instead of a send/receive pair (see Exercise 10.2). Using a call invocation, though, precludes clients from performing other work while waiting for the server to give back results.

In general, a call invocation provides a cleaner interface than does a send/receive pair. In particular, the passing of results back to the invoker is an implicit part of a call invocation. Using a send/receive pair, on the other hand, requires declaring a local operation to which results get sent and passing a capability for that operation. Using a call invocation also allows invocations of value-returning operations within expressions. However, send/receive pairs are useful when a client wants to do some work between initiating a request for service and picking up results from that request.

10.3 Return, Reply, and Forward Statements

The return, reply, and forward statements provide additional flexibility in handling remote procedure calls. They appear in the body of a proc and alter the way results are passed back to the invoking process. They can also be used, with similar meanings, as part of the rendezvous mechanism, as discussed later in Chapter 11.

Return

We have already seen the return statement in the context of sequential procedures and procs (see Chapter 4). Its meaning there is consistent with its more general meaning, which we give here.

Recall from Section 10.1 the view of a call invocation to a proc: it causes a new process to be created to service the invocation. A return statement, then, terminates both the call invocation and the process that executes the return. Any results of the invocation—variable and result parameters and the return value—are returned to the invoker.

Sometimes it is useful to allow a proc to be invoked by either call or send. For example, the proc might update a display screen. In some cases invoking processes will want to wait for the update to complete; in others they will not. Such a proc might execute a return statement. If the proc was invoked by send, the return statement just terminates the process that executes the return. Since a send invocation terminates immediately after its parameters are sent to the proc, any results from the proc are not actually returned.

Reply

The reply statement is used by a proc to continue execution after servicing an invocation of the proc. It has the form

```
reply
```

Like a return statement, a reply statement terminates the invocation being serviced by the enclosing proc, if it was called. However, a process that executes a reply statement continues executing with the statement following the reply. Such a process may continue to reference the formals until it leaves their scope; however, no subsequent change to formal parameters or to the return value is reflected back to the caller. A reply to a send invocation has no effect; a subsequent reply to an invocation for which a reply has already been executed also has no effect.

The reply statement may appear in top-level initialization code in a resource or global. Such code is executed by an implicitly created initialization process (see Appendix E for details). If that process executes `reply`, then resource or global creation completes, and the creator and initialization process execute concurrently. The final code in a resource or global is also executed by an implicitly created finalization process. A `reply` executed by that process is ignored.

As a simple example of reply, consider the code outline below. The reply statement in `f` terminates the invocation from `p`. At that point, the return value, `80`, is copied back and assigned to `z`, and process `p` continues execution with its next statement. The process executing `f` continues execution, too, with the statements following `reply`. It modifies the value of `y` and then terminates. That modification has no effect on the caller; in particular, it does not change `z`.

```
resource fun()
  op f(x: int) returns y: int
  process p
    ...; z := f(10); ...
  end
  proc f(x) returns y
    y := x*8
    reply
    y := 0
  end
end
```

The following more realistic example of a reply also demonstrates one of its common uses—programming what is called *conversational continuity*. A client process creates a server process and wishes to carry out a private conversation with it, i.e., send further requests for work to it. This interaction can be accomplished by having the server process execute `reply`, passing back a capability (or capabilities) for local operations. The following code outline illustrates this technique:

```
resource conversation()
  op server(n: int) returns c: cap (s: string[10])
  process client(i := 1 to ...)
    var t[20]: string[10]
      ...
    var c: cap (s: string[10])
    c := server(20)
    fa i := 1 to 20 -> send c(t[i]) af
  end
  proc server(n) returns c
    op line(s: string[10])
    c := line
    reply   # pass back capability for line
    fa i := 1 to n ->
      var s: string[10]
      receive line(s)
      # do something with s, e.g., print it
    af
  end
end
```

Here a client process creates a server process, passing it n, the number of lines that the client will later send it. The server first assigns a capability for its local operation, line, and returns that to its client by executing a reply. The reply allows both the client and the server to continue execution. The client sends n messages to its server; the server receives n messages from its client. The use of a local operation here ensures that only a server's client can send it messages.

A communication structure similar to the one used above is employed in the following example to implement a parallel sorting algorithm. Sorting is performed by an array of worker processes connected in a pipeline fashion. Each worker keeps the smallest value it sees, and passes all others on to the next worker. For n input values, a total of n workers are eventually executing. The first worker sees all n input values; the last sees just one value. After seeing all the values it will receive, each worker passes back the smallest value it saw.

```
resource pipeline_sort()
  op print_array(a[1:*]: int)
  op sort(var a[1:*]: int)
  op result(pos, value: int) {send}   # results
  optype pipe(value: int) {send}       # values to sort
  op worker(m: int) returns p: cap pipe {call}

  process main_routine
    var n: int
    writes("number of integers? "); read(n)
    var nums[1:n]: int
    write("input integers, separated by white space")
    fa i := 1 to n -> read(nums[i]) af
    write("original numbers")
    print_array(nums)
    sort(nums)
    write("sorted numbers")
    print_array(nums)
  end

  # Print elements of array a
  proc print_array(a)
    fa i := 1 to ub(a) -> write(a[i]) af
  end

  # Sort array a into non-decreasing order
  proc sort(a)
    if ub(a) = 0 -> return fi
    var first_worker: cap pipe
```

```
        # Call worker; get back a capability for its
        # pipe operation; use the pipe to send all values
        # in a to the worker.
        first_worker := worker(ub(a))
        fa i := 1 to ub(a) ->
          send first_worker(a[i])
        af
        # Gather the results into the right places in a
        fa i := 1 to ub(a) ->
          var pos, value: int
          receive result(pos, value); a[pos] := value
        af
    end

    # Worker receives m integers on mypipe from its
    # predecessor.  It keeps smallest and sends
    # others on to the next worker.  After seeing all
    # m integers, worker sends smallest to sort,
    # together with the position (m) in array a in
    # which smallest is to be placed.
    proc worker(m) returns p
      var smallest: int     # the smallest seen so far
      op mypipe: pipe
      p := mypipe
      reply  # invoker now has a capability for mypipe
      receive mypipe(smallest)
      if m > 1 ->
        # create next instance of worker
        var next_worker: cap pipe # pipe to next worker
        next_worker := worker(m-1)
        fa i := m-1 downto 1 ->
          var candidate: int
          receive mypipe(candidate)
          # save new value if it is smallest
          # so far; send other values on
          if candidate < smallest ->
            candidate :=: smallest
          fi
          send next_worker(candidate)
        af
      fi
      send result(m, smallest)  # send smallest to sort
    end
  end pipeline_sort
```

Each worker, other than the last one, creates the next worker in the pipeline. A worker uses a reply statement to pass a capability for its `mypipe` operation back to its invoker. The first worker passes the capability back to the process executing `sort`; each other worker passes it back to the previous worker.

Above, the worker processes are created dynamically, so exactly as many as are required (n) are created. This necessitates the use of local operations (`mypipe`) and capabilities for these operations. Exercise 10.8 explores a more static version of this problem.

Forward

The forward statement defers replying to a called invocation and instead passes on this responsibility. The fact that an invocation was forwarded is transparent to the original invoker.

The forward statement names an operation and contains a list of expressions separated by commas:

```
forward operation ( expr, expr, ... )
```

Execution of forward takes the operation invocation currently being serviced, evaluates a possibly new set of arguments, and invokes the named operation. An invocation can be forwarded to any operation having the same signature, including the operation being serviced! (See Exercise 10.11.) If the invocation being serviced was called, the caller remains blocked until the new invocation has been serviced (to completion).

After executing forward, the forwarding process continues with the next statement just as if it had replied to the forwarded invocation. A subsequent forward of the same invocation is treated as if it were a send invocation from the forwarding process. A subsequent reply to a forwarded invocation has no effect. Similarly, a subsequent return from within the block handling the invocation has no effect on the caller if the invocation was called, although it has the usual effect of causing the executing process to exit that block.

While within the block handling a forwarded invocation, the forwarding process may still reference formal parameters. However, no subsequent changes to variable or result parameters or to the return value will be seen by any other process.

As a simple (contrived) example, consider the following program fragment:

```
resource fun()
  op f(x: int) returns z: int
  op g(y: int) returns z: int
  process p
    var a := f(1); write(a)
  end
```

```
        proc f(x) returns z
          forward g(2*x)
            ...  # continue executing, perhaps changing z
        end
        proc g(y) returns z
          z := y+10
        end
    end
```

First, process p invokes f. The process executing f doubles its argument x, forwards the invocation to g, and then continues executing; the process may assign to z, but this has no effect on the result returned to process p. Forwarding to g causes a new process to be created; it adds 10 to its argument and returns the value to p, which is waiting for its invocation of f to return. The overall effect, then, is that variable a is assigned 12.

A more realistic example of the use of forward is the following. Client processes make requests for service to a central allocator process. The allocator assigns a server process to the request by forwarding the invocation to it. To be more concrete, the allocator might represent a file server to which clients pass the names of files. The allocator determines on which server the requested file is located and forwards the client's request to the server, which typically would be located on a different machine. Chapter 17 explores this example and its use of forward in detail.

Exercises

10.1   Consider the Stack resource in Section 10.1. Give a detailed explanation of how two processes, each executing on behalf of an invocation of push, can overflow the array, despite the explicit top<size test.

10.2   Show how to rewrite the client-server model in resource cs4 (see the end of Section 9.2) using a call statement instead of send and receive statements. Assume clients do no work between the send and receive.

10.3   Suppose proc p is declared as

```
        op p(x: int) returns y: int
        proc p(x) returns y
          y := x*x
        end
```

Show how to rewrite p and calls to it using send/receive pairs.

10.4   Suppose proc p is declared as in Exercise 10.3, and consider the following:

```
        var a[N]: int
        co (i := 1 to N) a[i] := p(a[i]) oc
```

(a) Show how to rewrite p and the concurrent calls to it using send/receive pairs. Discuss the need and desire for a concurrent invocation statement in SR.

(b) Discuss the complications that arise if the concurrent invocation statement contains postprocessing code, possibly including exit and next statements.

10.5   Suppose proc p is declared as

```
op p(x: int) returns y: int
var z := 0
proc p(x) returns y
   y := x*x
   reply
   z +:= y
end
```

Show how to rewrite p and calls to it using send/receive pairs. Discuss the need and desire for a reply statement in SR.

10.6   Suppose proc p is declared as

```
op p(rep: cap (z: int); x: int)
proc p(rep, n)
   reply
   send rep(n+1000)
end
```

Also suppose that p is invoked as

```
process q
   ...
   op rep(z: int)
   p(rep, 33)
   var z :int
   receive rep(z)
   ...
end
```

Show how to rewrite p and calls to it using send/receive pairs.

10.7   Recode the `conversation` resource (see Section 10.3) so that clients are in a different resource than servers.

10.8   Show how to code the `pipeline_sort` program (see Section 10.3) using an array of operations instead of local operations. Assume exactly N values are to be sorted, where N is a declared constant rather than an input value.

10.9   Recode the `pipeline_sort` program (see Section 10.3) so that workers are not passed the number of numbers to expect. Instead they are passed a sentinel (e.g., 0) after all legitimate numbers.

10.10   Repeat the previous exercise, but assume each worker is sent a special done message (represented by a new operation declared local to the worker) after all legitimate numbers.

10.11   Write a factorial procedure that is (technically) not iterative or recursive. Use a forward statement to achieve the effect of a loop or a recursive procedure call. Do not use a loop or a recursive call.

10.12   A *monitor* is a modular synchronization mechanism [Hoare 1974] (see also [Andrews 1991]). It exports a collection of procedures that are called by processes that want to communication and synchronize. The procedures execute with mutual exclusion and use what are called condition variables for condition synchronization.

Show how to simulate a monitor using RPC and semaphores. Illustrate your simulation by converting one of the monitors in [Hoare 1974] or [Andrews 1991] into an SR global or resource. What are the differences between using a global and a resource to implement a monitor?

## CHAPTER 11

Rendezvous

A rendezvous, like a remote procedure call, involves two processes: an invoking process and a process that handles the invocation. However, the invocation is handled by an existing process; a new process is *not* created as a result of the invocation. As with remote procedure call, rendezvous is synchronous from the invoking process's perspective, and the two processes can be located on different virtual or physical machines.

Rendezvous, like SR's other synchronization mechanisms, is accomplished through the use of operations. The invoking process uses a call invocation of an operation to initiate a rendezvous. The operation is one that is serviced by an existing process executing what is called an input statement.* SR's input statement allows a process to wait for one of several operations to be invoked. It also allows a process to base its decision as to which invocation to service on the values of the invocation parameters.

This chapter first discusses the general form of the input statement and gives a few simple examples. We then show how the receive statement is an abbreviation for a common form of input statement. In Chapter 9 the receive statement was used to service send invocations; `receive` can also be used to service call invocations, which results in synchronous message passing. The remainder of the chapter describes other aspects of the input statement—synchronization expressions, scheduling expressions, conditional input, and servicing arrays of operations—and its use with other statements such as exit and reply. Although we focus on rendezvous, we also show how the input statement can be used to handle send invocations.

---

*This kind of rendezvous is sometimes called an extended rendezvous to contrast it with the simple rendezvous of synchronous message passing, as in CSP [Hoare 1978].

11.1 The Input Statement

The input statement is SR's most complicated statement in that it has many optional parts that can affect its execution. On the other hand, it is also SR's most powerful statement, as we shall see. In this section we describe the input statement's general form and give a few simple examples. Subsequent sections explore the parts in detail and give numerous additional examples.

General Form and Semantics

An input statement contains one or more operation commands separated by brackets that form boxes:

in *op_command* [] *op_command* [] ... ni

Each operation command specifies an operation to service, an optional synchronization clause, an optional scheduling clause, and a block of code. An operation command servicing an operation without a return value has the general form

operation (*formal_id_list*)
   st *synch_expr* by *sched_expr* -> *block*

An operation command servicing an operation with a return value has the general form

operation (*formal_id_list*) returns *result_id*
   st *synch_expr* by *sched_expr* -> *block*

The identifiers are new names for the parameters and return value. The keyword st (such-that) introduces the *synchronization expression.** It specifies which invocations of the operation are acceptable. The keyword by introduces the *scheduling expression.* It dictates the order in which invocations are serviced.

In general, an input statement can service any operation declared in a scope that includes the statement. The same operation can even appear in more than one operation command (see Exercises 11.9, 11.10, and 11.11). However, an input statement that services an operation declared in a global can service only operations declared in that same global. Thus, if a resource imports a global, it cannot contain an input statement that services both an operation exported by the global and one declared within the resource; these operations must be serviced by separate input statements.

---

* The and or & operators can also be used in place of the st keyword.

Although not shown above, the operation in an operation command can be an element of an array of operations, in which case it must be subscripted to indicate the particular operation to be serviced. Furthermore, a quantifier can be used to specify that any one of a group of elements of an operation array is to be serviced. Arrays of operations and quantifiers are discussed later.

A process executing an input statement is in general delayed until some invocation is selectable. An invocation is *selectable* if the boolean-valued synchronization expression for the corresponding operation is true (or is omitted). In general, the oldest selectable invocation is serviced. However, if the corresponding operation command contains a scheduling expression, the invocation that is serviced is the oldest one that is selectable and that also minimizes the scheduling expression. Both synchronization and scheduling expressions can reference invocation parameters, thereby allowing selection to be based on their values. If no invocations are pending for an input statement, the process executing that statement delays until a selectable invocation is received.

An invocation is serviced by executing the corresponding block. The input statement terminates when that block terminates. If the invocation was called, the corresponding call statement also terminates at that time.

The operation commands in an input statement can be followed by an else command, which has the form

```
[] else -> block
```

This block of code is executed if no invocation is selectable. Thus a process will never delay when it executes an input statement containing an else command.

For readers familiar with Ada, SR's input statement combines and generalizes aspects of Ada's **accept** and **select** statements. In particular, an input statement is like a **select** statement in which each arm is an **accept** statement. Also, SR's else command is similar to Ada's **otherwise** clause in a **select** statement. The notable differences between SR's and Ada's rendezvous mechanisms are (1) SR allows synchronization expressions to reference parameters of operation invocations, whereas Ada does not, and (2) SR includes a scheduling expression, which Ada does not. These make the input statement much more expressive and powerful, but they do add some implementation overhead when used (see Appendix E).

Simple Input Statements

As a first example of an input statement, consider the code outline below. The two processes, p and q, interact via a rendezvous through operation f. Process p calls f(y) and then waits until process q receives y and increments its local variable z; that is, p delays until q reaches the end of the command block associated with f. If process q arrives at its input statement and finds no pending invocations of f, it delays until p invokes f.

```
resource main()
  op f(x: int)
  process p
    var y: int;  ...
    call f(y)
    ...
  end
  process q
    var z: int;  ...
    in f(x) -> z +:= x ni
    ...
  end
end
```

The following code outline presents a slightly more complicated example of an input statement:

```
resource main()
  op f(x: int), g(u: real) returns v: real
  process p1
    var y: int;  ...
    call f(y)
    ...
  end
  process p2
    var w: real;  ...
    w := g(3.8)
    ...
  end
  process q
    var z: int;  ...
    in f(x) -> z +:= x
    [] g(u) returns v -> v := u*u-9.3
    ni
    ...
  end
end
```

Here three processes interact via two rendezvous: p1 and q interact through operation f, and p2 and q interact through operation g, which has a return value. The input statement allows process q to service either an invocation of f or an invocation of g. When q reaches its input statement, it finds one of three states:

- An invocation of only one of f or g is pending—q will service the operation that has pending invocations.

- Invocations of both f and g are pending—q will service the invocation that arrived first.

- No invocations are pending—q delays until either f or g is invoked.

After invoking f, process p1 delays until its invocation is serviced by process q, i.e., until q reaches the end of the block in the corresponding operation command. Similarly, after invoking g, process p2 delays until its invocation is serviced by process q. As programmed above, only one rendezvous will actually occur; if the input statement were embedded in a loop and executed twice, both would occur but in an unpredictable order.

The next example shows how input statements can be nested, even when they service the same operation. It also demonstrates that the formal identifiers used in an input statement need not match the parameter identifiers used in the corresponding operation declaration. Consider the following code outline:

```
resource main()
  op swap(var x: int)
  process p1
    var y: int
    call swap(y)
    ...
  end
  process p2
    var z: int
    call swap(z)
    ...
  end
  process q
    in swap(x1) -> in swap(x2) -> x1 :=: x2 ni ni
    ...
  end
end
```

Processes p1 and p2 both invoke swap to exchange values. Process q uses a nested input statement to service one invocation of swap within another. It services one of the calls of swap with the outer input statement and another with the nested input statement. In the innermost block, q has access to the parameters of both invocations of swap because they have been given different local names.

11.2   Receive Statement Revisited

The receive statement, introduced in Chapter 9, is an abbreviation for a simple form of input statement. For example,

```
receive f(v1, v2)
```

is equivalent to the following input statement:

```
in f(p1, p2) -> v1 := p1; v2 := p2 ni
```

In the input statement, each variable that appears in the receive statement is assigned the value of the corresponding parameter. Variables are assigned to in left-to-right order. If the same variable appears more than once (which is bad programming practice), only the last assignment is visible.

The receive statement was used in Chapter 9 to service send invocations. It can also service call invocations. The effect is what is called *synchronous message passing*: The calling process delays until a receiving process accepts its message. For example, suppose foo is an operation used by two processes as follows:

```
process A                process B
  ...                      ...
  call foo(v)              receive(x)
  ...                      ...
end                      end
```

Assume foo is used only by these two processes and that there are no pending invocations. Then the first process to arrive at its communication statement delays until the other arrives; the value of v is then assigned to variable x, and both processes continue execution. When call and receive are used as above, they are like the output and input commands, respectively, in CSP [Hoare 1978] and Occam [May 1983, INMOS 1984].

The input statement has been used thus far in this chapter to service call invocations. It can also service send invocations (even if the block in the operation command is not empty). As an example of the use of send invocations with the receive form of input statements, consider the following code for a process that allocates a single unit of some resource:

```
# single unit allocator
do true ->
  receive request(); receive release()
od
```

It repeatedly services two operations, `request` and `release`, in that order. To gain access to the resource, a process calls `request`. To release its access to the resource, a process could call `release`. However, there is no need for a releasing process to wait for the allocator to service its release (unlike the request). Therefore, sending to `release` is better.

The receive statement can be used for simple forms of process interaction, but the input statement must be used for more complicated forms. A receive statement does not provide a process the means to wait for one of several operations to be invoked, in contrast to the input statement in the second resource `main` in Section 11.1. It also does not allow synchronization and scheduling expressions, which are discussed in subsequent subsections. Finally, the receive statement cannot be used to service an operation that has a return value or variable or result parameters; receive supports only one-way information flow from the invoker to the receiving process.

Consider, for example, the following code fragment that implements a single slot buffer (mailbox):

```
op deposit(item: int), fetch() returns item: int
process manager
  var buffer: int
  do true ->
    in deposit(item) -> buffer := item ni
    in fetch() returns item -> item := buffer ni
  od
end
```

The `manager` process repeatedly services a `deposit` operation and then a `fetch` operation. Thus synchronization to the single slot buffer is provided by "flow of control." For example, if an item has just been deposited into the buffer, the manager can service only a `fetch`, not another `deposit`. The first input statement above can be written more concisely with a receive statement:

```
receive deposit(buffer)
```

The second input statement cannot be written in this way, however, since `fetch` has a return value.

Using a call invocation serviced by an input statement can simplify some send/receive interactions. For example, some of the client-server models in Section 9.2 can be simplified. In particular, both the code that used an array of operations (resource cs2) and the code that used capabilities (resource cs3) can be rewritten as follows:

```
resource cs()
  op request(...)
  const N := 20   # number of processes
  process client(i := 1 to N)
    ...
    call request(...)
    ...
  end
  process server
    do true ->
      in request(...) ->
        # handle request; assign to result parameters
      ni
    od
  end
end
```

The send/receive pair in the client has been replaced by a call invocation of request. The request operation now has result parameters, in which values are passed back. The server uses an input statement to service each request. When the server reaches the end of the input statement, it implicitly passes results back. This structure, though, precludes clients from performing other work while waiting for the server to give back results.

The request operation above is serviced by a single server process. Hence invocations of request are serviced one at a time, i.e., with mutual exclusion. If request had been implemented by a proc instead of an input statement, instances of the proc could execute concurrently but then the programmer would have to program mutual exclusion, using semaphores, for example.

Section 9.5 discussed how shared operations can be used with send and receive statements. The operations that are invoked as part of rendezvous—or more generally, serviced by input statements—follow the same rules. In particular, an operation declared in a resource (or body of a global) can be serviced by input statements in multiple processes in that resource (or global). An operation declared in the spec of a global g can be serviced by processes in g or in any resource or global that imports g. Processes obtain access to pending invocations in a first-come, first-served order.

11.3 Synchronization Expressions

A boolean-valued synchronization expression can be used to control which invocation an input statement services next. Consider the following input statements:

```
in a(x) st c > 0 -> ... ni

in a(x) st x = 3 -> ... ni

in a(x) st x = 3 -> ...
[] b(y,z) st y = f(z) -> ...
ni
```

The first input statement services an invocation of a only when the value of variable c is positive. The second input statement services only invocations of a whose parameter x is equal to 3. The third input statement services the same invocations as the second, as well as invocations of b whose parameters satisfy the condition y = f(z), where f represents a user-defined or predefined operation.

It is important to emphasize that synchronization expressions can reference invocation parameters. That ability leads to straightforward solutions to many synchronization problems, as we shall see later in this chapter and in Part III. However, it is more expensive to implement such synchronization expressions since it requires searching the queue of pending invocations (see Appendix E). This tradeoff between expressive power and implementation cost is a fundamental aspect of language design.

As a more realistic application of a synchronization expression, consider a process that manages a multiple unit resource. Each client process requests or releases a single unit at a time. The single-unit allocator code given in Section 11.2 would not work here because the manager now needs to be able to service either a request operation or a release operation. A two-arm input statement with a synchronization expression can be used for that purpose:

```
# multiple unit allocator for M units
var avail := M
do true ->
  in request() st avail>0 -> avail--
  [] release() -> avail++
  ni
od
```

The synchronization expression with request, avail>0, ensures that a resource is only allocated to a requesting process if at least one unit of the resource is available. If a process requests a resource and none is available, the invocation is not serviced—and the caller delays—until a resource becomes available.

The next example presents a solution to the classic bounded buffer problem. The `bounded_buffer` resource provides two operations: `deposit` and `fetch`. A producer process calls `deposit` to insert an item into the buffer; a consumer process calls `fetch` to retrieve an item from the buffer. An input statement synchronizes how invocations of `deposit` and `fetch` are serviced to ensure that messages are fetched in the order in which they were deposited, are not fetched until deposited, and are not overwritten. The code is as follows:

```
resource bounded_buffer
  op deposit(item: int)
  op fetch() returns item: int
body bounded_buffer(size: int)
  var buf[0:size-1]: int
  var count := 0, front := 0, rear := 0
  process worker
    do true ->
      in deposit(item) st count < size ->
          buf[rear] := item
          rear := (rear+1) % size
          count++
      [] fetch() returns item st count > 0 ->
          item := buf[front]
          front := (front+1) % size
          count--
      ni
    od
  end
end
```

The worker process loops around a single input statement, which services `deposit` and `fetch`. The synchronization expressions in the input statement ensure that the buffer does not overflow or underflow. For example, a producer is delayed if the buffer is full and a consumer is delayed if the buffer is empty.

The bounded buffer resource is somewhat similar to the stack resource we saw in Sections 5.1 and 10.1. Except for the names of the operations, their specs are nearly identical. They differ, though, in that the stack operations enforce a last-in, first-out discipline whereas the bounded buffer operations enforce a first-in, first-out discipline. The bodies of the two resources also differ in how overflow and underflow are handled. For the stack those invocations are handled as errors; for the bounded buffer those invocations are not serviced until they can be handled without error. Thus a bounded buffer is a synchronized queue. The same technique used for programming the bounded buffer can be used to program a synchronized stack (see Exercise 11.13).

The readers/writers problem is another classic synchronization problem [Courtois et al. 1971]. There are two classes of processes that want to access a database (or file or set of shared variables). Reader processes only examine the database; hence they can execute concurrently with each other. Writer processes update the database; to keep the database consistent, they must have exclusive access to it. Suppose that reader processes call operation `start_read` before reading the database and call (or send to) operation `end_read` when done. Similarly, writer processes call `start_write` before and call (or send to) `end_write` after writing to the database. The following process implements the specified reader/writer exclusion:

```
process RW_allocator
  var nr := 0, nw := 0
  do true ->
    in start_read() st nw = 0 -> nr++
    [] end_read() -> nr--
    [] start_write() st nr = 0 and nw = 0 -> nw++
    [] end_write() -> nw--
    ni
  od
end
```

Variables `nr` and `nw` count the number of active readers and writers, respectively. Reader processes can start reading when there are no active writers; a writer process can start writing when there are no active readers or writers. The process above implements what is called a *readers' preference* solution. Namely, if there is a steady stream of readers, the value of `nr` will always be positive, and hence a writer may never get to access the database. The solution can be modified to give writers preference or to guarantee eventual access to all processes (see Exercise 11.14).

One predefined function dealing with operations is particularly useful in synchronization expressions. It is denoted by the prefix operator ?. The expression `?f` returns the number of pending invocations of operation `f`; it can be used only within the scope of `f`. This function can, for example, be used to give preference to servicing invocations of one operation over another:

```
# preference to servicing invocations of f over g
in f(...) -> ...
[] g(...) st ?f = 0 -> ...
ni
```

The synchronization expression on the second arm of the input statement says that an invocation of g should be serviced only if no invocations of f are pending. Thus the above input statement gives preferential service to invocations of f over those of g.

11.4 Scheduling Expressions

A scheduling expression can be used to control which invocation—of those whose synchronization expression is true—an input statement services next. Preference is given to the selectable invocation that minimizes the value of the scheduling expression; If there is more than one such invocation, the oldest is selected. The type of a scheduling expression may be any ordered type—such as int—or real. Scheduling expressions, like synchronization expressions, make it easy to solve many problems, but they do incur an implementation cost since all pending invocations have to be examined.

Consider the following three input statements:

```
in a(x) by x -> ... ni

in a(x) st x mod 2 = 0 by -x -> ... ni

in a(x) st x mod 2 = 0 by -x -> ...
[] b(y,z) by y+z -> ...
ni
```

The first input statement services invocations of a, giving preference to those with smaller values of x. The second services only invocations of a whose parameter x is even, giving preference to those with larger values of x. The third input statement services the same invocations of a, in the same order, as the second input statement or services invocations of b, giving preference to those with smaller values of y+z.

Exactly which invocation the third input statement services depends on what invocations are pending and when they arrived. The most interesting case occurs when invocations of a for which x is even and invocations of b are both pending. Of those invocations, the one that arrived first determines which operation is serviced. If that operation is a, the invocation of a with the largest even x value is serviced (even if there are earlier invocations of b). Otherwise the invocation of b with the smallest value of y+z is serviced. Several invocations might tie in minimizing the scheduling expression, in which case the one that arrived first is serviced.

A more realistic example of the use of a scheduling expression is a variant of the single unit allocator given in Section 11.2. Suppose each requesting process includes in its request the length of time it expects to use the resource; the allocator gives preference to the request with the smallest time.

The following implements this shortest-job-next (SJN) allocation scheme:

```
# single unit allocator; SJN variant
do true ->
    in request(usage_time) by usage_time -> skip ni
    receive release()
od
```

The scheduling expression of the input statement causes invocations of `request` to be serviced in increasing order of the value of `usage_time`.

11.5 Exit And Next Statements

As shown earlier, the exit statement forces early termination of a do or for-all statement or a concurrent invocation statement. The next statement forces return to the loop control of such statements. Exit and next statements may also appear within an input statement that is nested within a loop or a concurrent invocation statement. In these cases execution of an exit or next statement also forces the input statement to terminate.

For example, consider the following code outline, which illustrates a common server structure:

```
process server
    do true ->
        in work(...) -> ... [] done() -> exit ni
    od
end
```

A client process repeatedly makes requests for service by invoking `work`, usually by a call invocation. When a client is through using the server, it so informs the server by invoking `done`. The server process repeatedly services invocations of `work`. When it services an invocation of `done`, it exits the do loop; the exit statement also terminates the invocation of `done`. We will see this structure again in later examples.

11.6 Conditional Input

An input statement's last operation command can be an else command. As described earlier, the block of code associated with the else command is executed if none of the input statement's operation guards is true; when that block terminates, so does the input statement. The use of an else command supports *conditional input* since the executing process has control over whether it waits for an operation to be invoked.

For example, consider the following program fragment:

```
in a() -> x := 1 [] else -> x := 2 ni
```

If an invocation of a is present, the executing process executes the first assignment; otherwise it executes the second assignment. If only one process services invocations of a, the above input statement is equivalent to*

```
if ?a > 0 -> receive a(); x := 1
[] else -> x := 2
fi
```

However, if more than one process receives invocations of a, then the above two input statements are not equivalent because a process executing the second statement could evaluate ?a, find it positive, and yet block at the receive statement. (Other processes could grab all pending invocations after ?a is evaluated.) In contrast, an input statement with an else command never causes a process to block.

Conditional input is useful in a number of situations. One is illustrated by the following code outline:

```
do true ->
  # do some work.
  in done() -> exit [] else -> skip ni
od
```

Here a process repeatedly does some work and then checks for an invocation of the done operation, indicating that it should terminate. If no such invocation is present, the process just continues with the next loop iteration.

A second situation in which conditional input is useful is typified by the following code fragment:

```
# service all invocations of a for which x = t
do true ->
  in a(x) st x = t -> ... [] else -> exit ni
od
```

The overall effect of the do loop is to service all pending invocations of a whose parameter x is equal to t. On each iteration of the loop, the input statement services one such invocation, if there is one, or exits the loop.

---

*It is equivalent if a is invoked by send. However, if a is invoked by call, the caller continues before 1 is actually assigned to x. This difference does not matter if x is local to the process executing the receive statement; it might matter if x is shared.

11.7   Arrays of Operations

Input statements (or semaphore `P` statements or receive statements) can also be used to service arrays of operations. A particular element of an array of operations is serviced by specifying its index. For example, suppose `N` is a constant and consider the following program outline:

```
op f[N](x: int)
process q(i := 1 to N)
   ...
   in f[i](x) -> ... ni
   ...
end
```

Each process services one element of the array `f`.

An input statement can service any one of a group of elements of an operation array by specifying a quantifier. For example, consider the following input statement:

```
# wait for any one of signal[1:4] to be invoked
in (i := 1 to 4) signal[i]() -> skip ni
```

The scope of the quantifier variable extends to the end of the command block. Thus in the above, `i` could be used within the command block. Its value would indicate which element of `signal` is being serviced.

11.8   Return, Reply, and Forward Statements

Return, reply, and forward statements can be used within input statements. The meaning of return is similar to its meaning within a proc (see Section 10.3); the only difference is what happens to the process executing return. The meanings of reply and forward are identical to their meanings within a proc.

A return statement within an input statement transmits results to the invoker of the operation being serviced—if it was called—and terminates the input statement. The process executing `return` continues execution with the statement following the input statement. (The process executing `return` terminates when the return statement is not within an input statement.)

A reply statement within an operation command of an input statement transmits results to the invoker, if the invocation was called. The replying process continues execution with the statement following the reply. A forward statement defers replying to a called invocation and instead passes on this responsibility to another operation. The forwarding process continues execution with the statement following the forward.

The following example illustrates the use of a reply statement within an input statement. It provides another example of conversational continuity, which was introduced in resource conversation in Section 10.3. The problem considered here uses a sieve of processes to find prime numbers. The solution is structurally similar to the pipeline_sort resource in Section 10.3. The algorithm is a parallel implementation of what is called the sieve of Eratosthenes. Worker processes pass numbers down a pipeline. Each worker filters out multiples of its prime number and passes the next prime number on to the next worker, which it must create. In this example, however, a given worker does not know in advance how many numbers it will receive. Therefore, each worker also provides a termination operation, which its invoker uses to inform it to terminate.

```
# finds primes from 2 through n
resource sieve()
  type Wrets = rec(feed: cap(num: int); done: cap())
  op worker() returns c: Wrets

  begin # initial code to start up pipeline
    var n: int, c : Wrets
    writes("find primes 2 ... n? "); read(n)
    c := worker()
    fa i := 2 to n -> send c.feed(i) af
    send c.done()
  end

  # Each worker receives a stream of integers.
  # It keeps the first, discards multiples, and
  # passes the rest onto the next worker, its child.
  proc worker() returns c
    op filter(x: int), done(); var n: int
    c.feed := filter; c.done := done
    reply
    receive filter(n)
    write(n)
    var child: Wrets, child_exists := false
    do true ->
      in filter(y) ->
        if y % n != 0 ->
          if not child_exists ->
            child := worker(); child_exists := true
          fi
          send child.feed(y)
        fi
```

```
              [] done() ->
                 exit
              ni
           od
           if child_exists -> send child.done() fi
        end worker
     end sieve
```

Each worker provides two local operations, `filter` and `done`; it returns capabilities for these to its creator via the reply statement. A worker services invocations of `filter` from its creator until an invocation of `done` is sent, at which point it exits its loop and informs its child, if any, to terminate. The use of the termination message is another example of the structure we saw in Section 11.5.

Exercises

11.1 Semaphores in SR are provided using abbreviations for operations and for send and receive statements. In turn, receive statements are abbreviations for input statements.

(a) Rewrite the critical section resource `CS` given in Section 8.1 to use operations and send and input statements.

(b) Rewrite the barrier synchronization resource `barrier` given in Section 8.2 to use operations and send and input statements.

11.2 Consider the nested input statements used for swapping in Section 11.1:

```
        in swap(x1) -> in swap(x2) -> x1 :=: x2 ni ni
```

Suppose SR required the formal identifiers used in an operation command to match those in the corresponding operation declaration. Show how to rewrite the nested input statement so it conforms to such a rule.

11.3 Consider again the code for swapping in the previous exercise. Show how processes p1 and p2 can exchange values without involving a third process.

11.4 Rewrite the `pipeline_sort` resource given in Section 10.3 so it uses input statements instead of receive statements.

11.5 (a) Consider the single unit allocator given in Section 11.2, which repeatedly services `request` and `release` operations in that order. Explain why the following is an incorrect solution to the problem:

```
        do true ->
           in request() -> in release() -> skip ni ni
        od
```

(b) Modify the code in part (a) so it keeps the same nested structure but correctly solves the problem.

11.6 Consider again the single unit allocator given in Section 11.2. Explain why the following is an incorrect solution to the problem:

```
do true ->
  in request() -> skip [] release() -> skip ni
od
```

11.7 Show how to rewrite the second input statement in the single slot buffer code (see Section 11.2) to use receive (and send). Also show what an invocation of fetch must now look like.

11.8 Rewrite the code in resource stream_merge (see Section 9.1) so that it does not use an end of stream marker. Instead, have each sending process invoke an additional operation that signifies end of stream.

11.9 An operation may appear in more than one operation command in an input statement. Consider the following program fragment:

```
op a(i: int)
process foo
  do true ->
    in a(i) st i >= 0 -> write("arm 1", i)
    [] a(i) st i <= 0 -> write("arm 2", i)
    ni
  od
end
```

What will be printed if a(-1) is invoked? What if a(0) is invoked? What if a(1) is invoked? Explain your answers.

11.10 Let S1 and S2 denote statement lists, and let B1 and B2 denote boolean expressions. Are the following two input statements equivalent?

```
in f(x) st B1 -> S1 [] f(x) st B2 -> S2 ni

in f(x) -> if B1 -> S1 [] B2 -> S2 fi ni
```

Give a convincing argument why they are, or a specific example demonstrating why they are not.

11.11 Consider the multiple unit allocator given in Section 11.3. Initially there are M units of the resource, as shown. Suppose there are W worker processes that call request and release. The units could represent a bag of tasks for the workers to process. In this case, a worker calls request to get a task from the bag and calls release to put a new task in the bag. Also, the allocator is an administrator process that manages the bag of tasks.

Suppose the workers and allocator are the only processes and that each worker has the following code outline:

```
do true ->
  request()
  release()   # zero or more times per request
od
```

Assume that eventually `request` is called M more times than `release`, i.e., that eventually the bag is empty and all tasks have been processed.

As programmed, the processes will deadlock. Modify the code in the multiple unit allocator so that it terminates the computation by executing `stop`. Hint: Service an operation in more than one operation command.

11.12   Modify the `bounded_buffer` resource (see Section 11.3) so that it also provides `current_size` and `query` operations. The former returns the current number of elements in the buffer; the latter returns a boolean indicating whether a specified number is an element of the buffer.

11.13   Program a stack resource that provides synchronized push and pop operations in the same spirit as the `bounded_buffer` resource (see Section 11.3).

11.14   The readers/writers scheduling process `RW_allocator` (see Section 11.3) gives preference to readers.

(a) Modify the process to give preference to writers; i.e., if a writer wants to start writing, it gets to do so before a reader gets to start reading. Hint: Use the `?` operator.

(b) Modify the process so scheduling is fair; i.e., any reader or writer that wants to access the database is able to do so eventually, assuming every process eventually calls `end_read` or `end_write`.

11.15   The readers/writers scheduling process `RW-allocator` (see Section 11.3) uses a four-arm input statement and synchronization expressions. Show how to convert that input statement into code that has the same effect but that does not use synchronization expressions. Hint: Use nested input statements plus additional statements.

11.16   Consider again the input statement that uses a quantifier given in Section 11.7. First, show how that code can be rewritten without using a quantifier. Now suppose that `signal` is declared with an upper bound of n, which is read from input, and that the input statement is to service any one of `signal[1:n]`. Does your rewriting technique used above generalize to this case? Explain why or why not.

11.17   Consider the output of the code in the prime sieve algorithm (see Section 11.8). Is it printed in order or might it be interleaved? Explain.

11.18   Consider again the prime sieve algorithm (see Section 11.8). Modify the code so that after the pipeline is set up, it can be searched for a given number. Use a separate local operation, `search`, within each worker to service requests for searching; when called, it should return the worker's prime number. Also use a separate local operation, `search_done`, within each worker; when it is called, the worker should terminate.

11.19   Repeat the previous exercise for the pipeline sort algorithm introduced in Section 10.3.

11.20   Consider again the prime sieve algorithm (see Section 11.8). Modify the code
        so that an explicit `done` message is not needed. Instead pass a special number
        (e.g., zero) to `filter`. Which technique is more general and cleaner?

11.21   Consider the following operation declarations and input statement:

```
op a(x: real), b(y: char)
  ...
in a(x) -> ... [] b(y) -> ... ni
```

        Assume that these operations are invoked only by call. Show how the input
        statement can be replaced by a receive statement. Also show how `a` and `b`
        must now be invoked.

11.22   Consider the following input statement from the prime sieve algorithm (see
        Section 11.8):

```
in filter(...) -> ...
[] done() -> exit
ni
```

        It services all invocations of `filter` and then an invocation of `done`. Suppose
        that the semantics of SR's input statement were that invocations are handled
        in a non-deterministic order instead of in first-come, first-served order. Given
        these non-deterministic semantics, show how the above input statement would
        need to be written so that all invocations are handled in the same order as
        they are now.

11.23   The following sort procedure uses an operation to sort an array:

```
procedure sort(var a[1:*]: int)
  op list(x: int)
  fa i := lb(a) to ub(a) -> send list(a[i]) af
  fa i := lb(a) to ub(a) ->
    in list(x) by x -> a[i] := x   ni
  af
end
```

        Explain how it works. Its running time appears to be linear, i.e., order n,
        where n is the size of `a`. Of course, a general linear-time sorting algorithm is
        not possible. Explain the discrepancy.

11.24   In extended forms of CSP [Hoare 1978], guards in if and do statements can
        contain both input and output commands; thus a process can be waiting either
        to receive input or to send output. SR does not allow invocations to appear in
        guards of input statements; on the other hand, `send` is non-blocking. Ada's
        select statement allows either invocation statements (calls) or **accept**
        statements (input), but not both; Ada does not have an asynchronous
        invocation statement.

        Discuss the tradeoffs between these three approaches. Are there differences in
        expressive power? In implementation cost?

11.25 *Dutch National Flag.* A collection of colored balls is distributed among n processes. There are at most n different colors of balls. The goal is for the processes to exchange balls so that eventually, for all i, process i holds all balls of color i. Assume process identities and colors are integers between 1 and n.

The number of balls in the collection is unknown to the processes. A process might start holding no balls if that is how the balls were initially distributed. Process i will finish holding no balls if no balls of color i appear in the collection.

Write code for the processes. Assume interprocess communication forms a ring: Process i is allowed to give a ball only to process $i+1$ (with wrap-around from process n to process 1). Processes are allowed to pass only messages that contain a single ball or control information (but not counts of the number of balls).

## CHAPTER 12

Virtual Machines

So far we have implicitly assumed that programs execute within a single address space on a single physical machine. This chapter describes the SR mechanisms that allow programs to contain multiple address spaces, which can execute on multiple physical machines. These additional mechanisms thus support truly distributed programming.

The SR model of computation allows a program to be split into one or more address spaces called *virtual machines*. Each virtual machine defines an address space on one physical machine. Virtual machines are created dynamically, in a way similar to the way resources are created. When a virtual machine is created, it can be placed on a specific physical machine.

How a virtual machine is used is reflected in how its resource instances and globals are created. As before, a resource instance is created using the create statement; however, an optional clause in the create statement specifies the virtual machine on which the new resource instance is to be located. Processes, variables, and operations in a resource instance exist entirely within a single virtual machine. Also as before, globals are created automatically as needed; however, one instance of a global is created on *each* virtual machine that needs it.

Communication between virtual machines is transparent. For example, a send invocation from one virtual machine to an operation serviced within a resource instance located on a different virtual machine has the same syntax and semantics as a send invocation to an operation serviced on the same virtual machine. The syntax and semantics of call invocations is also independent of virtual machine location.

This chapter describes the SR mechanisms for creating and destroying virtual machines, including how to place them on different physical machines. It also describes how resource instances and globals are created on virtual machines. Finally, we discuss how the implementation-dependent mechanisms for input/output and accessing command-line arguments work in programs that employ multiple virtual machines. As usual, we present several example programs that employ multiple virtual and physical machines. Additional, more realistic examples appear in Chapter 13 and Part III. Some of the rules for the mechanisms described in this chapter are motivated by implementation concerns (see Appendix E).

12.1 Program Start-Up and Execution Overview

As stated in Chapter 5, execution of a program begins with the implicit creation of one instance of the program's main resource. To be more precise, program execution begins with the implicit creation of a virtual machine, on which one instance of the program's main resource is then created. This main virtual machine executes on the physical machine from which program execution was initiated.

When a virtual machine is created, it is essentially empty: It contains no resource instances or globals. (It does, however, contain a copy of the object code, as described in Appendix D.) The main virtual machine is therefore empty when it is first created; however, it is special in that one instance of the program's main resource is immediately and automatically created on it. Code in the main resource, or in resource instances or globals created directly or indirectly by the main resource, can create additional virtual machines, which can be located on other physical machines. Resource instances and globals can then be created on those virtual machines.

Termination of a program with multiple virtual machines is similar to that for a program with only a single virtual machine. As before, a program terminates when all processes have terminated, a deadlock has occurred, or a stop statement is executed. Also, the globals and main resource on the main virtual machine are destroyed (unless stop is executed with a non-zero exit status). However, other resources and globals are not destroyed implicitly. Moreover, the effect of a stop statement is not instantaneous; i.e., all parts of a distributed program do not halt immediately.

12.2 Creating Virtual Machines

A virtual machine is created by creating an instance of the `vm` pseudo-resource, which is a special, predefined resource. In this case, the create statement returns a capability of type `cap vm`. For example, consider

```
var c: cap vm
c := create vm()
```

This code fragment creates a new virtual machine and assigns a capability for that virtual machine to variable `c`.

By default, a new virtual machine is placed on the same physical machine as its creator. A new virtual machine instance can be placed on a specific physical machine (network node) by using the following form of `create`:

```
create vm() on expr
```

The expression specifies a physical machine as a string or an integer. When the expression is a string, it is the name of a physical machine, which is, of course, installation dependent. When *expr* is an integer, it represents a physical machine; the mapping between the value of such an expression and a specific machine is also defined by the implementation. Section 12.6 and Appendix D contain more details on this mapping.

As an example, suppose the following code fragment is executed on a physical machine named `ivy`:

```
var c1, c2, c3: cap vm
c1 := create vm()
c2 := create vm() on "carob"
c3 := create vm() on "holly"
```

It creates three virtual machines and assigns capabilities for them to `c1`, `c2`, and `c3`. The first virtual machine is created on `ivy` since no explicit physical machine was specified. The second is created on a physical machine named `carob` and the third on `holly`.

12.3 Creating Resources and Globals

Resource instances must be created explicitly using create expressions, as described in Chapter 5. By default, a resource instance is created on the same virtual machine as its creator. The following form of create creates an instance of the specified resource on the specified (existing) virtual machine:

```
create res_name ( arguments ) on expr
```

The value of the expression is a capability for the virtual machine on which an instance of the specified resource is to be created.

For example, consider the following, which uses `c1` and `c2` from above:

```
create r(34) on c1
create r(22) on c2
create r(70)
```

This code fragment creates three instances of resource r. The first is created on virtual machine c1, the second on c2, and the third on the same virtual machine as the creator.

Recall from Chapter 5 that a global is created implicitly when it is first imported. Globals are virtual machine specific: Each virtual machine contains its own instance of a global, if one is needed. In particular, an instance of a global g is created implicitly on a virtual machine the first time another resource or global on that virtual machine imports g.

Since globals are virtual machine specific, variables and operations declared in a global's spec are local to that virtual machine. That is, sharing of variables and operations is restricted to those resource instances and globals on the same virtual machine. The examples in Section 12.5 illustrate this point.

12.4 Destroying Virtual Machines

A virtual machine, and all activity within it, can be destroyed using a destroy statement. Its form is

```
destroy expr
```

The type of the expression is cap vm; typically, the expression is simply a virtual machine capability variable. This form of the destroy statement is the same, except for the expression's type, as that used for destroying resource instances.

When a virtual machine is destroyed, first creation of new resources in the virtual machine is prevented. Then each existing resource in the virtual machine is implicitly destroyed; its final code is executed as described in Chapter 5. Next each existing global in the virtual machine is implicitly destroyed; its final code is as described in Chapter 5. (Thus final code in a global can perform any cleanup activities needed when a virtual machine is destroyed.) Finally, the address space of the virtual machine is destroyed.

As happens when resource instances are destroyed, execution of a destroy statement causes a run-time error if the expression has the value null or if the virtual machine has already been destroyed. Execution of a destroy statement has no effect if the expression has the value noop.

12.5 Examples of Multiple Machine Programs

The following examples present programs composed from a global and two kinds of resources, one of which is the main resource. The global and non-main resource are the same in each program; only the main resource differs.

The global is as follows:

```
global glob
  var x := 0
  sem mutex := 1 #   for exclusive access to x
body glob
  final
     write(x)
  end
end
```

If the global is used on the main virtual machine, its final code is executed when the program terminates. If it is used on another virtual machine, its final code is executed if that virtual machine is explicitly destroyed.

The non-main resource is as follows:

```
resource foo(N, n: int; c: cap())
  import glob
  process p(i := 1 to N)
     P(mutex); x +:= n; V(mutex)
     send c()
  end
end
```

Each of the N instances of process p adds n to the shared variable x; the update is protected by using mutex, the semaphore (shared operation) declared in glob. Each process then sends a message to the operation pointed to by capability c, which is a resource parameter.

As a first example, consider the following main resource:

```
resource main1()
  import foo
  const N := 5
  op done()
  var foo1, foo2: cap foo
  foo1 := create foo(N, 1, done)
  foo2 := create foo(N, 2, done)
  fa i := 1 to 2*N -> receive done() af
  destroy foo1; destroy foo2
end
```

It creates two instances of foo, then gathers done messages from every process p in each instance, and finally destroys the two instances of foo. At this point the program terminates.

The above program executes on a single virtual machine. Therefore, only one instance of `glob` is created. When the program terminates, the instance of `glob` is destroyed and the program outputs the single number 15. (The five processes in `foo1` each add 1 to x; the five in `foo2` each add 2 to x.)

As a second example, consider the following main resource:

```
resource main2()
  import foo
  const N := 5
  op done(); var vmcap: cap vm
  var foo1, foo2: cap foo
  foo1 := create foo(N, 1, done)
  vmcap := create vm()
  foo2 := create foo(N, 2, done) on vmcap
  fa i := 1 to 2*N -> receive done() af
  destroy foo1; destroy foo2
  destroy vmcap
end
```

The code here differs from `main1` in that it creates a second virtual machine on which it places the second instance of `foo`.

Since `main2` executes on two virtual machines, an instance of `glob` is created on each. The effect is to create separate instances of x and `mutex` on each virtual machine. The program outputs first the number 10—when the second virtual machine is destroyed—and then the number 5—when the program terminates.

This program executes on a single physical machine. If desired, the second virtual machine can be placed on a different physical machine by changing the statement that creates it as follows:

```
vmcap := create vm() on "holly"
```

However, the program's output remains the same, i.e., first 10 and then 5.

In the examples, parameter c of resource `foo` is a capability for the operation `done` declared in the main resource. It is worth noting that invocations of c might cross virtual and physical machine boundaries. In `main2`, for example, the invocations of c from the second instance of `foo` go from the explicitly created virtual machine (pointed at by `vmcap`) to the original one. Those invocations also go from one physical machine to another if the second virtual machine is on a different physical machine, which can be accomplished as shown above. No change to the send or receive statements is required for such intermachine invocations.

12.6 Predefined Functions

A number of predefined functions deal with virtual and physical machines. The first, `locate`, is used to alter the default interpretations of physical machine numbers, which are used when creating virtual machines (see Section 12.2). By convention, program execution commences on machine 0, and other integers have default meanings that depend on the local network configuration.

The form of an invocation of `locate` is

```
locate(n, hostname)
```

The effect is to associate integer `n` with the machine specified by string expression `hostname`. This association between `n` and `hostname` affects the subsequent meaning of machine `n` on *all* virtual machines in the program. In most cases it is advisable to set up explicit associations using `locate` rather than depending on the default mappings.

The `locate` function provides a convenient way to use a contiguous range of integers to specify machine locations. The use of machine names can thereby be localized to just the invocations of the locate function, rather than being part of each creation of a virtual machine, thus making programs more portable. Consider, for example, the following program fragment:

```
const hosts[2]: string[10] := ("holly", "carob")
fa i := 1 to 2 -> locate(i, hosts[i]) af
  ...
fa i := 1 to 3 ->
  vmcap[i] := create vm() on ((i+1) mod 2 + 1)
af
```

The invocations of `locate` within the for-all loop associate the numbers 1 and 2 with the machines named `holly` and `carob`, respectively. These numbers, instead of the two installation-specific machine names, can then be used throughout the program. As shown above, their values are used within a subsequent for-all loop that places two virtual machines on `holly` and one on `carob`. If the program were ported to another installation with different machine names, only the initialization of the `hosts` array would need to be changed; the create statements would not need to be changed.

Two other predefined functions deal with virtual or physical machines. The function `mymachine` returns the number of the physical machine on which it is executed. Similarly, the function `myvm` returns a capability for the virtual machine on which it is executed.

12.7 I/O and Command-Line Arguments

As described in Chapter 6, the mechanisms for dealing with input/output and command-line arguments are implementation dependent. In the current implementation of SR, these mechanisms behave differently in multiple virtual machine programs than in single virtual machine programs.

The initially created virtual machine inherits the standard input (`stdin`), standard output (`stdout`), and standard error (`stderr`) streams from the command that starts execution of an SR program. Other virtual machines created by the program inherit `stdout` and `stderr` from the initial virtual machine, but for them `stdin` is connected to the file `/dev/null`.

Except for this initial duplication of `stdout` and `stderr`, input/output is virtual machine specific. In particular, capabilities for files that have been opened on one virtual machine will not be valid on another. (The current implementation does not check for such misuse, however, which makes abusive programs susceptible to crashes or other unexpected results.)

The functions that access command-line arguments—i.e., `numargs` and `getarg`—are valid only from the main virtual machine. Thus, command-line arguments cannot be accessed directly from other virtual machines. If they are needed on another machine, they have to be passed from the main virtual machine, e.g., as parameters to a resource created on the other machine.

Exercises

12.1 Extend `main2` (see Section 12.5) so that it places the first instance of `foo` on a new virtual machine located on the physical machine `carob`. How many instances of `glob` are now created, and what does the program output?

12.2 Explain what the differences would be in the executions of `main1` and `main2` (see Section 12.5) if the two destroy statements were replaced by a stop statement.

12.3 In a multiple virtual machine program, standard output from all virtual machines appears by default on the main virtual machine's `stdout` file. Thus output can be interleaved and therefore difficult to comprehend. In a multiple window or multiple terminal environment, output from each virtual machine can instead be directed to its own window or terminal.

(a) Demonstrate how to do so in your environment. As a concrete example, use `main2` or a variant that does more output.

(b) Adapt your solution so that each virtual machine takes its input from its own window or terminal.

## Chapter 13

The Dining Philosophers

This chapter presents three solutions to the classic dining philosophers problem [Dijkstra 1968b]. This problem is interesting because it raises aspects of resource allocation problems that real operating and distributed systems must deal with. In particular, avoiding deadlock and starvation (or lack of fairness) are important goals in solutions to this and similar problems.

Our three solutions employ many SR communication mechanisms and illustrate different ways to structure solutions to synchronization problems. They also illustrate how to use virtual machines so that a program can execute on several physical machines. Unlike the other chapters in this part, this chapter introduces no new language mechanisms. It does, however, show mechanisms used in different combinations than seen earlier.

In the dining philosophers problem, n philosophers (typically five) sit around a circular table set with n forks, one between each pair of philosophers. Each philosopher alternately thinks and eats. To eat, a philosopher must first acquire the forks to its immediate left and right. After eating, a philosopher places the forks back on the table.

This problem can be solved in several ways in SR. In our three solutions, philosophers are represented by processes. The solutions differ in how forks are managed, as shown in the following table:

Approach	Servant(s)
centralized	one servant
distributed	one servant per fork
decentralized	one servant per philosopher

The first approach is to have a single, centralized servant process that manages all n forks. The second approach is to distribute the forks among n servant processes, with each servant managing one fork. The third approach is to decentralize control but employ one servant per philosopher instead of one servant per fork.

13.1 Centralized Solution

This approach employs a single servant process that manages all n forks. Each philosopher requests two forks from the servant, eats, and then releases the forks back to the servant. This interaction for n equals 5 is illustrated in Figure 13.1. In the figure a P represents a philosopher, the S represents the servant, and the lines represent communication.

Our solution employs three resources: Servant, Philosopher, and Main. They are compiled in that order due to the order of their imports. One instance of Main is created when execution of the program begins. It first prompts for input giving the number of philosophers (n) and the number of "sessions" each philosopher is to execute (t). The Main resource then creates one instance of Servant and n instances of Philosopher. The instance of Servant is passed the number of philosophers. Each instance of Philosopher is passed a capability for the instance of Servant, the philosopher's identity, and the number of sessions.

```
resource Main()
  import Philosopher, Servant
  var n, t: int
  writes("how many Philosophers? "); read(n)
  writes("how many sessions per Philosopher? ")
  read(t)
  # create the Servant and Philosophers
  var s: cap Servant
  s := create Servant(n)
  fa i := 1 to n ->
    create Philosopher(s, i, t)
  af
end
```

Each philosopher alternately eats and thinks for t sessions. Before eating, a philosopher calls the servant's getforks operation; after eating, it calls the servant's relforks operation. The Servant resource services invocations of getforks and relforks from all instances of Philosopher. Each instance of Philosopher passes its id to these operations to allow the servant to distinguish between philosophers. A philosopher is permitted to eat when neither of its neighbors is eating.

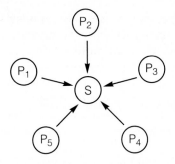

Figure 13.1. Structure of centralized solution.

```
resource Philosopher
  import Servant
body Philosopher(s: cap Servant; id, t: int)
  process phil
    fa i := 1 to t ->
      s.getforks(id)
      write("Philosopher", id, "is eating")    # eat
      s.relforks(id)
      write("Philosopher", id, "is thinking") # think
    af
  end
end

resource Servant
  op getforks(id: int)   # called by Philosophers
  op relforks(id: int)
body Servant(n: int)
  process server
    var eating[1:n] := ([n] false)
    do true ->
      in getforks(id) st not eating[(id mod n) + 1]
          and not eating[((id-2) mod n) + 1] ->
              eating[id] := true
      [] relforks(id) ->
              eating[id] := false
      ni
    od
  end
end
```

The `Servant` resource is passed the number of philosophers (n) as a resource parameter. It uses this value to allocate the array `eating`, which indicates the status of each philosopher. The `server` process continually services the operations `getforks` and `relforks`. The synchronization expression on `getforks` uses the invocation parameter `id` together with n to determine, using modular arithmetic, whether either of a philosopher's neighbors is eating. If neither neighboring philosopher is eating, `server` grants the philosopher requesting forks permission to eat and updates the philosopher's entry in `eating`.

The above solution is deadlock-free since, in effect, `getforks` allocates both forks at the same time. However, a philosopher can starve if its two neighbors "conspire" against it, i.e., if at any time at least one of them is eating.

The above program executes on a single virtual machine and, therefore, on a single physical machine. It can be easily modified, though, so that each philosopher executes on a different virtual machine. Only `Main`'s loop needs to be changed as follows:

```
fa i := 1 to n ->
  var vmcap: cap vm
  vmcap := create vm()
  create Philosopher(s, i, t) on vmcap
af
```

The loop can be further modified so that each virtual machine is on a different physical machine. For example, in the loop above, the assignment that creates virtual machines can be changed to

```
vmcap := create vm() on i
```

As described in Section 12.6, the meaning of physical machine number i is installation dependent, and in general the `locate` function should be used to associate machine numbers with machine names. In particular, the create statement above assumes that machines numbered 1 through n are available for executing the user's program. Whether or not that is true depends on the local computing environment. In general, though, it is not true, necessitating the use of `locate`.

To illustrate this point further, suppose that only three physical machines—carob, `holly`, and `ivy`—are available. To distribute the load somewhat evenly on those machines, the following loop can be placed in `Main` before the code that creates the servant and philosophers:

```
fa i := 1 to n ->
  if i mod 3 = 0 -> locate(i, "carob")
  [] i mod 3 = 1 -> locate(i, "holly")
  [] i mod 3 = 2 -> locate(i, "ivy")
  fi
af
```

An equivalent, more general way to achieve the same effect is

```
var hosts[0:2]: string[20]
hosts[0] := "carob"
hosts[1] := "holly"
hosts[2] := "ivy"
fa i := 1 to n ->
  locate(i, hosts[i mod (ub(hosts)-lb(hosts)+1)])
af
```

The elements of hosts are initialized using distinct assignments, rather than an array constructor, because the string expressions have different lengths.

To complete this series of examples, the above code and the loop on the previous page that creates virtual machines can be combined, without using locate, as follows:

```
var hosts[0:2]: string[20]
hosts[0] := "carob"
hosts[1] := "holly"
hosts[2] := "ivy"
fa i := 1 to n ->
  var vmcap: cap vm
  vmcap := create vm() on
                hosts[i mod (ub(hosts)-lb(hosts)+1)]
  create Philosopher(s, i, t) on vmcap
af
```

This code uses the machine name (a string), instead of an integer machine number, directly in the on clause. (The locate function is still useful when a program does not want to use an installation's default machine numbers.)

To port a program containing code such as that in the above loops to another installation, only the hosts array needs to be changed to contain the local machine names. In fact, that array might be defined in a global and imported as needed.

13.2 Distributed Solution

The centralized solution to the dining philosopher's problem is deadlock-free, but it is not fair. Also, the single servant could act as a bottleneck because all philosophers need to interact with it. In contrast, the distributed solution employs one servant per fork, and it is deadlock-free and fair. Each philosopher interacts with two servants to obtain the forks it needs. A philosopher that is hungry may eat after it obtains a fork from each of the servants. This interaction is illustrated in Figure 13.2.

Our solution for this approach again employs three resources: `Servant`, `Philosopher`, and `Main`. They are again compiled in that order. The `Main` resource is similar to `Main` in the centralized solution. It differs in that `Main` now creates n instances each of `Philosopher` and `Servant` and passes capabilities for the latter to the former so they can communicate with each other.

```
resource Main()
  import Philosopher, Servant
  var n, t: int
  writes("how many Philosophers? "); read(n)
  writes("how many sessions per Philosopher? ")
  read(t)
  var s[1:n]: cap Servant
  # create the Servants
  fa i := 1 to n ->
    s[i] := create Servant(i)
  af
  # create the Philosophers; to prevent deadlock,
  # they are passed capabilities for their servants
  # in an asymmetric fashion
  fa i := 1 to n-1 ->
    create Philosopher(s[i], s[i+1], i, t)
  af
  create Philosopher(s[1], s[n], n, t)
end
```

The asymmetric way in which capabilities for servants are passed as resource parameters to instances of `Philosopher` makes deadlock easy to avoid, as discussed later.

The `Philosopher` resource is also similar to its counterpart in the centralized solution. The differences are that it is now passed capabilities for two `Servants`, and it now invokes `getfork` and `relfork` in each of those two `Servants`.

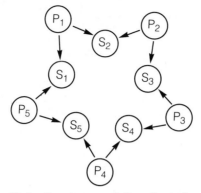

Figure 13.2. Structure of distributed solution.

```
resource Philosopher
  import Servant
body Philosopher(l, r: cap Servant; id, t: int)
  process phil
    fa i := 1 to t ->
      l.getfork(); r.getfork()
      write("Philosopher", id, "is eating")    # eat
      l.relfork(); r.relfork()
      write("Philosopher", id, "is thinking") # think
    af
  end
end
```

The `server` process in each instance of `Servant` continually services invocations of first `getfork` and then `relfork` from its two associated instances of `Philosopher`. This ensures that the servant's fork is allocated to at most one philosopher at a time. A philosopher is permitted to eat when it obtains a fork from each of its two servants.

```
resource Servant
  op getfork(), relfork()
body Servant(id: int)
  process server
    do true ->
      receive getfork(); receive relfork()
    od
  end
end
```

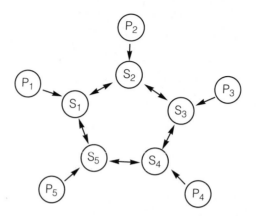

Figure 13.3. Structure of decentralized solution.

The distributed solution is deadlock-free. When `Main` creates instances of `Philosopher`, it passes them capabilities for their left and right servants. The order of these capabilities is switched for the last philosopher (i.e., the `Philosopher` passed an id of n). Thus the last philosopher requests its right fork first, whereas each other philosopher requests its left fork first. This avoids the typical deadlock scenario in which each philosopher picks up one of its forks and then requests its other fork. A more formal way to state this property, as defined in operating systems texts, is that requests from philosophers cannot form a cycle in the resource (i.e., fork) allocation graph. Unlike the centralized solution, the distributed solution also prevents starvation since forks are allocated one at a time and invocations of `getfork` are serviced in order of their arrival.

13.3 Decentralized Solution

The decentralized solution employs one servant per philosopher. Each philosopher interacts with its own personal servant; that servant interacts with its two neighboring servants. Each individual fork either is held by one of the two servants that might need it or is in transit between them. A philosopher that is hungry may eat when its servant holds two forks. This interaction is illustrated in Figure 13.3.

The specific algorithm that the servants employ is adapted from [Chandy & Misra 1984]. It has the desirable properties of being deadlock-free and fair. The basic solution strategy also has applications to other, realistic problems such as file replication, distributed database consistency, and distributed mutual exclusion.

Our decentralized solution once again employs `Servant`, `Philosopher`, and `Main` resources. `Main` is similar to its counterpart used in the distributed solution. The differences are that `Main` in this solution passes different combinations of capabilities—to support the communication structure in Figure 13.3—and it sends each instance of `Servant` the initial values for its local variables.

```
resource Main()
  import Philosopher, Servant
  var n, t: int
  writes("how many Philosophers? "); read(n)
  writes("how many sessions per Philosopher? ")
  read(t)
  var s[1:n]: cap Servant
  # create the Servants and Philosophers
  fa i := 1 to n ->
    s[i] := create Servant(i)
    create Philosopher(s[i], i, t)
  af
  # give each Servant capabilities for
  # its two neighboring Servants
  fa i := 1 to n ->
    send s[i].links(s[((i-2) mod n) + 1],
                    s[(i mod n) + 1])
  af
  # initialize each Servant's forks;
  # initialization is asymmetric to prevent deadlock;
  # see Servant resource for parameters' meanings.
  send s[1].forks(true, false, true, false)
  fa i := 2 to n-1 ->
    send s[i].forks(false, false, true, false)
  af
  send s[n].forks(false, false, false, false)
end
```

Capabilities for a philosopher's servant are passed to the philosopher as resource parameters. On the other hand, capabilities for a servant's neighbor are passed to it via a separate operation, `links`. This dissimilarity results from the fact that `Main` has to create the instances of `Servant` before it passes them the capabilities for each other. Here the servants are arranged circularly; therefore, no order of creation would allow this code to pass capabilities for servants as resource parameters to instances of `Servant`.

As in the previous solutions, each philosopher alternately eats and thinks for t sessions. Before eating, a philosopher calls the `getforks` operation in its personal instance of Servant; after eating, it calls the relforks operation in that Servant. Thus Philosopher here is almost identical to Philosopher in the centralized solution. The only difference is that a philosopher no longer passes its identity to getforks or relforks. Each philosopher now interacts with a single servant, whereas in the centralized solution, the one servant is shared by all philosophers.

```
resource Philosopher
  import Servant
body Philosopher(s: cap Servant; id, t: int)
  process phil
    fa i := 1 to t ->
      s.getforks()
      write("Philosopher", id, "is eating")    # eat
      s.relforks()
      write("Philosopher", id, "is thinking") # think
    af
  end
end
```

Instances of Servant service invocations of getforks and relforks from their associated instance of Philosopher. They communicate with neighboring instances of Servant using the needL, needR, passL, and passR operations. A philosopher is permitted to eat when its servant has acquired two forks. A servant may already have both forks when getforks is called, or it may need to request one or both from the appropriate neighbor.

Two variables are used to record the status of each fork: haveL (haveR) and dirtyL (dirtyR). Starvation is avoided by having servants give up forks that are dirty; a fork becomes dirty when it is used by a philosopher. Further details on the servant's algorithm are in [Chandy & Misra 1984].

```
resource Servant
  # operations invoked by associated philosopher
  op getforks() {call}, relforks() {call}
  # operations invoked by neighboring servants
  op needL() {send}, needR() {send},
    passL() {send}, passR() {send}
  # initialization operations invoked by Main
  op links(l, r: cap Servant),
    forks(haveL, dirtyL, haveR, dirtyR: bool)
body Servant(id: int)
  var haveL, dirtyL, haveR, dirtyR: bool
  var l, r: cap Servant
  op hungry() {send}, eat() {send}
```

```
      proc getforks()
        send hungry() # tell server Philosopher is hungry
        receive eat() # wait for permission to eat
      end
      process server
        receive links(l, r)
        receive forks(haveL, dirtyL, haveR, dirtyR)
        do true ->
          in hungry() ->
              # ask for forks I don't have; I ask my
              # right neighbor for its left fork,
              # and my left neighbor for its right fork
              if ~haveR -> send r.needL() fi
              if ~haveL -> send l.needR() fi
              # wait until I have both forks
              do ~(haveL and haveR) ->
                in passR() ->
                    haveR := true; dirtyR := false
                [] passL() ->
                    haveL := true; dirtyL := false
                [] needR() st dirtyR ->
                    haveR := false; dirtyR := false
                    send r.passL(); send r.needL()
                [] needL() st dirtyL ->
                    haveL := false; dirtyL := false
                    send l.passR(); send l.needR()
                ni
              od
              # let my Philosopher eat;
              # then wait for it to finish
              send eat(); dirtyL := true; dirtyR := true
              receive relforks()
          [] needR() ->
              # neighbor needs my right fork (its left)
              haveR := false; dirtyR := false
              send r.passL()
          [] needL() ->
              # neighbor needs my left fork (its right)
              haveL := false; dirtyL := false
              send l.passR()
          ni
        od
      end
    end Servant
```

Notice the various combinations of operation invocation and servicing that are employed. For example, `getforks` provides a procedural interface and hides the fact that getting forks requires sending a `hungry` message and receiving an `eat` message. Also, server processes use a send to invoke the need and pass operations serviced by neighboring servers; a call cannot be used for this because deadlock could result if two neighboring servers invoked each other's operations at the same time. The declaration of each operation includes a call or send restriction to specify—and enforce—the correct usage.

A philosopher and its servant are represented as separate resources. This structure provides a clean separation of their functionalities. However, they can be combined into a single resource (see Exercise 13.6).

The structure of the servants and their interaction in the above example is typical of that found in some distributed programs, such as those that implement distributed voting schemes. Such a program might contain a collection of voter processes, each of which can initiate an election. After a voter process initiates an election, it tallies the votes from the other voters. While a voter process is waiting for votes to arrive for its election, it must also be able to vote in elections initiated by other voter processes. This kind of communication can be accomplished easily only by using an asynchronous send.

In the above example, when a servant is attempting to acquire both forks for its philosopher, it might give up a fork it already possesses (because the fork is dirty). In this case it passes the fork to its neighbor and then immediately requests the fork's return. To reduce the number of messages exchanged, the request for the fork's return could be combined with the passing of the fork. In particular, the pass operations could be parameterized with a boolean that indicates whether or not the servant, when its philosopher has finished eating, should automatically pass the fork back to its neighbor (see Exercise 13.7).

Exercises

13.1 Give a solution to the dining philosophers problem in which all processes reside in a single resource and use semaphores to synchronize. (No servant process is needed.)

13.2 Repeat the previous exercise, but define the semaphores within a global and represent each philosopher as its own resource instance.

13.3 Modify the code in the distributed solution so that each philosopher is created on its own virtual machine and the one servant used by that philosopher is created on the same virtual machine. Show how to modify your solution so that each virtual machine executes on its own physical machine.

13.4 Modify the code in the decentralized solution so that each philosopher and its servant is created on a separate virtual machine. Show how to modify your solution so that each virtual machine executes on its own physical machine.

13.5 Rewrite the code for the decentralized solution so that it uses only call invocations. (Good luck!)

13.6 Show how, in the decentralized solution, to combine philosophers and servants into a single resource, as suggested at the end of Section 13.3. Can this also be done in the distributed solution?

13.7 Show how to write the variant of the decentralized solution suggested at the end of Section 13.3 to reduce message passing.

13.8 A philosopher and its servant are represented as separate processes in the decentralized solution. Can they be combined into a single process? If so, show how. If not, explain why not.

13.9 In all the dining philosopher solutions, the operations to release one or both forks have been invoked using calls. For each solution, state whether it will work if those calls are replaced by sends. Justify your answer.

13.10 Run each solution to the dining philosophers problem.

(a) Evaluate the performance of the different solutions. Which is fastest? Which is slowest? How much does performance differ? Explain the reasons for your answers.

(b) Does the order in which philosophers eat differ? If so, explain why. If not, explain why not.

13.11 *Distributed mutual exclusion.* Given are n user processes, each of which repeatedly executes a critical section of code and then a non-critical section. At most one process at a time is permitted to execute its critical section of code.

Develop centralized, distributed, and decentralized solutions to this problem. The structures of your solutions should be similar to those for the dining philosophers problem. The centralized solution should have one "servant" process with which all n users interact. The distributed solution should have n servant processes; each user process should interact with all n servants. The decentralized solution should also have n servant processes, but each user should interact with just one servant; the servants should also interact with each other.

PART **III**

Applications

Parts I and II described SR's sequential and concurrent programming mechanisms and gave numerous, mostly small examples. In this part we examine several larger applications. These are representative of the kinds of parallel and distributed programming problems SR can be used to solve. The solutions also illustrate several process interaction paradigms that occur in concurrent programs. Each interaction paradigm is an example or model of an interprocess communication pattern and associated programming technique that can be used to solve a variety of problems. The exercises at the end of each chapter explore additional problems that can be solved using these paradigms.

Chapters 14 and 15 examine two problems that are representative of those that arise in scientific computing: matrix multiplication and iterative solutions to partial differential equations (PDEs). In both cases we develop solutions that use shared variables and ones that use message passing. We also discuss performance issues, including the effect of memory caches and the tradeoffs between task size and communication and synchronization overhead. In Chapter 16 we examine the classic traveling salesman problem, which is representative of combinatorial problems. Again we present both centralized and distributed solutions and discuss performance tradeoffs. The final two chapters in Part III present further examples of concurrent programs. In Chapter 17 we develop a simple command interpreter and distributed file system. Chapter 18 develops an implementation of a discrete event simulation package.

CHAPTER 14

Parallel
Matrix Multiplication

Matrix computations lie at the heart of most scientific computing problems. Matrix multiplication is one of the most basic of these computations. In Chapter 1 we presented a simple, but inefficient, parallel algorithm for matrix multiplication. Here we develop four realistic algorithms. Two employ shared variables and hence are suitable for execution on shared-memory multiprocessors. The other two algorithms employ message passing and hence are suitable for execution on distributed-memory systems. Each algorithm also illustrates a different programming technique and a different combination of SR mechanisms.

As in Section 1.3, the problem is to compute the product of two $n \times n$ real matrices a and b. This requires computing n^2 inner products, one for each combination of a row of a and a column of b. On a massively parallel, synchronous multiprocessor, all inner products could be computed in parallel with reasonable efficiency since, by default, every processor executes the same sequence of instructions at the same time. However, on an asynchronous multiprocessor each process has to be created and destroyed explicitly, and each inner product requires relatively little computation. In fact, the parallel program in Section 1.3 would be much slower than a sequential program since the cost of creating and destroying processes would far outweigh any benefits derived from parallel execution.

To execute efficiently on an asynchronous multiprocessor, each process in a parallel program must perform quite a bit of work relative to the amount of time it takes to create the process and the amount of time the process spends communicating and synchronizing with other processes. A common way to describe the amount of sequential work that a process performs is in terms of the number of basic steps—or *grains*—of the parallel computation. Choosing an appropriate grain size is a ubiquitous and important problem in parallel computing because the grain size determines each process's sequential execution time, which must be much greater than the concurrency and communication overhead. The exact balance depends, of course, on the underlying hardware and on the concurrent programming mechanisms that are employed. This chapter develops four matrix multiplication algorithms that employ different combinations of communication and synchronization mechanisms. Each can readily be modified to alter the balance between sequential execution time and concurrency overhead.

14.1 Prescheduled Strips

Our first algorithm uses real matrices `a[N,N]`, `b[N,N]`, and `c[N,N]`. Assume that these are shared variables, and we wish to use `PR` processes to compute the product of `a` and `b` and store it in `c`. For simplicity we also assume that `N` is a multiple of `PR`; for example, `N` might be 100 and `PR` might be 10.

To balance the amount of computation performed by each process, each should compute N^2/PR inner products. The simplest way to do this is to assign each process responsibility for computing the values for all elements in a strip of matrix `c`, as shown in Figure 14.1. In particular, let `S` be `N/PR`. Then the first process computes the values of the first `S` rows of `c`, the second computes the values of the next `S` rows of `c`, and so on. This kind of approach is sometimes called prescheduling because each process is assigned in advance a certain number of "chores," i.e., inner products in this case.

To implement this algorithm in SR, we use one global and one resource, which are compiled in that order. The global declares the shared constants `N`, `PR`, and `S` and reads values for `N` and `PR` from the command line. It then computes `S`; if `N` is not a multiple of `PR`, the global prints an error message and stops the program.

```
global sizes
  var N := 10      # matrix size, default 10
  var PR := 2      # number of processes, default 2
  var S: int       # strip size
body sizes
  getarg(1, N); getarg(2, PR); S := N/PR
  if N mod PR != 0 ->
    write("N must be a multiple of PR"); stop (1)
  fi
end
```

Variables `N` and `PR` are given default initial values; these are used if there are

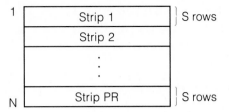

Figure 14.1. Assigning processes to strips.

no command-line arguments. (Calling `getarg` has no effect if there is no corresponding argument.)

The resource declares the matrices and an array of PR processes to compute the inner products. It also contains a process that implements a barrier synchronization point and final code to print results.

```
resource mult()
  import sizes
  var a[N,N], b[N,N], c[N,N]: real
  sem done := 0, continue := 0

  var start := age()  # determine start time
  process strip(p := 1 to PR)
    const R := (p-1)*S + 1  # starting row of strip
    # initialize parts of a and b
    fa i := R to R+S-1, j := 1 to N ->
      a[i,j] := 1.0; b[i,j] := 1.0
    af
    # barrier to wait for all initialization
    V(done); P(continue)
    # compute S*N inner products
    fa i := R to R+S-1, j := 1 to N ->
      var inner_prod := 0.0  # local accumulator
      fa k := 1 to N ->
        inner_prod +:= a[i,k]*b[k,j]
      af
      c[i,j] := inner_prod
    af
  end

  process coordinator
    fa i := 1 to PR -> P(done) af
    fa i := 1 to PR -> V(continue) af
  end
```

```
final  # print results
  var finish := age()  # determine finish time
  write("execution time for", PR, "processes was",
        finish-start, "milliseconds")
  fa i := 1 to N ->
    fa j := 1 to N -> writes(c[i,j], " ") af
    write()
  af
end
end
```

Each instance of process strip first initializes its bands of matrices a, b, and c. For simplicity we have initialized all elements of a and b to 1.0; in general, initial values would come from a prior computation or from external files.

Because all elements of a and b must be initialized before they are used by other processes, we need to implement a barrier synchronization point. Here we have simply used two semaphores and a coordinator process. The coordinator first waits for all PR instances of strip to signal semaphore done, then it signals semaphore continue PR times. Since the barrier is executed only once, this approach is reasonable for this program. In general, however, one will want to use one of the more efficient barriers described in [Andrews 1991] or [Mellor-Crummey & Scott 1991].

The final code in mult is executed when all instances of strip have terminated. That code prints the results. This use of final code frees the programmer from having to program termination detection.

To determine the execution time of the program, we have used two calls of the predefined age function: one just before the strip processes are created, and a second at the start of the final code. The difference between the two values returned by age is the time, in milliseconds, that the SR program has been executing.

Many shared-memory multiprocessors employ caches, with one cache per processor. Each cache contains the memory blocks most recently referenced by the processor. (A block is typically a few contiguous words.) The purpose of caches is to increase performance, but they have to be used with care by the programmer or they can actually decrease performance (due to cache conflicts). Hill and Larus [1990] give three rules-of-thumb programmers need to keep in mind:

- Perform all operations on a variable, especially updates, in one process (processor).

- Align data so that variables updated by different processors are in different cache blocks.

- Reuse data quickly when possible so it remains in the cache and does not get "spilled" back to main memory.

Since SR stores matrices in row-major order (i.e., by rows), the above program uses caches well. Each `strip` process reads one distinct strip of a and writes one distinct strip of c, and it references elements of a and c by sweeping across rows. Every process references all elements of b, but that is unavoidable. (If b were transposed, so that columns were actually stored in rows, it too could be referenced efficiently.)

14.2 Dynamic Scheduling: A Bag of Tasks

The algorithm in the previous section statically assigned an equal amount of work to each `strip` process. If the processes execute on homogeneous processors without interruption, they would be likely to finish at about the same time. However, if the processes execute on different-speed processors, or if they can be interrupted—e.g., in a timesharing system—then different processes might complete at different times. To dynamically assign work to processes, we can employ a shared bag of tasks, as in the solution to the adaptive quadrature problem in Section 9.5. Here we present a matrix multiplication program that implements such a solution. The structure of the solution is illustrated in Figure 14.2.

As in the previous program, we employ one global and one resource. The global declares the matrix size N and the number of worker processes W, and reads values for these variables from the command line.

```
global sizes
  var N := 10    # matrix size, default 10
  var W := 2     # number of workers, default 2
body sizes
  getarg(1, N); getarg(2, W)
end
```

As before, the shared variables are given default initial values.

The resource, `mult`, imports `sizes` and declares shared matrices a, b, and c; the sizes of these matrices again depend on N. The resource then declares an operation, `bag`, which is shared by the `worker` processes in the resource. The initialization code in `mult` sets all elements of a and b to 1.0 and sends each row index to `bag`. After initialization has completed, the worker processes are created. Each worker process repeatedly receives a row index i from `bag` and computes N inner products, one for each element of row i of result matrix c.

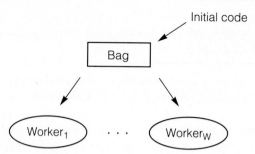

Figure 14.2. Replicated workers and bag of tasks.

```
resource mult()
  import sizes
  var a[N,N], b[N,N], c[N,N]: real
  op bag(row: int)

  # initialize the arrays and bag of tasks
  fa i := 1 to N, j := 1 to N ->
      a[i,j] := 1.0; b[i,j] := 1.0
  af
  fa i := 1 to N -> send bag(i) af

  process worker(id := 1 to W)
     var i: int     # index of row of c to compute
     do true ->
       receive bag(i)     # get a task from the bag
       fa j := 1 to N ->
         var inner_prod := 0.0
         fa k := 1 to N ->
             inner_prod +:= a[i,k]*b[k,j]
         af
         c[i,j] := inner_prod
       af
     od
  end

  final
    fa i := 1 to N ->
      fa j := 1 to N -> writes(c[i,j], " ") af
      write()
    af
  end
end mult
```

The computation terminates when `bag` is empty and all worker processes are blocked waiting to receive from it. At this point, the final code is executed; it prints out the values in `c`.

This program has been executed on a Sequent Symmetry multiprocessor using 1, 2, 4, and 8 workers and processors. It shows nearly perfect speedup—over the one worker and one processor case—for reasonable-size matrices, e.g., when `N` is 100 or more. In this case the amount of computation per iteration of a worker process far outweighs the overhead of receiving a message from the bag. Like the previous program, this one uses caches well since SR stores matrices in row-major order, and each worker fills in an entire row of `c`. If the bag of tasks contained column indices instead of row indices, performance would be much worse because workers would encounter cache update conflicts.

14.3 A Distributed Broadcast Algorithm

The program in the previous section can be modified so that the workers do not share the matrices or bag of tasks. In particular, each worker (or address space) could be given a copy of `a` and `b`, and an administrator process could dispense tasks and collect results (see Exercise 14.3). With these changes, the program could execute on a distributed-memory machine.

This section and the next present two additional distributed algorithms. To simplify the presentation, we use N^2 processes, one to compute each element `c[i,j]`. Initially each such process also has the corresponding values of `a` and `b`, i.e., `a[i,j]` and `b[i,j]`. In this section we have each process broadcast its value of `a` to other processes on the same row and broadcast its value of `b` to other processes on the same column. In the next section we have each process interact only with its four neighbors. Both algorithms are inefficient as given since the grain size is way too small to compensate for communication overhead. However, the algorithms can readily be generalized to use fewer processes, each of which is responsible for a block of matrix `c` (see Exercises 14.7 and 14.8).

Our broadcast implementation of matrix multiplication uses three components: a global, a resource to compute elements of `c`, and a main resource. They are compiled in that order. The global declares and reads a command-line argument for the matrix size `N`, as follows:

```
global sizes
  var N := 6     # matrix size, default 6
body sizes
  getarg(1, N)
end
```

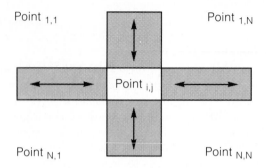

Figure 14.3. Broadcast algorithm interaction pattern.

Instances of resource `point` carry out the computation. The main resource creates one instance for each value of `c[i,j]`. Each instance exports three operations: one to start the computation, one to exchange row values, and one to exchange column values. Operation `compute` is implemented by a `proc`; it is invoked by a send statement in the main resource and hence executes as a process. The arguments of the `compute` operation are capabilities for other instances of `point`. Operations `rowval` and `colval` are serviced by receive statements; they are invoked by other instances of `point` in the same row `i` and column `j`, respectively.

The N^2 instances of `point` interact as shown in Figure 14.3. The `compute` process in `point` first sends its value of `aij` to the other instances of `point` in the same row and receives their elements of `a`. The `compute` process then sends its value of `bij` to other instances of `point` in the same column and receives their elements of `b`. After these two data exchanges, `point(i,j)` now has row `i` of `a` and column `j` of `b`. It then computes the inner product of these two vectors. The final code prints out the value of `cij`. It is executed when the resource instance is destroyed explicitly. (Only the initial instance of the main resource is destroyed implicitly.)

```
resource point     # one instance per point
   op compute(rlinks[*], clinks[*]: cap point)
   op rowval(sender: int; value: real)
   op colval(sender: int; value: real)
body point(i, j: int)
   import sizes
   var aij := 1.0, bij := 1.0, cij := 0.0
   var row[N], col[N]: real
   row[j] := aij; col[i] := bij
```

```
proc compute(rlinks, clinks)
  # broadcast aij to points on same row
  fa k := 1 to N st k != j ->
    send rlinks[k].rowval(j, aij)
  af
  # acquire other points from same row
  fa k := 1 to N st k != j ->
    receive rowval(sender, row[sender])
  af
  # broadcast bij to points on same column
  fa k := 1 to N st k != i ->
    send clinks[k].colval(i, bij)
  af
  # acquire other points from same column
  fa k := 1 to N st k != i ->
    receive colval(sender, col[sender])
  af
  # compute inner product of row and col
  fa k := 1 to N -> cij +:= row[k]*col[k] af
end compute

final writes(cij, " ") end
end point
```

The main resource creates N^2 instances of `point` and gets back a capability for each, which it stores in matrix `pcap`. It then invokes the `compute` operations, passing each instance of `point` capabilities for other instances in the same row and column. We use the slice `pcap[i,1:N]` to pass row i of `pcap` to `compute`. Similarly, we use the slice `pcap[1:N,j]` to pass column j to `compute`.

```
resource main()
  import sizes, point
  var pcap[N,N]: cap point
  # create points
  fa i := 1 to N, j := 1 to N ->
    pcap[i,j] := create point(i, j)
  af
  # give each point capabilities for its neighbors
  fa i := 1 to N, j := 1 to N ->
    send pcap[i,j].compute(pcap[i,1:N], pcap[1:N,j])
  af
```

```
        final
          fa i := 1 to N ->
            fa j := 1 to N -> destroy pcap[i,j] af
            write()    # output a newline character
          af
        end
      end main
```

When the program terminates, the final code in `main` is executed. It destroys instances of `point` in row-major order, which causes the elements of `c` to be printed in row-major order.

As noted, this program can readily be modified to have each instance of `point` start with a block of `a` and a block of `b` and compute all elements of a block of `c`. It also can be modified so that the blocks are not square, i.e., strips can be used. In either case the basic algorithmic structure and communication pattern is identical. The program can also be modified to execute on multiple virtual machines: The main resource first creates the virtual machines and then creates instances of `point` on them.

14.4 A Distributed Heartbeat Algorithm

In the broadcast algorithm, each instance of `point` acquires an entire row of `a` and an entire column of `b` and then computes their inner product. Also, each instance of `point` communicates with all other instances on the same row and same column. Here we present a matrix multiplication algorithm that employs the same number of instances of a `point` resource. However, each instance holds only one value of `a` and one of `b` at a time. Also, each instance of `point` communicates only with its four neighbors, as shown in Figure 14.4. Again, the algorithm can readily be generalized to work on blocks of points and to execute on multiple virtual machines.

As in the broadcast algorithm, we will use N^2 processes, one to compute each element of matrix `c`. Again, each initially also has the corresponding elements of `a` and `b`. The algorithm consists of three stages [Manber 1989]. In the first stage, processes shift values in `a` circularly to the left; values in row `i` of `a` are shifted left `i` columns. Second, processes shift values in `b` circularly up; values in column `j` of `b` are shifted up `j` rows. The result of the initial rearrangement of the values of `a` and `b` for a 3×3 matrix is

```
a[1,2], b[2,1]    a[1,3], b[3,2]    a[1,1], b[1,3]

a[2,3], b[3,1]    a[2,1], b[1,2]    a[2,2], b[2,3]

a[3,1], b[1,1]    a[3,2], b[2,2]    a[3,3], b[3,3]
```

Point _{1,1}   Point _{1,N}

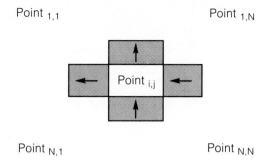

Point _{N,1}   Point _{N,N}

Figure 14.4. Heartbeat algorithm interaction pattern.

In the third stage, each process multiplies one element of a and one of b, adds the product to its element of c, shifts the element of a circularly left one column, and shifts the element of b circularly up one row. This compute-and-shift sequence is repeated N-1 times, at which point the matrix product has been computed.

We call this kind of algorithm a *heartbeat algorithm* because the actions of each process are like the beating of a heart: first send data out to neighbors, then bring data in from neighbors and use it. To implement the algorithm in SR, we again use one global and two resources, as in the broadcast algorithm. The global is identical to the one used in the broadcast algorithm:

```
global sizes
   var N := 6     # matrix size, default 6
body sizes
   getarg(1, N)
end
```

The computation is carried out by N^2 instances of a point resource, which exports three operations as in the broadcast algorithm. However, here the compute operation is passed capabilities for only the left and upward neighbors, and the rowval and colval operations are invoked by only one neighbor. Also, the body of point implements a different algorithm, as shown on the next page.

```
resource point      # one instance per point
   op compute(left, up: cap point)
   op rowval(value: real), colval(value: real)
body point(i, j: int) separate
```

```
body point
  import sizes
  var aij: real := i, bij: real := j, cij := 0.0

  proc compute(left, up)
    # shift values in aij circularly left i columns
    fa k := 1 to i ->
      send left.rowval(aij); receive rowval(aij)
    af
    # shift values in bij circularly up j rows
    fa k := 1 to j ->
      send up.colval(bij); receive colval(bij)
    af
    cij := aij*bij
    fa k := 1 to N-1 ->
      # shift aij left, bij up, then multiply
      send left.rowval(aij); send up.colval(bij)
      receive rowval(aij); receive colval(bij)
      cij +:= aij*bij
    af
  end

  final writes(cij, " ") end
end point
```

The main resource creates instances of `point` and passes each capabilities
for its left and upward neighbors. When the computation terminates, the
final code destroys the instances.

```
resource main()
  import sizes, point
  var pcap[N,N]: cap point

  procedure prev(index: int) returns lft: int
    lft := (index-2) mod N + 1
  end

  # create points, then give each capabilities
  # for its left and upward neighbors
  fa i := 1 to N, j := 1 to N ->
    pcap[i,j] := create point(i, j)
  af
  fa i := 1 to N, j := 1 to N ->
    send pcap[i,j].compute(pcap[i,prev(j)],
                           pcap[prev(i),j])
  af
```

```
      final
        # destroy points, which output the results
        fa i := 1 to N ->
          fa j := 1 to N -> destroy pcap[i,j] af
          write()
        af
      end
    end main
```

Function `prev` in `main` uses modular arithmetic so that instances of `point` on the left and top borders communicate with instances on the right and bottom borders, respectively.

Exercises

14.1   Add explicit termination detection code to the program in Section 14.1.

14.2   Modify the prescheduled strip algorithm so that `N` does not have to be a multiple of `PR`.

14.3   Change the bag of tasks program so that it does not use shared variables.

14.4   The `compute` process in resource `point` in Section 14.3 contains the following receive statement:

```
        receive rowval(sender, row[sender])
```

This statement is within a for-all statement.

(a) Write an equivalent input statement for the receive statement.

(b) Explain why the receive statement cannot be simplified to the following, assuming the declaration of `rowval` is changed to omit the `sender` field:

```
        receive rowval(row[k])
```

14.5   Suppose a and b are 5×5 matrices. Determine the location of each value of a and b after the two shift stages of the heartbeat algorithm in Section 14.4.

14.6   Determine the total number of messages that are sent in the distributed broadcast algorithm and the size of each. Do the same for the distributed heartbeat algorithm. Explain the differences.

14.7   Modify the broadcast algorithm so that each instance of `point` is responsible for a block of points. Use PR^2 processes, where `N` is a multiple of `PR`.

14.8   Modify the heartbeat algorithm so that each instance of `point` is responsible for a block of points. Use PR^2 processes, where `N` is a multiple of `PR`.

14.9   Compare the performance of the various programs presented in this chapter or those that you developed in answering the above exercises.

14.10   Modify the programs in this chapter to read input values from files.

14.11   Implement matrix multiplication using a grid of filter processes [Hoare 1978, Andrews 1991].

14.12   Implement Gaussian elimination (see Exercise 7.13) using the techniques illustrated in this chapter.

## CHAPTER 15

Solving PDEs:
Grid Computations

Partial differential equations (PDEs) are used to model a variety of different kinds of physical systems: weather, airflow over a wing, turbulence in fluids, and so on. Some simple PDEs can be solved directly, but in general it is necessary to approximate the solution at a finite number of points using iterative numerical methods. In this chapter we show how to solve one specific PDE—Laplace's equation in two dimensions—by means of a grid computation, which employs what is called a finite-difference method. As in the previous chapter, we present several solutions that illustrate a variety of programming techniques and their realizations in SR.

Laplace's equation is an example of what is called an elliptic partial differential equation. The equation for two dimensions is the following:

$$\frac{\partial^2 \Phi}{\partial x^2} + \frac{\partial^2 \Phi}{\partial y^2} = 0$$

Function Φ represents some unknown potential, such as heat or stress.

Given a fixed spatial region and solution values for points on the boundaries of the region, our task is to approximate the steady-state solution for points within the interior. We can do this by covering the region with an evenly spaced grid of points, as shown in Figure 15.1. Each interior point is initialized to some value. The steady-state values of the interior points are then calculated by repeated iterations. On each iteration the new value of a point is set to a combination of the old and/or new values of neighboring points. The computation terminates when every new value is within some acceptable difference ε of every old value.

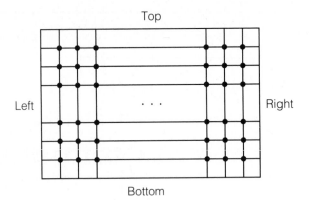

Figure 15.1. Approximating Laplace's equation using a grid.

There are several stationary iterative methods for solving Laplace's equation—Jacobi iteration, Gauss-Seidel, and successive over-relaxation (SOR). In Jacobi iteration, the new value for each point is set to the average of the old values of the four neighboring points. Jacobi iteration can be parallelized readily because each new value is independent of the others. Although Jacobi iteration converges more slowly than other methods, we will use it in this chapter since it is easier to program. In any event, parallel computations that use other iterative methods employ basically the same communication and synchronization patterns.

15.1 A Data Parallel Algorithm

A data parallel algorithm is an iterative algorithm that repeatedly and in parallel manipulates a shared array [Hillis & Steele 1986]. This kind of algorithm is most closely associated with synchronous (SIMD) multi-processors, but it can also be used on asynchronous multiprocessors. Here we present a data parallel implementation of Jacobi iteration. It illustrates uses of SR's concurrent (`co`) statement.

The main loop in a data parallel implementation of Jacobi iteration repeatedly executes three phases:

```
do true ->
    compute new values for all grid points
    replace old values by new values
    check for convergence; exit if converged
od
```

To implement this computation in SR, we use two globals and a main resource, which are compiled in the order presented below. (The second global could be eliminated by including its code as part of the resource. However, it is reused in the next section.) The first global declares and initializes the grid size:

```
global size
  var N := 8     # grid size, default 8
body size
  getarg(1, N)
end
```

Variable N is the number of rows and columns in the grid of interior points; i.e., points whose steady-state value is to be computed.

The second global declares and initializes an array that contains old and new grid values, two variables that are used to index grid, and the convergence criterion epsilon. The current (old) grid values are grid[cur] and the next (new) grid values are grid[nxt]. The code later in this section reads values from the old grid and writes values to the new grid on each iteration. At the end of each iteration, the code replaces the old values by the new values by simply swapping nxt and cur, which is more efficient than copying grid[nxt] to grid[cur]. The global also exports a procedure that is called to print the current grid.

```
global data
  import size
  var grid[2][0:N+1,0:N+1]: real
  var cur := 1, nxt := 2; var epsilon: real
  op print()     # called to print the grid
body data
  grid := ([2] ([N+2] ([N+2] 0.0)))
  var l, t, r, b: real
  writes("enter 4 border values (l, t, r, b): ")
  read(l, t, r, b)
  fa i := 0 to N+1 ->
    grid[cur][i,0]   := l; grid[nxt][i,0]   := l
    grid[cur][0,i]   := t; grid[nxt][0,i]   := t
    grid[cur][i,N+1] := r; grid[nxt][i,N+1] := r
    grid[cur][N+1,i] := b; grid[nxt][N+1,i] := b
  af
  writes("enter epsilon: "); read(epsilon)

  proc print()
    write()   # leave a blank line
```

```
          fa i := 1 to N ->
            fa j := 1 to N -> writes(grid[cur][i,j]," ") af
            write()
          af
        end print
      end data
```

Array `grid` consists of two matrices. Each matrix has N+2 rows and columns so the boundary values can be stored within the matrix. This avoids having to treat the boundaries as special cases in the main computation. For simplicity each interior grid point is initialized to zero; for faster convergence each should be initialized to a value that somewhat approximates the expected final value.

The main resource contains arrays to hold intermediate results, three local procedures, and a main loop. The main loop has three phases, as outlined above. The first phase is implemented by a `co` statement that makes N^2 calls of `update`. The second phase is implemented by a swap statement, which switches the roles of the two grids. The third phase is implemented by a second `co` statement that makes N calls of `check_diffs` and by an if statement that exits the loop if the grid values have converged.

```
        resource jacobi()
          import data, size
          var diff[1:N,1:N]: real      # differences

          procedure update(i, j: int)
            grid[nxt][i,j] := (grid[cur][i-1,j] +
                  grid[cur][i,j-1] + grid[cur][i+1,j] +
                  grid[cur][i,j+1]) / 4
            diff[i,j] := abs(grid[nxt][i,j] - grid[cur][i,j])
          end

          procedure check_diffs(i: int)
            fa j := 2 to N ->
              diff[i,1] := max(diff[i,1], diff[i,j])
            af
          end

          var iters := 0, maxdiff: real
          do true ->      # iterate until convergence
            iters++
            # compute new values for all grid points
            co (i := 1 to N, j := 1 to N) update(i,j) oc
            # replace old values by new values
            nxt :=: cur
```

```
            # check for convergence; exit if converged
            maxdiff := 0.0
            co (i := 1 to N) check_diffs(i) ->
                  maxdiff := max(maxdiff, diff[i,1])
            oc
            if maxdiff <= epsilon -> exit fi
         od
         write("convergence after", iters, "iterations")
         print()                    .
      end jacobi
```

After the first co statement terminates, matrix diff contains the differences
between all old and new grid points. The role of the second co statement is to
determine the maximum difference. It does so by calling N instances of
check_diffs in parallel, one for each row i. Each instance of check_diffs
stores the maximum difference of the elements in its row in diff[i,1].
When each call of check_diffs completes, the postprocessing clause in the
second co statement updates local variable maxdiff, which contains the
maximum of all the differences. If this value is at most epsilon, we exit the
loop and print the results.

15.2 Prescheduled Strips

The main loop in the algorithm in the previous section repeatedly creates
numerous processes and then waits for them to terminate. Process
creation/destruction is much more time consuming than most forms of
interprocess synchronization, especially when processes are repeatedly
created and destroyed. Hence we can implement a data parallel algorithm
much more efficiently on an asynchronous multiprocessor by creating
processes once and using barriers to synchronize execution phases. (See
[Andrews 1991] for further discussion of this topic.) We can make the
implementation even more efficient by having each process handle several
points of the grid, not just one.

   This section presents a parallel algorithm for Jacobi iteration that uses a
fixed number of processes. As in the matrix multiplication algorithm in
Section 14.1, each process is responsible for a strip of the grid. In particular,
for an N × N grid, we use PR processes, with each responsible for S rows of the
grid. The solution also illustrates one way to implement a monitor [Hoare
1974] in SR.

   Our program employs three globals and a main resource, compiled in the
order shown below. The first global (see next page) declares and initializes N,
PR, and S. For simplicity, we require that N be a multiple of PR.

```
global size
  var N := 8     # grid size
  var PR := 2    # number of processes
  var S: int     # strip size
body size
  getarg(1, N); getarg(2, PR); S := N/PR
  if (N mod PR) != 0 ->
    write("N must be a multiple of PR"); stop(1)
  fi
end
```

The second global declares and initializes the grids and convergence criterion. It is identical to global `data` (see Section 15.1).

The third global implements a barrier synchronization point for `PR` processes. It is essentially a monitor, with mutual exclusion and condition synchronization implemented using semaphores. In particular, the global exports one operation `barrier`. Processes call `barrier` when they reach a barrier synchronization point. All but the last to arrive block on a semaphore. The last to arrive awakens those that are sleeping and resets the local variables.

```
global barrier_synch
  import size
  op barrier()
body barrier_synch
  var cnt := 0, sleep := 1
  sem mutex := 1, delay[1:2] := ([2] 0)

  proc barrier()
    P(mutex)
    cnt++
    if cnt < PR ->
        var mysleep := sleep
        V(mutex); P(delay[mysleep])
    [] else ->
        cnt := 0
        fa i := 1 to PR-1 -> V(delay[sleep]) af
        sleep := 3-sleep  # switch delay semaphores
        V(mutex)
    fi
  end
end barrier_synch
```

Two delay semaphores are needed to prevent processes that are quick to arrive at the next barrier synchronization point from "stealing" signals intended for processes that have not yet left the previous barrier. Their use is analogous to the use of an array of condition variables in a monitor. Variable sleep indicates which element of delay a process is to block on; its value alternates between 1 and 2. Before blocking, a process copies the current value of sleep into a local variable; this is necessary since the value of sleep could otherwise change before the process blocks (see Exercise 15.7).

The main resource implements parallel Jacobi iteration using PR processes. As before, each process repeatedly executes three phases: computing new values, replacing old values by new ones, and checking for convergence. These are implemented in pretty much the same way as in the data parallel algorithm. To ensure that all processes complete one phase before beginning the next, the first and last are followed by a barrier synchronization point.

```
resource jacobi()
  import data, size, barrier_synch
  var maxdiff[1:PR]: real     # differences
  var iters := 0

  process strip(p := 1 to PR)
    const r := (p-1)*S + 1     # starting row of strip
    var mdiff: real
    do true ->
      # if process 1, count iterations
      if p = 1 -> iters++ fi
      # compute new values for strip of grid
      # use local variable to hold maximum difference
      mdiff := 0.0
      fa i := r to r+S-1, j := 1 to N ->
        grid[nxt][i,j] := (grid[cur][i-1,j] +
               grid[cur][i,j-1] + grid[cur][i+1,j] +
               grid[cur][i,j+1]) / 4
        mdiff := max(mdiff,
               abs(grid[nxt][i,j] - grid[cur][i,j]))
      af
      maxdiff[p] := mdiff
      barrier()
      # if process 1, swap roles of grids
      if p = 1 -> nxt :=: cur fi
      # check for convergence and possibly terminate
      fa i := 1 to PR ->
        mdiff := max(mdiff, maxdiff[i])
      af
```

```
        if mdiff <= epsilon -> exit fi
        barrier()
      od
    end strip

    final
      write("convergence after", iters, "iterations")
      print()
    end
  end jacobi
```

As commented in the code, only the first process counts the number of iterations (all will execute the same number since all use the same convergence criterion). Also, only the first process executes the swap statement that switches the roles of the grids. Variable `iters` is global to the processes so that it is accessible to the final code.

To avoid cache update conflicts, each `strip` process uses a local variable to accumulate the maximum difference between old and new values in its strip of the grid. Only at the end of phase one of its main loop does a process store into shared array `maxdiff`. In the second phase, each process then reads these shared values to determine the maximum difference in the entire grid; again it uses local variable `mdiff` to avoid writing into shared variables.

15.3 A Distributed Heartbeat Algorithm

The previous two programs for Jacobi iteration use shared variables. In this section we present a distributed program that uses message passing. The program again employs PR processes, and each is responsible for a strip of S rows of the grid. Also, each process repeatedly executes the same three phases: updating grid points, copying new values into old, and checking for termination. These phases are realized differently, however, as is end-of-phase synchronization.

In a distributed SR program that might execute on multiple virtual machines, we cannot use globals to store shared data since each virtual machine gets a distinct copy of each global. Hence we will use two resources and no globals. The first resource, `jacobi`, implements the computation proper. The second, `main`, creates PR instances of `jacobi` and then starts the computation in each instance. During each iteration of the computation, instances of `jacobi` exchange the boundaries of their strip of the grid.

The `jacobi` resource exports three operations: `toprow`, which is used to acquire a new top boundary; `bottomrow`, which is used to acquire a new bottom boundary; and `compute`, which is used to start the computation. Each instance of `jacobi` is also parameterized with several values, most of which were stored in globals in the previous two programs.

The body of `jacobi` contains four parts: variable declarations, initialization code, a proc that performs the computation, and final code.

```
resource jacobi
  import main
  op toprow([*] real), bottomrow([*] real)
  op compute(up, down: cap jacobi; coord: cap main)
body jacobi(id, N, PR, S: int; l, t, r, b: real)
  var grid[2][0:S+1,0:N+1]: real
  var cur := 1, nxt := 2
  var diff: real     # max difference

  # initialize grids
  grid := ([2] ([S+2] (1, [N] 0.0, r)))
  if id = 1 ->  # top for process 1
    grid[cur][0] := grid[nxt][0] := ([N+2] t)
  fi
  if id = PR ->  # bottom for process PR
    grid[cur][S+1] := grid[nxt][S+1] := ([N+2] b)
  fi

  proc compute(up, down, coord)
    do true ->
      # compute new values for grid points
      diff := 0.0
      fa i := 1 to S, j := 1 to N ->
        grid[nxt][i,j] := (grid[cur][i-1,j] +
               grid[cur][i,j-1] + grid[cur][i+1,j] +
               grid[cur][i,j+1]) / 4
        diff := max(diff, abs(grid[nxt][i,j] -
                                grid[cur][i,j]))
      af
      # replace old values by new ones, and
      # exchange top and bottom rows with neighbors
      cur :=: nxt
      send up.bottomrow(grid[cur][1,*])
      send down.toprow(grid[cur][S,*])
      if id != 1 -> receive toprow(grid[cur][0,*]) fi
      if id != PR ->
        receive bottomrow(grid[cur][S+1,*])
      fi
      # check for termination
      if coord.terminate(diff) -> exit fi
    od
  end compute
```

```
        final
          fa i := 1 to S ->
            fa j := 1 to N -> writes(grid[cur][i,j]," ") af
            write()
          af
        end
      end jacobi
```

Each instance of `jacobi` is responsible for a strip of `S` rows and `N` columns of the grid. As before, array `grid` contains two matrices, and each has two extra rows and columns to hold the values on the edges of the strip. The extra columns contain boundary values, which do not change. However, the extra rows contain values computed on each iteration by the instances of `jacobi` responsible for adjacent strips. Hence each instance exchanges these rows with its neighbors on each iteration. The instances responsible for the topmost strip and bottommost strip have only one neighbor, so they exchange only one row. As we shall see, capability `up` is set to `noop` for the topmost strip, and `down` is set to `noop` for the bottommost strip; this makes the corresponding send statements have no effect.

The main resource exports one operation, `terminate`, which is called by instances of `jacobi` to check for termination. The body of `main` contains five parts: variable declarations and initialization, code to create instances of `jacobi`, code to start the computation, a loop that checks for termination, and final code.

```
      resource main
        import jacobi
        op terminate(diff: real) returns ans: bool
      body main()
        var N := 8      # grid size
        var PR := 2     # number of processes
        var S: int      # strip size
        # read command-line arguments, if present
        getarg(1, N); getarg(2, PR); S := N/PR
        if (N mod PR) != 0 ->
          write("N must be a multiple of PR"); stop(1)
        fi
        # read boundary values and epsilon
        var l, t, r, b, epsilon: real
        writes("enter 4 border values (l, t, r, b): ")
        read(l, t, r, b)
        writes("enter epsilon: "); read(epsilon)
```

```
# create instances of jacobi()
var jcap[1:PR]: cap jacobi
if PR = 1 ->
  jcap[1] := create jacobi(1,N,PR,S,l,t,r,b)
[] else ->
  jcap[1] := create jacobi(1,N,PR,S,l,t,r,0.0)
  fa i := 2 to PR-1 ->
    jcap[i] := create jacobi(i,N,PR,S,l,0.0,r,0.0)
  af
  jcap[PR] := create jacobi(PR,N,PR,S,l,0.0,r,b)
fi

# start the computation
if PR = 1 ->
   send jcap[1].compute(noop,noop,myresource())
[] else ->
  send jcap[1].compute(noop,jcap[2],myresource())
  fa i := 2 to PR-1 ->
    send jcap[i].compute(jcap[i-1],
                         jcap[i+1],myresource())
  af
  send jcap[PR].compute(jcap[PR-1],
                        noop,myresource())
fi

# do termination checks until convergence
var iters := 0
do true ->
  iters++
  # wait for all processes to call terminate, then
  # service invocation with largest value for diff
  in terminate(diff) returns ans
        st ?terminate = PR by -diff ->
          ans := diff <= epsilon
          fa i := 1 to PR-1 ->
            in terminate(diff2) returns ans2 ->
              ans2 := ans
            ni
          af
          if ans -> exit fi
  ni
od
```

```
        final  # print results
          write("convergence after", iters, "iterations")
          fa i := 1 to PR -> destroy jcap[i] af
        end
      end main
```

The initialization code is identical to that in the previous programs. The other parts are different because this is a distributed program.

The code that starts the computation invokes the `compute` operation in each of the PR instances of `jacobi`. Each instance is passed three capabilities: two for neighboring instances and one for the main resource. Since the first and last instances of `jacobi` have only one neighbor, each is passed one `noop` capability.

The loop in `main` that checks for termination illustrates an interesting use of nested input statements. On each iteration of its computational loop, each instance of `jacobi` calls `terminate(diff)`, where `diff` is the maximum difference it found. The outer input statement in `main` uses a synchronization expression (`?terminate = PR`) to wait for all PR instances of `jacobi` to call `terminate`. It then uses a scheduling expression (`-diff`) to service the invocation that has the maximum value for parameter `diff`. If this maximum is at most `epsilon`, the computation has converged, so `ans` is set to true; otherwise `ans` is set to false.

The inner input statement is used to service and return the value of `ans` to the PR-1 other invocations of `terminate`. Note that the formal and result identifiers in the nested input statement are different from those in the outer input statement. In this case the formal identifier could be the same since it is not used in the body of the inner input statement. However, the result identifier, `ans2`, must be different so that the value of `ans` can be returned.

The final code in `main` is executed after all processes terminate. It destroys each instance of `jacobi`, which in turn causes the final code in each instance to print its portion of the result.

15.4 Using Multiple Virtual Machines

The program in the previous section will execute on one virtual machine. Here we show how to extend it to employ multiple virtual machines, which can be on multiple physical machines.

To use multiple virtual machines, we need to make only a few changes to the main resource; `jacobi` does not need to change at all. In particular, we need to create virtual machines before we create instances of `jacobi`. Let `hosts` be the name of a file that contains a list of at least PR strings, each of which is the name of a physical machine. Then the following code will create a virtual machine on each of the named host machines:

```
# create virtual machines
var fd: file, hostname: string[50]
fd := open("hosts", READ)
var vmcap[1:PR]: cap vm
fa i := 1 to PR ->
  read(fd, hostname)
  vmcap[i] := create vm() on hostname
af
```

We can create instances of jacobi on the different virtual machines by appending location specifications to the resource creation statements. To place each instance on a different virtual machine, we would change the resource creation code in the main resource in Section 15.3 to:

```
# create instances of jacobi()
var jcap[1:PR]: cap jacobi
if PR = 1 ->
    jcap[1] := create jacobi(1,N,PR,S,
                             1,t,r,b) on vmcap[1]
[] else ->
    jcap[1] := create jacobi(1,N,PR,S,
                             1,t,r,0.0) on vmcap[1]
    fa i := 2 to PR-1 ->
      jcap[i] := create jacobi(i,N,PR,S,
                               1,0.0,r,0.0) on vmcap[i]
    af
    jcap[PR] := create jacobi(PR,N,PR,S,
                              1,0.0,r,b) on vmcap[PR]
fi
```

No further changes to the distributed program are required.

Exercises

15.1   Copy the four programs in this chapter into files and compile them. (Source files containing the programs come with the SR distribution.) Construct a set of experiments to determine the relative performance of the four programs. Experiment with different problem sizes, numbers of processes, and numbers of processors. Explain the results you observe.

15.2   (a) Develop a program for Jacobi iteration that uses a bag of tasks and replicated workers, as illustrated in Section 14.2. Experiment with different problem sizes, tasks sizes, and numbers of workers.

(b) Compare the results of your experiments to the results of the experiments conducted in Exercise 15.1. Explain any differences you observe.

15.3   Consider the data parallel program in Section 15.1.

(a) Modify the program to employ only PR processes per concurrent statement. Assume that N is a multiple of PR.

(b) Compare the performance of your answer to (a) to the performance of the original program. Experiment with different values of PR. Explain your results.

15.4   The second concurrent statement in resource jacobi in Section 15.1 uses postprocessing code to accumulate the maximum difference. Modify the resource so that it does not use postprocessing code.

15.5   Rewrite the convergence-checking code in resource jacobi in Section 15.1 so that only one process checks for convergence. If that process finds that the maximum difference is at most epsilon, it should inform the others.

15.6   In resource jacobi in Section 15.1, the last concurrent statement is followed by an if statement. Suppose the if statement were moved into the postprocessing code of the concurrent statement. Would the resulting program be correct? Explain.

15.7   Consider the global barrier_synch (see Section 15.2), which implements a barrier.

(a) Suppose local variable mysleep is not used. In particular, delete its declaration and change the P operation to P(delay[sleep]). Explain why the resulting code is incorrect. Hint: When could context switches occur?

(b) Suppose the array of delay semaphores is replaced by a single semaphore (and variable sleep is deleted). Explain why the resulting code is incorrect when used by the code in resource jacobi (see Section 15.2). Is there any situation in which the modified code would correctly implement a barrier?

15.8   In the convergence-checking code in resource jacobi in Section 15.2, every strip process calculates the maximum value in maxdiff[*].

(a) Modify the program so that only one process computes the maximum and other processes wait until that value has been computed.

(b) Compare the performance of your answer to (a) with the original code for various numbers of strip processes. Which is faster? Why? How does performance depend on the number of processes?

15.9   The distributed program in Section 15.3 partitions the grid into strips and assigns one instance of jacobi to each strip. Suppose instead that the grid is partitioned into blocks; e.g., a 100×100 point grid is partitioned into 16 blocks of 25×25 points each. Modify the program to implement this approach.

15.10   The main resource in Section 15.3 exports operation terminate, which is invoked by instances of resource jacobi in Section 15.3. Modify the two resources so that instead terminate is declared in the body of main and is passed as a resource parameter to instances of jacobi. Hint: Use an operation capability.

15.11 The `main` resource in Section 15.3 implements convergence checking. Modify the program in Section 15.3 so that the instances of `jacobi` interact only with each other to check for convergence. In particular, delete the block of code in `main` between the comment `# do termination` ... and the final code.

15.12 The termination checking code in resource `main` in Section 15.3 uses the `?` operator. Show how to rewrite the code in the following ways so as not to use the `?` operator.

(a) Change the interface to the `terminate` operation and/or introduce another operation.

(b) Do not change the interface to the `terminate` operation. Instead use the forward statement.

(c) Do not change the interface to the `terminate` operation or use the forward statment. Instead use additional processes.

(d) Use recursion to simulate nested input statements, but do not use any of the above "tricks."

15.13 Gauss-Seidel and successive over-relaxation (SOR) are two additional iterative methods for solving Laplace's equation. With Gauss-Seidel, on each iteration, new values for points are computed sequentially; each new value is the average of two values from the current iteration and two from the previous iteration. In particular, new values are computed by the following loop:

```
fa i := 1 to N, j := 1 to N ->
  grid[i,j] := (grid[i-1,j] + grid[i,j-1] +
                grid[i+1,j] + grid[i,j+1]) / 4
af
```

Note that `grid` is updated in place, unlike in Jacobi iteration.

SOR is a generalization of Gauss-Seidel that also averages in the previous value of a point. With SOR, new values are computed by

```
fa i := 1 to N, j := 1 to N ->
  grid[i,j] := omega*(grid[i-1,j] + grid[i,j-1] +
                      grid[i+1,j] + grid[i,j+1]) / 4
             + (1-omega)*grid[i,j]
af
```

Variable `omega` is called the over-relaxation parameter. For optimum convergence it usually is chosen to be between 1 and 2. (If `omega` is 1, SOR simplifies to Gauss-Seidel.)

Write sequential SR programs to implement Jacobi iteration, Gauss-Seidel, and SOR. Compare the performance of your programs. For a given set of initial values, which converges most rapidly? How does the rate of convergence depend on the initial values? How does the performance of SOR depend on the value of `omega`?

15.14   The Gauss-Seidel and SOR methods defined in the previous problem have to be applied sequentially in order to converge. Both methods update points in place, which can lead to chaos if the points were all updated concurrently. However, both can be parallelized by a using a red/black (checkerboard) partitioning scheme that partitions the grid of points into blocks. For example, partition a 100×100 point grid into 16 blocks of 25×25 points each. Next color each block red or black in a checkerboard fashion; i.e., adjacent blocks have different colors. Assign a process to each block or, better yet, to each set of two or four blocks. On each iteration of the main computation, concurrently update all red blocks, then concurrently update all black blocks. Within a block use Gauss-Seidel or SOR to update points sequentially.

(a) Implement a parallel algorithm for red/black SOR. Use shared variables and a value of 1.5 for `omega`.

(b) Implement a distributed algorithm for red/black SOR. Use message passing and a value of 1.5 for `omega`.

(c) Construct a set of experiments to determine the performance of your two programs. Compare their performance to the corresponding programs in this chapter that use Jacobi iteration.

15.15   The following region-labeling problem arises in image processing. Given is integer array `image[n,n]`. The value of each entry is the intensity of a pixel. The neighbors of a pixel are the four pixels that surround it, i.e., the elements of `image` to the left, right, above, and below it. Two pixels belong to the same region if they are neighbors and they have the same value. Thus a region is a maximal set of pixels that are connected and that all have the same value.

The problem is to find all regions and assign every pixel in each region a unique label. In particular, let `label[n,n]` be a second matrix, and assume that the initial value of `label[i,j]` is `n*i + j`. The final value of `label[i,j]` is to be the largest of the initial labels in the region to which pixel `[i,j]` belongs.

(a) Write a shared-variable program to solve this problem. Divide the image into fixed-size sub-images, and assign one process to each sub-image.

(b) Write a recursive, divide-and-conquer algorithm to solve this problem. Start with the entire image and recursively fork processes to assign labels to sub-images; stop recursing when you reach a sub-image of some prespecified size. When subprocesses terminate, combine their labeled sub-images into a larger labeled image.

(c) Write a distributed program to solve this problem; use a heartbeat algorithm. Divide the image into sub-images of some prespecified size, and assign one process to each sub-image.

(d) Write a program to solve this problem using the bag-of-tasks paradigm. Divide the image into sub-images of some prespecified size, and put these "tasks" into a bag. Worker processes repeatedly take tasks from this bag, label the corresponding sub-image, and put the labeled sub-images into a second bag. Other workers repeatedly take pairs of adjacent sub-images from the second bag, combine them into a larger labeled image, and put the combined image back into the second bag. The computation terminates when the entire image has been properly labeled. Implement the bags by means of operations that are shared by the worker processes.

(e) Repeat part (d), but do not use shared bags of tasks. Instead, have one or two administrator processes implement the bags.

(f) Write a program to solve this problem using a data parallel algorithm. First, for each pixel determine whether it is on the boundary of a region. Second, have each boundary pixel determine which neighbors are also on the boundary; in essence, for each region this produces a doubly linked list connecting all pixels that are on the boundary of that region. Third, using the lists, propagate the largest label of any of the boundary pixels to the others that are on the boundary. (The pixel in a region that has the largest label will be on its boundary.) Finally, propagate the label for each region to pixels in the interior of the region.

(g) Construct a set of experiments to compare the performance of the programs you wrote for previous parts of this problem. Experiment with different image sizes and numbers of processes. Explain the results you observe.

## CHAPTER 16

The Traveling Salesman Problem

The traveling salesman problem is the classic "hard" combinatorial search problem. Given are n cities and a matrix dist[1:n,1:n] of intercity distances. The value in dist[i,j] is the distance from city i to city j, e.g., the airline miles. We assume there is a path from each city to every other.

A salesman starts in city 1 and wishes to visit every city exactly once, ending back in city 1. The problem is to determine a path that minimizes the distance the salesman must travel. Thus we need to find a permutation of integers 1 to n such that the sum of the distances between adjacent pairs of cities—plus the distance back to city 1—is minimized.

For n cities, there are (n-1)! different paths starting and ending in city 1. Unless n is small, this number is, of course, very large. Thus we need to look for ways to cut down on the amount of computation that has to be performed and for ways to use parallelism to speed up the computation.

This chapter presents three solutions to the traveling salesman problem. To simplify the programs, we develop exact solutions, i.e., ones that find a minimum cost tour. In practice, finding an exact solution is infeasible except for small values of n (e.g., 15 or so). Consequently, many heuristics have been developed to generate approximate solutions to the traveling salesman and similar optimization problems. A few are considered in the exercises; see [Lawler et al. 1985] and [Johnson 1990] for descriptions of those heuristics and numerous others.

The first solution is a sequential program that uses depth-first search to examine all feasible paths. A path is feasible if it is not (yet) longer than the best complete path that has been computed so far. The second solution is a parallel program that uses the bag-of-tasks paradigm. In particular, partial paths are stored in an operation queue shared by several worker processes;

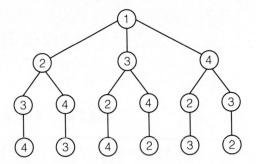

Figure 16.1. Search tree for four cities.

each worker repeatedly extracts a partial path and extends it with cities that have not yet been visited. The final, distributed solution modifies the second program to use only message passing.

All three solutions illustrate techniques for solving branch-and-bound algorithms, which arise in numerous applications such as searching game trees and solving optimization problems.

16.1 Sequential Solution

To find the shortest path that visits all cities exactly once, we have to consider every possible tour. If we start in city 1, there are n-1 possible cities we could visit next. From each of these, there are n-2 possible cities to visit third, and so on. We can thus represent all possible tours by a tree, with city 1 at the root. The tree has depth n (the number of cities) and (n-1)! leaves (the number of different tours). Figure 16.1 illustrates a search tree for four cities.

The standard way to examine all paths in a tree such as this is to use depth-first search, which is realized by a recursive, backtracking algorithm. We must follow a path all the way to a leaf node, then go part way back up the tree and follow a path to a different leaf node, and so on. For example, if we search from left to right in the tree in Figure 16.1, we would visit the four cities in the following order:

$$(1, 2, 3, 4), \ (1, 2, 4, 3), \ (1, 3, 2, 4), \ (1, 3, 4, 2), \ (1, 4, 2, 3), \ (1, 4, 3, 2)$$

In the traveling salesman problem, the goal is to find the shortest tour. It is not necessary to consider a tour that is known to be longer than the shortest complete tour that has been found so far. We can use this fact to "prune" infeasible paths from the tree. The larger the number of cities, the more dramatic the effect pruning can have. For example, on sample data for ten cities, we have seen pruning reduce execution time by a factor of ten.

Below we present a sequential SR program to solve the traveling salesman problem. Our solution has two globals and a main resource, compiled in the order presented below. The first global reads two command-line arguments: the number of cities and the name of a file that contains the distance matrix.

```
global Arguments
  var n: int, fname: string[20]
body Arguments
  getarg(1, n); getarg(2, fname)
end
```

We should check the return value from `getarg`, but we have not done so for the sake of brevity.

The second global exports the distance matrix, a variable that contains the length of the shortest path so far, and an operation that is called to update the shortest path.

```
global Shared
  import Arguments
  var dist[1:n,1:n]: int              # distances
  var shortest: int := 2**30          # best so far
  op update(path[1:*], length: int)
body Shared
  var fd: file := open(fname, READ)
  fa i := 1 to n, j := 1 to n ->
    read(fd, dist[i,j])
  af
  var shortest_path[1:n]: int

  # update shortest length and path, if necessary
  proc update(path, length)
    if length < shortest ->
      shortest := length; shortest_path := path
    fi
  end

  final
    write("the shortest path has length", shortest)
    write("the cities on the shortest path are:")
    fa i := 1 to n -> writes(" ",shortest_path[i]) af
    write()
  end
end
```

The final code prints the result once the program terminates. Above, `length` is used as the name of a parameter; it is also the name of a predefined function. It is legal to redeclare the name of a predefined function—except for `new`, `low`, and `high`—but the function is then hidden.

The main resource contains initialization code and two procedures. The computation is carried out by procedure `tsp`. The initialization code invokes `tsp` once for each partial path of length 2; `tsp` in turn recursively examines all other feasible paths. Auxiliary procedure `visit` is used to extend a path by a city, if that city has not yet been visited.

```
resource Main()
  import Arguments, Shared

  # if city is not in path, add it and return true;
  # otherwise return false
  procedure visit(path[1:*], city: int)
    returns ok: bool
      fa i := 2 to ub(path) st path[i] = city ->
        ok := false; return
      af
      ok := true
  end

  # using recursion and backtracking, examine all
  # paths that could be the shortest
  procedure tsp(path[1:*], length: int)
    var hops := ub(path)
    if hops = n ->      # complete tour, see if best
        length +:= dist[path[n],1]
        update(path, length)
    [] hops < n ->      # visit cities not yet in path
        fa city := 2 to n st visit(path, city) ->
          var newpath[1:hops+1], newlength: int
          newpath[1:hops] := path
          newpath[hops+1] := city
          newlength := length +
              dist[newpath[hops],newpath[hops+1]]
          # recurse if newpath possibly the best
          if newlength < shortest ->
            tsp(newpath, newlength)
          fi
        af
    fi
  end tsp
```

```
      var path[1:2] := (1, 0)
      fa i := 2 to n ->
        path[2] := i; tsp(path, dist[1,i])
      af
   end Main
```

The for-all loops in `visit` and `tsp` both contain such-that clauses. By using these clauses, we avoid having to put the loop body inside an if statement.

16.2   Replicated Workers and a Bag of Tasks

In the traveling salesman problem, paths are independent, so we could evaluate all of them in parallel. However, this would lead to far too much concurrency for most problem sizes and machines. An alternative is to employ a fixed number of worker processes that share a bag of tasks.

Each task contains a partial path, the number of cities (hops) on the path, and the path's length. We will initially put `n-1` tasks in the bag, representing the `n-1` tours starting at city 1. Each worker repeatedly takes a task from the bag and extends the path with every city that has not yet been visited. If a new path is too long, it is discarded. If a path does not include all cities and it is not yet too long, the worker puts the new path and its length back into the bag of tasks. If a path includes all cities and it might be shorter than the shortest path found so far, the worker updates the shortest path.

Our program for this algorithm has two globals and two resources. The first global reads command-line arguments: the number of cities, the name of a file containing distances, and the number of worker processes to employ.

```
   global Arguments
      var n, w: int, fname: string[20]
   body Arguments
      getarg(1, n); getarg(2, w); getarg(3, fname)
   end
```

The second global again exports the distance matrix, the length of the shortest path, and a procedure to update the shortest path. Here it also exports an operation that implements the bag of tasks.

```
   global Shared
      import Arguments
      op bag(path[1:*], hops, length: int)    # tasks
      var dist[1:n,1:n]: int                   # distances
      var shortest: int := 2**30               # best so far
      op update(path[1:*], length: int)
```

```
body Shared
  var fd: file; fd := open(fname, READ)
  fa i := 1 to n, j := 1 to n ->
    read(fd, dist[i,j])
  af
  var shortest_path[1:n]: int
  sem mutex := 1

  proc update(path, length)
    P(mutex)  # get lock for shared variables
      if length < shortest ->
        shortest := length; shortest_path := path
      fi
    V(mutex)  # release lock
  end

  final
    write("the shortest path has length", shortest)
    write("the cities on the shortest path are:")
    fa i := 1 to n -> writes(" ",shortest_path[i]) af
    write()
  end
end Shared
```

The body of `Shared` is nearly identical to `Shared` in the sequential solution (see Section 16.1). The difference is that since `update` alters shared variables and might be called by more than one worker at a time, its body needs to execute as a critical section.

Tours are computed by instances of the `Worker` resource. It contains a worker process and a procedure that the worker calls to extend a given path by another city. On each iteration, the worker process receives a new task from the shared bag. The task is a partial tour, which the worker extends by each city that has not yet been visited. If a complete tour is found that might be the best, the worker calls the shared procedure `update`. Again, we use the length of the shortest tour found so far to avoid searching infeasible paths.

```
resource Worker()
  import Arguments, Shared

  # visit city if it has not yet been visited
  procedure visit(city: int; var path[1:*]: int;
      hops: int; length: int) returns newlength: int
    fa i := 2 to hops st path[i] = city ->
      newlength := 0; return
    af
```

```
      newlength := length + dist[path[hops], city]
      path[hops+1] := city
   end

   process worker
      var path[1:n], hops, length, newlength: int
      do true ->
        receive bag(path, hops, length)
        fa city := 2 to n ->
          newlength := visit(city, path, hops, length)
          if newlength = 0 -> next fi  # city visited
          if hops+1 < n and newlength < shortest ->
              # put partial tour back into bag
              send bag(path, hops+1, newlength)
          [] hops+1 = n ->
              # add distance back to city 1
              newlength := newlength + dist[path[n],1]
              if newlength < shortest ->
                # this tour is possibly the best
                update(path, newlength)
              fi
          fi
        af
      od
   end
end Worker
```

The main resource puts n-1 tasks into the bag and then creates w instances of the Worker resource.

```
   resource Main()
      import Arguments, Shared, Worker
      # put first set of partial tours into bag
      var path[1:n]: int := (1, [n-1] 0)
      fa i := 2 to n ->
        path[2] := i
        send bag(path, 2, dist[1,i])
      af
      # create worker processes
      fa i := 1 to w -> create Worker() af
   end Main
```

Since we do not need to communicate with instances of Worker or to destroy them, we do not need to save the capabilities returned by create.

If there are more than a small number of cities (e.g., more than ten), this program generates a huge number of partial tours. In fact the size of the bag could become so large that the program will run out of memory. A better approach is to put some fixed number of tasks in the bag to start—say partial tours of length three. Then on each iteration a worker process extracts one partial tour and uses the sequential algorithm of the previous section to examine all paths starting with that partial tour. In addition to decreasing the amount of storage required for the bag, this approach also increases the amount of computation a worker does every time it accesses the bag.

16.3 Manager and Workers

The program in the previous section employs two global components, which contain shared variables and operations. However, globals cannot be shared across virtual machines. Instead each gets its own copy.

Here we present a distributed program that does not use globals. Again we employ instances of a `Worker` resource. However, the bag of tasks and shortest path are maintained by a `Manager` resource, which also serves as the main resource. The workers and manager use asynchronous message passing, RPC, and rendezvous to communicate with each other.

As in the previous section, the `Worker` resource contains a process and a local procedure. Also, the worker process repeatedly gets a partial tour from the bag and extends it with all cities that have not yet been visited. However, a worker process cannot simply receive a new task from the bag because `bag` is not a shared operation in a global. Instead `bag` is exported and serviced by the manager. To get a new task, a worker calls `getjob`, which is another operation exported by the manager.

Another difference between the `Worker` resource below and the one in Section 16.2 is that the length of the shortest path is not directly accessible in a shared variable. Instead the manager keeps track of the shortest path. Any time it changes, the manager sends the new value to the `updatemin` operation exported by each instance of `Worker`.

```
resource Worker
  import Manager
  op updatemin(length: int)
body Worker(n, dist[*,*]: int; cm: cap Manager)

  # visit city if it has not yet been visited
  procedure visit(city: int; var path[1:*]: int;
      hops: int; length: int) returns newlength: int
    fa i := 2 to hops st path[i] = city ->
      newlength := 0; return
    af
```

```
        newlength := length + dist[path[hops], city]
        path[hops+1] := city
    end

    process worker
      var path[1:n], hops, length, newlength: int
      var shortest := 2**30     # shortest known about
      do true ->
        # see if there is a better shortest tour
        do ?updatemin > 0 ->
          receive updatemin(length)
          shortest := min(length, shortest)
        od
        # get a job and process it
        cm.getjob(path, hops, length)
        fa city := 2 to n ->
          newlength := visit(city, path, hops, length)
          if newlength = 0 -> next fi  # city visited
          if hops+1 < n and newlength < shortest ->
              # put partial tour back into bag
              send cm.bag(path, hops+1, newlength)
          [] hops+1 = n ->
              # add distance back to city 1
              newlength := newlength + dist[path[n],1]
              if newlength < shortest ->
                # tell manager this tour possibly best
                send cm.newmin(path, newlength)
                shortest := newlength
              fi
          fi
        af
      od
    end
  end Worker
```

At the start of each iteration, the worker process checks to see if there is a pending invocation of updatemin, which indicates that there is a new shortest path.

The manager resource exports three operations: bag, which contains the bag of tasks; getjob, which is called by workers to get new tasks; and newmin, which is called by workers when they think they have found a new shortest path. The body of the manager first reads the command-line arguments and file of distances. It then creates w instances of Worker. The manager passes each instance the values of n and dist since these are no longer in a global. The manager also passes a capability for itself so that the workers can invoke the manager's operations. Unlike in the resource Main used in Section 16.2, the manager needs capabilities for the workers because it needs to invoke their updatemin operations.

Operation getjob is serviced by a proc, which simply receives a task from operation bag into the result parameters of getjob. Operation newmin is serviced by an input statement in process manager. When manager receives a new shortest path, it uses a concurrent statement to broadcast the length of that path to the workers.

Two (or more) workers could, at about the same time, find what they believe to be new shortest paths. The input statement in manager uses a scheduling expression to service the invocation of newmin that has the smallest value of parameter length. This can decrease the number of times that the manager needs to broadcast a new value of shortest to the workers.

```
resource Manager
  import Worker
  op bag(path[1:*], hops, length: int)  # tasks
  op getjob(res path[1:*], hops, length: int)
  op newmin(path[1:*], length: int)
body Manager()

  var n, w: int, fname: string[20]
  getarg(1, n); getarg(2, w); getarg(3, fname)
  var dist[1:n, 1:n]: int         # distances
  var shortest: int := 2**30      # best so far
  var shortest_path[1:n]: int
  var fd: file; fd := open(fname, READ)
  fa i := 1 to n, j := 1 to n ->
    read(fd, dist[i,j])
  af

  # create worker resources
  var cw[1:w]: cap Worker
  fa i := 1 to w ->
    cw[i] := create Worker(n, dist, myresource())
  af

  proc getjob(path, hops, length)
    receive bag(path, hops, length)
  end
```

```
        process manager
          # put first set of partial tours into bag
          var path[1:n]: int := (1, [n-1] 0)
          fa i := 2 to n ->
            path[2] := i
            send bag(path, 2, dist[1,i])
          af
          do true ->
            # wait for candidate for shortest path
            in newmin(path, length) by length ->
              if length < shortest ->
                shortest := length
                shortest_path := path
                # broadcast new minimum to all workers
                co (i := 1 to w)
                  send cw[i].updatemin(shortest)
                oc
              fi
            ni
          od
        end

        final
          write("the shortest path has length", shortest)
          write("the cities on the shortest path are:")
          fa i := 1 to n -> writes(" ",shortest_path[i]) af
          write()
        end
      end Manager
```

Using the techniques shown in Section 15.4, we can readily extend the above program to execute on multiple virtual machines. For example, we could have `Manager` and each instance of `Worker` execute on a different virtual machine, which in turn could be on a different physical machine.

Exercises

16.1 Modify the sequential program in Section 16.1 so that it does not prune infeasible paths. Compare the execution time of your program and the one given in the text.

16.2 The program in Section 16.1 employs two globals. Explain why the two globals cannot be combined into one.

16.3   Copy the program in Section 16.2 into a file and compile it. Generate test data
for various numbers of cities. (If you have access to an airline guide, you
might want to use actual air distances between various cities.)

(a) Analyze the performance of the program for various sets of input data and
various numbers of worker processes. Determine how large a number of cities
you can handle without running out of storage for the bag of tasks.

(b) Modify the program as suggested at the end of Section 16.2. In particular,
initialize the bag with some fixed number of tasks and have each worker use
the sequential algorithm to extend a partial tour with all feasible tours.
Analyze the performance of this program for various sets of input data and
various numbers of worker processes. Compare the performance of this
program to that of the program in Section 16.2.

16.4   Copy the program in Section 16.3 into a file and compile it. Generate test data
for various numbers of cities.

(a) Analyze the performance of the program for various sets of input data and
various numbers of worker processes.

(b) Compare the performance of this program to the program in Section 16.2.

(c) Modify the program to have the manager and each worker execute on its
own virtual machine, and place these on different physical machines. Analyze
the performance of this program for various sets of input data and various
numbers of worker processes.

16.5   The distributed program in Section 16.3 terminates when the bag of tasks is
empty and all worker processes are blocked. Suppose SR did not support
automatic distributed termination detection. Modify the program to detect
termination explicitly; execute a stop statement when the bag is empty and all
workers are blocked. Hint: Modify the `Manager` resource, use an input
statement to service `getjob`, and use the `?` operator.

16.6   (a) Solve the traveling salesman problem by assigning one process to each
city. City 1 generates partial tours of length 2 that are sent to each other city.
When a city gets a partial tour, it extends it and sends it on to other cities.
When it gets a complete tour, it sends it back to city 1.

(b) Compare the performance of your program to the performance of the
program in Section 16.2. Explain any differences.

16.7   One heuristic algorithm for the traveling salesman problem is called the
nearest neighbor algorithm. Starting with city 1, first visit the city, say `c`,
nearest to city 1. Now extend the partial tour by visiting the city nearest to `c`.
Continue in this fashion until all cities have been visited, then return to city 1.

Write a program to implement this algorithm. Compare its performance to
that of the programs in the text. What is the execution time? How good or
bad an approximate solution is generated? Experiment with several tours of
various sizes.

16.8   Another heuristic is called the nearest insertion algorithm. First find the pair of cities that are closest to each other. Next find the unvisited city nearest to either of these two cities and insert it between them. Continue to find the unvisited city with minimum distance to some city in the partial tour, and insert that city between a pair of cities already in the tour so that the insertion causes the minimum increase in total length of the partial tour.

(a) Write a program to implement this algorithm. Compare its performance to that of the programs in the text. What is the execution time? How good or bad is the approximate solution that is generated? Experiment with several tours of various sizes.

(b) Compare the performance of this program to one that implements the nearest neighbor heuristic.

16.9   A third traveling salesman heuristic is to partition the plane into strips, each of which contains some bounded number B of cities. Worker processes in parallel find minimal cost tours from one end of the strip to the others. In odd-numbered strips the tours should go from the top to the bottom; in even-numbered strips they should go from the bottom to the top. Once tours have been found for all strips, they are connected together.

(a) Write a program to implement this algorithm. Compare its performance to that of the programs in the text. What is the execution time? How good or bad is the approximate solution that is generated? Experiment with several tours of various sizes.

(b) Compare the performance of this program to one that implements the nearest neighbor heuristic. Which is faster? Which gives a better solution?

16.10   Research heuristic algorithms and local optimization techniques for solving the traveling salesman problem. Start by consulting [Lawler et al. 1985] and [Johnson 1990]. Pick one or more of the better algorithms, write a program to implement it, and conduct a series of experiments to see how well it performs (both in terms of execution time and how good an approximate solution it generates).

16.11   Develop a program to generate prime numbers using a shared bag of tasks. The tasks are odd numbers that should be checked for primality. The workers check different candidates. Each worker should have a local table of primes that it uses to check candidates. When a worker finds a new prime, it should send it to all the other workers.

Execute your program for different ranges of primes and different numbers of workers. How does the performance differ?

16.12   The eight-queens problem is concerned with placing eight queens on a chess board in such a way that none can attack another. One queen can attack another if they are in the same row or column or are on the same diagonal.

Develop a parallel program to generate all 92 solutions to the eight-queens problem. Use a shared bag of tasks. Justify your choice of what constitutes a task. Experiment with different numbers of workers. Explain your results.

## CHAPTER 17

A Distributed
File System

The three previous chapters presented examples of parallel programs. There the purpose of each program was to compute a result for a given set of input. In this chapter we present an example of a distributed program in which one or more users repeatedly interact with the program. This kind of program is sometimes called a *reactive* program since it continuously reacts to external events. At least conceptually, the program never terminates.

Our specific example is a program, which we call DFS, that consists of a distributed file system and a user interface. DFS executes on one or more host computers. Each host provides a simple file system. Users interact with DFS through a command interpreter, which is modeled on UNIX and supports commands to create, examine, and copy files. Users identify files located on remote hosts by using names that include host names; these have the form `hostname:filename`. Thus DFS is similar to what is called a *network* file system. A user can log in to the system from any host and manipulate files on all hosts.

In this chapter we first give an overview of the structure of DFS. Then we present the implementations of the file system and user interface. The program employs the client/server process interaction pattern that is prevalent in distributed systems. It also illustrates several aspects of SR: multiple virtual machines, operation types, dynamic resource creation and destruction, UNIX file and terminal access, and the forward statement. Our main purpose is to illustrate how to program this kind of distributed system. Consequently, our implementation of DFS does some error checking, but it is by no means all that one would desire. Unlike the previous chapters in this part, each of which presents several solutions to a given problem, this chapter outlines only one way to program a distributed file system.

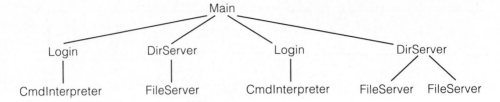

Figure 17.1. Snapshot of the structure of DFS.

17.1 System Structure

Our program for DFS consists of two globals and five resources. One global declares constants, data types, and operation types. The second global contains three "library" procedures. The resources and their roles are

`Main`	creates the directory and login servers
`Login`	handles login protocol and creates command interpreters
`CmdInterpreter`	implements commands to operate on files
`DirServer`	manages the files stored on one host
`FileServer`	provides access to an open file

The main resource creates one virtual machine on each host machine. On each virtual machine, `Main` then creates one instance of `DirServer` and one instance of `Login` for each terminal that can be used to talk to that host.

When a user successfully logs in, the corresponding instance of `Login` creates an instance of `CmdInterpreter`. Thus at any point in time there are as many instances of `CmdInterpreter` as there are active users.

To manipulate a file, a command interpreter first interacts with the instance of `DirServer` on the target machine (i.e., the one on which the file resides). Access to a file is provided by an instance of `FileServer`. A directory server creates a new instance of `FileServer` every time it opens a file for a command interpreter. The command interpreter then interacts directly with the file server to read and/or write data. When the file is closed, the file server destroys itself.

Figure 17.1 gives a snapshot of the structure of one possible execution of the DFS program. It assumes there are two host machines and that each has one terminal for user interaction. In the illustration there are two instances of `CmdInterpreter`, which means there are two active users. There are also three instances of `FileServer`, which means three files are being accessed. For example, the user on the leftmost machine might be copying a file from that machine to the other one (which uses two file servers), and the user on

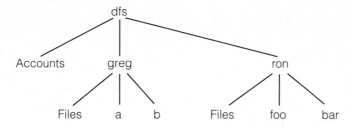

Figure 17.2. UNIX directory structure on one host.

the rightmost machine might be creating or reading a local file (which uses one file server).

To store system data and user files in DFS, we make use of the underlying UNIX file system. Before running DFS, we first need to create a directory named dfs in the user's home directory on each host machine. (A copy of DFS will execute in that directory.) In each of these dfs directories, there should be one file, Accounts, that contains a list of the names of authorized users of DFS. For each such user, there also needs to be one subdirectory in dfs. Each such subdirectory will be used by DFS to store a user's files. In addition, DFS employs one additional file, Files, in each user subdirectory; this contains a list of the names of the user's DFS files. For simplicity DFS assumes that the dfs directories and their files and subdirectories described above exist already; it does not create them as needed.

Figure 17.2 gives an example of the UNIX directory structure used by DFS on one host machine. There are two users and each has two files. The top-level structure is identical on each host machine; however, the user files stored on a particular host will, in general, differ.

17.2 Directory and File Servers

All five resources share the following constant and type definitions:

```
global Defs    # common definitions
  const USERS := 5, FILES := 10
  type name = string[20]
  type line = string[100]
  type file_descriptor =
    rec( r: cap fread; w: cap fwrite; c: cap fclose)
  optype fread(res ln: line) returns status: int
  optype fwrite(ln: line)
  optype fclose()
end Defs
```

The constants specify the maximum numbers of user accounts and files per user. The type declarations specify the types of user names, text lines, and file descriptors. The optype declarations define three types of operations on files. These operation types are defined in a global because, as we shall see, file operations are not exported by file servers. Rather, each instance of a file server process declares file operations locally and returns capabilities for them as the result of opening a file.

A second global defines three utility procedures used by the other components of DFS. A copy of the global, and hence the procedures, is created automatically on every virtual machine in our program.

```
global Utilities    # library procedures
  import Defs
  op get_arg(var cmdline: line) returns arg: name
  op parse_filename(arg: name; res mach, fname: name)
  op lookup(id: name; table[*]: name)
        returns index: int
body Utilities

  # extract next command-line argument, if any;
  # set cmdline to the remainder of the line
  proc get_arg(cmdline) returns arg
    var lc := length(cmdline)
    var f := 1     # position of first non-blank
    do f <= lc & cmdline[f] = ' ' -> f++ od
    if f > lc -> arg := ""; return fi
    var r := f     # position of end of argument
    do r < lc & cmdline[r+1] != ' ' -> r++ od
    arg := cmdline[f:r]
    cmdline := cmdline[r+1:lc]
  end

  # arg is "machine:filename" or "filename";
  # separate it into its two components
  proc parse_filename(arg, machine, fname)
    var i := 1     # position of colon in arg
    do i <= length(arg) & arg[i] != ':' -> i++ od
    if i > length(arg) ->     # no colon in arg
        machine := ""; fname := arg
    [] else -> machine := arg[1:i-1]
               fname := arg[i+1:length(arg)]
    fi
  end
```

```
      # if name id is in table, return its index;
      # otherwise return 0
      proc lookup(id, table) returns index
        fa i := 1 to ub(table) st id = table[i] ->
          index := i; return
        af
        index := 0
      end
    end Utilities
```

The first two procedures use SR's string-processing mechanisms. The third uses a such-that clause in a for-all statement to implement linear search.

Each instance of the directory server resource manages the DFS files on one host. The resource exports five operations:

```
    resource DirServer
      import Defs, Utilities, FileServer
      op fcreate(user, fname: name; m: accessmode)
          returns fd: file_descriptor
      op fopen(user, fname: name; m: accessmode)
          returns fd: file_descriptor
      op fremove(user, fname: name) returns result: bool
      op check(user: name) returns valid: bool
      op list(user: name; res files[FILES]: name)
          returns cnt: int
    body DirServer() separate
```

The first three operations are called to create a new file, open an existing file, and remove a file, respectively. Operation check is called by Login to determine whether a user has an account. Operation list returns the names of a user's files.

The body of DirServer implements these operations. First, however, it reads in the Accounts file stored in the local machine's dfs directory and reads in the list of each user's files. The fopen and check operations are implemented by procs since they do not need to execute with mutual exclusion. Multiple invocations of these operations can be serviced concurrently. However, the other three operations update shared resource variables and need to execute with mutual exclusion, so they are serviced by an input statement in a process. A forward statement is used at the end of the body of the fcreate operation. By using forward we avoid having the ds process delay until the file server's open operation has completed; this enables ds to service other requests while the file is being opened.

```
body DirServer
  var accounts[USERS]: name
  var files[USERS,FILES]: name
  var nfiles[USERS]: int

  # read in the names of users and their files
  var f: file
  f := open("dfs/Accounts", READ)
  var nusers := 0
  do read(f, accounts[nusers+1]) != EOF ->
    nusers++
  od
  fa u := 1 to nusers ->
    f := open("dfs/" || accounts[u] || "/Files",READ)
    if f = null -> nfiles[u] := 0; next fi
    var j := 1
    do read(f, files[u,j]) != EOF -> j++ od
    nfiles[u] := j-1
  af

  # create a file server and open file fname
  proc fopen(user, fname, m) returns fd
    var fscap := create FileServer()
    fscap.fopen(user, fname, m)
  end

  # check if user has an account
  proc check(user) returns valid
    valid := lookup(user, accounts) != 0
  end

  process ds
    do true ->
      in fcreate(user, fname, m) returns fd ->
        # look up user's index in accounts
        var u := lookup(user, accounts)
        # if necessary, add file to database
        var f := lookup(fname, files[u,*])
        if f=0 -> files[u, ++nfiles[u]] := fname fi
        # create file server and forward open to it
        var fscap := create FileServer()
        forward fscap.fopen(user, fname, WRITE)
      [] list(user, fls) returns cnt ->
        var u := lookup(user, accounts)
        fls := files[u]; cnt := nfiles[u]
```

```
            [] fremove(user, fname) returns result ->
                # look up user's index in accounts
                var u := lookup(user, accounts)
                # look up file name in database of files
                var f := lookup(fname, files[u,*])
                if f = 0 -> result := false; exit fi
                # remove file name from database
                files[u,f] := files[u,nfiles[u]]
                nfiles[u]--; result := true
          ni
        od
    end

    final
      fa i := 1 to nusers ->
        var f: file :=
          open("dfs/" || accounts[i] || "/Files",WRITE)
        fa j := 1 to nfiles[i] ->
          write(f, files[i,j])
        af
      af
    end
  end DirServer
```

The final code in `DirServer` writes out each user's list of files when execution of DFS terminates; this way the files are accessible the next time DFS is executed on the same hosts.

One instance of resource `FileServer` is created each time a file is opened. This resource exports just one operation, as follows:

```
    resource FileServer
      import Defs
      op fopen(user, fname: name; m: accessmode)
            returns fd: file_descriptor
    body FileServer() separate
```

The `fopen` operation is implemented by a proc. The body of the proc declares three local operations, which are invoked to read, write, and close the file. When `fopen` is called, it constructs a record containing capabilities for its local operations (assuming the file can be opened successfully). It assigns these to return variable `fd` and then executes a reply statement. At this point the client process that invoked `fopen` can proceed, and the remainder of the body of `fopen` continues executing as an independent server process. These two processes then engage in a conversation in which the client reads and writes the file. Eventually, the client invokes the `cl` (close) operation, at which point the file server closes the file and then destroys itself.

```
body FileServer
  proc fopen(user, fname, m) returns fd
    # local operations
    op rd: fread, wr: fwrite, cl: fclose
    var f := open("dfs/" || user || "/" || fname, m)
    if f = null ->    # cannot open file
      fd := file_descriptor(null, null, null)
      reply
      destroy myresource()
    fi
    fd := file_descriptor(rd, wr, cl)
    reply    # return result to invoker
    do true ->
      in rd(ln) returns status ->
          ln := ""    # to handle EOF properly
          status := read(f, ln)
      [] wr(ln) -> write(f, ln)
      [] cl() -> close(f); exit
      ni
    od
    destroy myresource()
  end
end FileServer
```

In our implementation of DFS, we employ one instance of `FileServer` for each open file. However, since the resource body does not contain any resource variables, we could employ fewer instances. For example, we could create just one instance of `FileServer` on each host machine. Then we could have different processes that are accessing files interact with different instances of the `fopen` proc. (We would also need to get rid of the destroy statements.)

17.3 User Interface

The remaining components of DFS are the user interface and the main resource. When a user of DFS first sits down at a terminal, that user is interacting with an instance of the `Login` resource. Each instance of `Login` reads from and writes to one terminal device. This could be a CRT display or a window on a workstation. The `Login` resource first opens the associated keyboard and display. (These are like two files that happen to have the same name.) Then Login waits for a user to attempt to log in to DFS. If the user is successful, Login creates an instance of the command interpreter and then waits for the command interpreter to terminate.

```
resource Login
   import Defs, DirServer, CmdInterpreter
body Login(myhost: int; device, host[*]: name;
           dscap[*]: cap DirServer)

   var ttyin, ttyout: file
   ttyin := open("/dev/" || device, READ)
   ttyout := open("/dev/" || device, WRITE)
   op done()

   process prompt
     write(ttyout, "Welcome to DFS\n")
     do true ->
       writes(ttyout, "login: ")
       var user: name
       read(ttyin, user)
       if not dscap[myhost].check(user) ->
         write(ttyout, "invalid login"); next
       fi
       var cicap: cap CmdInterpreter
       cicap := create CmdInterpreter(user, myhost,
                     ttyin, ttyout, host, dscap, done)
       receive done()
       destroy cicap
     od
   end
end Login
```

The terminal devices used by the DFS program are typically running UNIX shell processes. The name of each of these terminal devices needs to be given to DFS when it begins execution (see the Main resource later in this section). The name of each terminal device can be obtained by using the tty UNIX shell command. Furthermore, to prevent the shells from intercepting input intended for DFS, each shell process should be put to sleep before DFS executes by using the sleep UNIX shell command.

The command interpreter is the largest component of DFS. It implements two kinds of user commands: ones that deal with files and ones that deal with the current working directory. It also implements a logout command. These commands are modeled on UNIX commands. They are summarized in the following table:

`cr filename`	creates a new file by entering text
`cat filename`	prints the contents of a file
`cp filename1 filename2`	copies the first file into the second
`rm filename`	removes a file
`ls [machine]`	lists the files in a user's directory
`cd [machine]`	changes current working directory
`pwd`	prints machine name of current working directory
`exit`	logs out of a session

The `machine` argument is optional in the `ls` and `cd` commands. The default for `ls` is the current working directory, and the default for `cd` is to change to the original home directory.

A file name has the general form `machine:filename`, where `machine` is one of the hosts and `filename` is a file on that host. If the machine name (and colon) are omitted, a file name is interpreted relative to the current working directory.

The `CmdInterpreter` resource is the client of the file and directory server resources. It exports no operations. Its body implements the above user commands. Many of the commands have similar implementations, so we present below only part of the body of `CmdInterpreter`. The source for the complete implementation is included with the SR distribution.

The local procedures implement details of the file access commands. For example, the `cmd_cr` procedure given below implements the file-creation command by first creating a new file on the designated server machine and then reading terminal input and writing it to that file. The end of the input is indicated by a line with a single dot.

The command-interpreter process, `CI`, repeatedly writes a prompt and then reads and interprets a command. It uses a multi-guard if statement as a case statement. The last arm uses an else guard to catch all unrecognized cases. Our implementation of the command interpreter does a reasonable amount of error checking, but by no means all that one would, in general, desire to have.

```
resource CmdInterpreter
   import Defs, Utilities, Login, DirServer
body CmdInterpreter(user: name; myhost: int;
        ttyin, ttyout: file; host[*]: name;
        dscap[*]: cap DirServer; done: cap () )

   ...  # procedures for cat, rm, and cp (not shown)
```

```
# command "cr filename"
procedure cmd_cr(fname: name; server: int)
  var fd := dscap[server].fcreate(user,fname,WRITE)
  if fd.w = null ->
    write(ttyout, "cannot create file", fname)
    return
  fi
  # read from ttyin and write to fd
  write(ttyout, "Enter contents;",
                "Last line should be a single dot")
  var ln: line
  read(ttyin, ln)
  do ln != "." ->
    fd.w(ln); read(ttyin, ln)
  od
  fd.c()
end cmd_cr

# command interpreter process
process CI
  var cmdline: line, args[3]: name
  var cur_host := myhost
  do true ->
    # write prompt, then wait for input
    writes(ttyout, "% "); read(ttyin, cmdline)
    var cmd := get_arg(cmdline)
    if cmd = "cr" ->      # create a new file
        var arg := get_arg(cmdline)
        if arg = "" ->
          write(ttyout, "Usage: cr filename"); next
        fi
        var machine, fname: name
        parse_filename(arg, machine, fname)
        var server := cur_host  # the default
        if machine != "" ->
          server := lookup(machine,host)
          if server = 0 ->
            write(ttyout, "invalid host"); next
          fi
        fi
        cmd_cr(fname, server)
    [] cmd = "cat" ->     # print an existing file
        ...
```

```
    []  cmd = "rm" ->       # remove a file
        ...
    []  cmd = "cp" ->       # copy one file to another
        ...
    []  cmd = "ls" ->       # list current directory
        var machine := get_arg(cmdline)
        var server := cur_host      # default for ls
        if machine != "" ->
          server := lookup(machine,host)
          if server = 0 ->
            write(ttyout, "invalid host"); next
          fi
        fi
        var files[FILES]: name
        var nf := dscap[server].list(user, files)
        fa i := 1 to nf ->
          write(ttyout, files[i])
        af
    []  cmd = "pwd" ->      # print current directory
        write(ttyout, host[cur_host])
    []  cmd = "cd" ->      # change directory
        ...
    []  cmd = "exit" ->     # exit interpreter
        send done(); exit
    []  else -> write(ttyout, "invalid command")
    fi
  od
 end CI
end CmdInterpreter
```

The final component of DFS is the main resource, which gets everything started. It first reads the command-line arguments, which specify the host machines to use. Next Main creates one virtual machine on each of these hosts and one directory server on each virtual machine. Main then prompts for the names of each terminal that is to be used. After Main creates one instance of Login for each terminal, DFS is operational.

The terminal used to initiate execution of DFS is not one of the terminals within the system itself. Rather it serves as an "operator's console." The operator stops execution of DFS by entering an arbitrary string on the console. Upon reading the string, Main executes stop. At this point the final code in Main destroys the directory servers; their final code, in turn, updates DFS's record of user files.

```
resource Main()
  import Defs, DirServer, FileServer, Login

  # read machine names from the command line
  var nhosts := numargs()
  var host[nhosts]: name
  fa i := 1 to nhosts -> getarg(i, host[i]) af

  # create virtual machines, one per host;
  # each will execute in the home directory
  var vmcap[nhosts]: cap vm
  fa i := 1 to nhosts ->
    vmcap[i] := create vm() on host[i]
  af

  # create directory servers on each host
  var dscap[nhosts]: cap DirServer
  fa i := 1 to nhosts ->
    dscap[i] := create DirServer() on vmcap[i]
  af

  # prompt for names of terminal devices and
  # create a login server for each terminal
  fa i := 1 to nhosts ->
    writes("number of ttys for ", host[i], ": ")
    var nttys: int, device: name
    read(nttys)
    write("enter tty names")
    fa j := 1 to nttys ->
      read(device)
      create Login(i,device,host,dscap) on vmcap[i]
    af
  af

  write("DFS now executing; enter string to stop")
  var str: name; read(str)
  stop

  final    # destroy directory servers
    fa i := 1 to nhosts ->
      destroy dscap[i]
    af
  end
end Main
```

Exercises

17.1   Copy the source program for DFS into one or more files, compile it, and then execute the program. Use at least two machines and at least one terminal per machine. Experiment interacting with DFS and report on your experience. What features do you like, and why? What features do you not like, and why? What features do you miss having, and why?

17.2   Suppose the same user is logged in more than once on DFS. What happens if the user tries simultaneously to access the same file from more than one terminal? Consider each combination of file-access commands (cr, cat, cp, and rm).

17.3   In the body of the DirServer resource, the list operation is serviced by an input statement in process ds. Suppose list were serviced by a proc instead. Carefully explain what could go wrong.

17.4   Explain what can happen if the command-line arguments to DFS are not unique machine names.

17.5   Extend DFS so users can access each other's files. Define some protection scheme so that a user can control the way in which other users access his files.

17.6   Add commands and functionality to DFS, such as who and wc commands, a cat command with multiple arguments, tree-structured directories, pipes, I/O redirection, etc.

17.7   Add file caching to DFS.

17.8   Add automatic replication to DFS, so a user's files are the same on all hosts.

17.9   Add file locking to DFS to prevent several users from concurrently updating the same file. Permit concurrent reading, however.

## CHAPTER 18

Discrete Event
Simulation

A discrete event system is one in which state changes, or events, occur at discrete instants of time. The arrivals and departures of buses and passengers at a bus stop, for example, can be represented as such a system. The movements of planes on runways and between airports is another example of something that can be modeled as a discrete event system. In contrast, the flow of air over the wing of an aircraft cannot be modeled as a discrete system since the system state changes continuously. (Continuous systems can often be modeled by partial differential equations and hence simulated as shown in Chapter 15.)

A discrete event simulation is a program that models a discrete event system. The main components in a discrete event simulation are *simulation processes*, which represent active objects such as people and buses; *entities*, which represent passive objects such as a bus stop; and an *event scheduler*, which controls the order in which simulation activities occur. (An entity is often called a resource; we use the term "entity" to avoid confusion with SR's resource construct.)

Concurrent programming languages are well suited for programming discrete event simulations because processes in concurrent programs correspond closely to simulation processes. SR is especially well suited because its rich collection of synchronization mechanisms makes the interactions between the simulation components easy to program.

This chapter presents a simple discrete event simulation problem and describes an SR solution to it. The problem and a solution programmed in Ada originally appeared in [Bruno 1984]. The presentation in this chapter is based on [Olsson 1990].

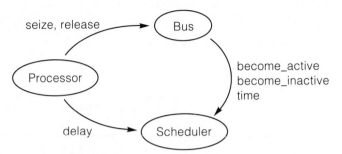

Figure 18.1. Resource interaction pattern.

18.1 A Simulation Problem

The specific problem we consider here is simulating one aspect of a simple multiprocessor architecture. Several processors compete to access a common memory bus. Each processor cyclically seizes the bus, transfers data on the bus, releases the bus, and then performs some other activity. Each processor is a simulation process, and the bus is an entity. The purpose of the simulation is to gather statistics on bus utilization and on delays encountered by the processors.

We use one resource to implement each simulation component. The main resource, `Processor`, contains one process for each processor in the system. The `Bus` resource implements the data bus. It exports `seize` and `release` operations, which the (simulated) processors call to seize and release the bus; it also exports a `print` operation, which is used to print the statistics `Bus` maintains.

The `Scheduler` resource implements the event scheduler. In particular, it maintains the simulation clock and event list. When no (simulated) processors are active, the scheduler picks the next event from the event list and updates the simulation clock to that event's time.

The `Scheduler` exports four operations. The processors call `delay` to simulate the passage of time during data transfers and other activity; the end of each such time period defines an event. The bus controller calls `become_inactive` to inform the scheduler that a processor has been blocked in its attempt to seize the bus. The bus controller calls `become_active` when the processor subsequently obtains access. These operations return the value of the simulation clock so that statistics can be gathered. This interaction between the scheduler and bus controller allows the scheduler to maintain a count of active processors. Bus controllers call the final `Scheduler` operation, `time`, to get the value of the simulation clock.

Figure 18.1 illustrates the interaction between the three resources. The details of the `Processor` and `Bus` resources are specific to this example.

However, the `Scheduler` resource provides functionality that is commonly required in any discrete event simulation. It is an abstract data type that could be reused; it could also be extended with additional functionality.

18.2 A Solution

This section presents and discusses these three resources. For pedagogic reasons, we first describe `Processor`, then `Bus`, and finally `Scheduler`. The resources would actually be compiled in the opposite order.

Processor Resource

The following is the simulation program's main resource, `Processor`:

```
resource Processor()
  import Scheduler, Bus
  var NUM_PROCESSORS := 3  # processors, default 3
  var TIME := 1000.0       # time to run simulation
  var sched: cap Scheduler, bus: cap Bus

  # get command-line arguments, if present
  getarg(1, NUM_PROCESSORS); getarg(2, TIME)
  # start up Scheduler, Bus, and processors
  sched := create Scheduler(NUM_PROCESSORS+1)
  bus := create Bus(sched)

  process processor(i := 1 to NUM_PROCESSORS)
    do true ->
      bus.seize()                    # grab the bus
      sched.delay(random(10.0))   # use the bus
      bus.release()                  # release the bus
      sched.delay(random(20.0))   # do something else
    od
  end

  # run the simulation for TIME clock ticks
  sched.delay(TIME)
  # print usages from bus, then stop the simulation
  bus.print()
  stop
end Processor
```

Program execution begins in `Processor`'s initial code. The code first handles optional command-line arguments that can override the default number of processors and the default length of time to run the simulation. Then it creates one instance each of the `Scheduler` and `Bus` resources, assigning their capabilities to `sched` and `bus`, respectively. A copy of `sched` is passed to `bus` when it is created so `bus` can invoke `sched`'s operations.

The initial code then implicitly creates `NUM_PROCESSORS` instances of `processor`. Next the initial code lets the simulation run for `TIME` simulation clock ticks by delaying itself for that long. After that delay it requests that statistics on bus utilization be output and then stops the simulation.

Each `processor` process interacts with `bus` and `sched` to simulate seizing the bus, using the bus for a random amount of time, releasing the bus, and then performing some other activity for a different random amount of time. The upper bounds on the delay intervals are fixed in the above program; in practice they too should be command-line arguments.

Bus Controller Resource

The `Bus` resource exports `seize`, `release`, and `print` operations. It is programmed as follows:

```
resource Bus
  op seize(), release(), print()
  import Scheduler
body Bus(sched: cap Scheduler)
  op try_seize(go_ahead: cap())

  process bus_manager
    # nreq is number of bus requests from processors
    # bus_time is total time bus is in use
    # wait_time is total waiting time of processors
    # free indicates whether the bus is free
    var nreq := 0, bus_time := 0.0, wait_time := 0.0
    var free := true
    # queue of processes blocked on seizing
    op block_list(go_ahead: cap())
    do true ->
      in try_seize(go_ahead) ->
          nreq++
          if free ->
              free := false
              bus_time -:= sched.time()
              send go_ahead()
          [] else ->
              wait_time -:= sched.become_inactive()
              send block_list(go_ahead)
          fi
```

```
                [] release() ->
                    if ?block_list > 0 ->
                        # awaken a waiting processor
                        wait_time +:= sched.become_active()
                        var go_ahead: cap ()
                        receive block_list(go_ahead)
                        send go_ahead()
                    [] else ->  # no processor waiting
                        free := true
                        bus_time +:= sched.time()
                    fi
                [] print() -> # compute and output statistics
                    var now := sched.time()
                    # average wait time and percent bus use
                    var avg_wait, pct_bus: real
                    avg_wait := (wait_time +
                                    now*?block_list) / nreq
                    if free ->
                        pct_bus := 100*bus_time / now
                    [] else ->
                        pct_bus := 100*(bus_time + now) / now
                    fi
                    # print statistics; code not shown
                ni
            od
        end bus_manager

        # provide a simple call interface for processors
        proc seize()
            op go_ahead()
            send try_seize(go_ahead)
            receive go_ahead()
        end
    end Bus
```

The seize operation is serviced by a proc, which hides the fact that seizing the bus requires sending a try_seize message and receiving a go_ahead message. The go_ahead operation is declared local to seize, so that a new instance of go_ahead is created for each instance of seize. A capability for go_ahead is sent to try_seize. That go_ahead capability will be invoked when the associated seize request can be satisfied, thus allowing seize to complete, and its caller to continue.

The try_seize, release, and print operations are repeatedly serviced by an input statement in the background process bus_manager. The `try_seize` operation determines if the bus is free. If so it allocates the bus and allows the invoker to proceed by invoking `go_ahead`. If not it saves the capability for the invoking process's `go_ahead` operation. The `release` operation awakens a waiting process, if one is present, by sending to that process's `go_ahead` operation; `release` marks the bus as free if no process is waiting. The `try_seize` and `release` operations also gather information on bus use and processor waiting time. The `print` operation outputs statistics based on that information.

The `bus_manager` process maintains two local variables `bus_time` and `wait_time` that record the total time the bus is in use and the total time that processes have waited to obtain access to the bus, respectively. One way to view `bus_time` is as the sum of the lengths of the intervals during which the bus is in use. The endpoints of such intervals are the simulation clock values of when the bus became busy and when it became free again; the lengths are then the differences in these two clock values. Thus process `bus_manager` *subtracts* the simulation clock from `bus_time` when the bus becomes busy, and it *adds* the simulation clock to `bus_time` when the bus later becomes free. The effect of this subtraction and addition is that `bus_time` is incremented by the length of the interval during which the bus is in use. Process `bus_manager` similarly maintains the variable `wait_time`.

The `bus_manager` maintains the queue of `go_ahead` capabilities for waiting processes by using the local `block_list` operation. An element is added to the end of the queue by sending to `block_list`. An element is removed from the front of the queue by receiving from `block_list`. The number of processes currently blocked in their attempts to seize the bus is therefore the number of pending invocations on `block_list`, i.e., the value of `?block_list`.

Scheduler Resource

The final resource, `Scheduler`, exports four operations. It code is as follows:

```
resource Scheduler
  op become_active() returns t: real
  op become_inactive() returns t: real
  op time() returns t: real
  op delay(t: real)
body Scheduler(num_tasks: int)
  op event_list(go_ahead: cap(); t: real)
  var clock := 0.0  # the simulation clock

  process event_manager
    # number of active simulation processes
    var active := num_tasks
```

```
              do true ->
                in become_active() returns t ->
                    active++; t := clock
                [] become_inactive() returns t ->
                    active--; t := clock
                [] time() returns t ->
                    t := clock
                [] event_list(go_ahead,t) st active=0 by t ->
                    clock := t; active++; send go_ahead()
                    # awaken any other processes scheduled
                    # for this same time
                    do true ->
                      in event_list(go_ahead,t) st t=clock ->
                          active++; send go_ahead()
                      [] else ->
                          exit  # exit do loop
                      ni
                    od
                ni
              od
            end event_manager

            # provide a simple call interface for processors
            proc delay(t)
              op go_ahead()
              send event_list(go_ahead, t+clock)
              send become_inactive()
              receive go_ahead()
            end
          end Scheduler
```

The `delay` operation is serviced by a proc for much the same reason that `seize` in the `Bus` resource is serviced by a proc. Here the proc hides the fact that delaying requires two sends and a receive.

   The other four operations—`become_active`, `become_inactive`, `time`, and `event_list`—are repeatedly serviced by an input statement in the background process `event_manager`. The code for both `become_active` and `become_inactive` simply updates the number of active simulation processes (`active`) and returns the value of the simulation clock (`clock`). The code for `time` returns the value of `clock`.

   Process `event_manager` services an invocation of `event_list` when no simulation processes are active. It advances the simulation to the next event on the event list and activates the associated simulation process. The guard on `event_list` uses a synchronization expression to ensure that no simulation processes are active, and it uses a scheduling expression to select from the event list the invocation with the smallest time `t`. The code for `event_list` then sets the simulation clock to the time in that invocation, increments `active`, and sends a `go_ahead` signal to the process associated with the invocation so that it may continue. Process `event_manager` then checks the event list for other events scheduled for the same time. Each iteration of `event_list`'s loop removes an invocation whose recorded time is identical to the current time, if one is present. The inner input statement employs a synchronization expression to select appropriate invocations. For each such invocation, the code increments `active` and sends the `go_ahead`, as above. The loop exits when the event list has no invocations with the current time.

18.3 Observations

The code in the `Bus` and `Scheduler` resources employs a technique of using the implicit queues of pending invocations associated with message passing instead of using explicit, programmer-defined queues. Thus operations are similar to data-containing semaphores (see Section 9.4). Using this technique can lead to more concise solutions to problems involving lists.

The `block_list` operation in `Bus`'s event manager process is used to maintain the list of processes that are blocked trying to seize the bus. Similarly, the `event_list` operation in `Scheduler` is used to maintain the list of events scheduled to occur in the future. However, these two operations are used differently. The `block_list` operation is local to, and is invoked only within, the `event_manager` process in `Bus`. On the other hand, `event_list` is global to `Scheduler` and multiple instances of `delay` append (send) elements to `event_list`. Processes accessing `event_list` are automatically synchronized. If the event list were coded instead to use an explicit, programmer-defined queue, then the processes accessing the queue would need to be synchronized explicitly.

Programs written in a language, such as SR, that provides a variety of synchronization mechanisms are in many cases simpler than those written in languages that provide only one form of synchronization. The simulation program presented in this chapter employs both rendezvous and asynchronous message passing. For example, consider how a process is delayed when it attempts a `seize` that cannot be satisfied immediately. It sends a message and waits for a `go_ahead`. The `bus_manager` sends the `go_ahead` when the bus becomes free; it does not need to respond immediately, as it would if it instead used a rendezvous. Of course, this kind of interaction can be programmed using rendezvous alone, but it is cumbersome (see Exercise 18.5).

The Scheduler resource illustrates the use of two other interesting SR language features not found in many concurrent programming languages. First, invocation parameters can be used in synchronization expressions. For example, the second input statement that services event_list in the Scheduler resource (see Section 18.2) selects invocations whose time parameter matches the current simulation clock. Second, invocations can be selected in an order dictated by their parameters. For example, the first input statement that services event_list in Scheduler uses a scheduling expression to select the invocation with the smallest time. These features of SR contribute to more concise solutions to many programming problems, of which discrete event simulation is just one example.

Exercises

18.1　Why does the initial code in Processor (see Section 18.2) pass NUM_PROCESSORS+1 instead of just NUM_PROCESSORS when it creates Scheduler.

18.2　Suppose the process declaration in Processor (see Section 18.2) were moved to the end of the resource, i.e., after the stop statement. Will the program work correctly? Explain.

18.3　The program in this chapter uses a stop statement to terminate. Modify the program so that it terminates without using a stop statement.

18.4　Suppose that the simulation program did not need to gather statistics. Show how that would simplify the code.

18.5　Program the bus controller resource Bus (see Section 18.2) using only rendezvous for synchronization. (Have fun!)

18.6　Program the inner input statement in resource Scheduler (see Section 18.2) without using a synchronization expression.

18.7　Program the outer input statement in Scheduler without using a scheduling expression.

18.8　The delay operation in Scheduler is serviced as a separate proc. Can it be serviced as an arm of the input statement in process event_manager? Explain your answer.

18.9　The Scheduler variable clock is shared between event_manager and instances of delay. Explain why it is safe for delay to add clock to t.

18.10　Consider the delay proc in Scheduler. Describe the effects of the following:

(a) Changing the first send (only) to a call.

(b) Changing the second send (only) to a call.

(c) Changing both sends to calls.

18.11   Explain why it would be easier to replace the `block_list` operation (in `Bus`) by an explicit, programmer-defined queue than it would be to do the same for `event_list` (in `Scheduler`).

18.12   Devise and execute various timing tests to determine the relative costs of maintaining a queue shared by several processes as an operation and as a programmer-defined linked list with explicit synchronization.

18.13   Show how to use an operation to maintain a stack.

18.14   Program a discrete event simulation that represents a simple cafeteria. Customers obtain food from a single food server and then pay for it at a single cashier. They then eat before repeating their activities. Reuse as much of the code presented in this chapter as you can.

18.15   Program a discrete event simulation that models the distributed solution to the dining philosophers problem (see Section 13.2). Use it to gather statistics on fork utilization and waiting times.

18.16   Program a simulation of passengers and buses arriving and departing from a bus stop.

18.17   Program a simulation of traffic on a grid of city streets. Assume there is a stop light at each intersection.

18.18   Program a simulation of the movements of planes on runways and between airports. Include gates from which planes depart and at which they arrive.

Language Synopsis

This appendix summarizes the general forms of the main SR constructs. Plurals and ellipses are used to indicate zero or more occurrences of items. Many items are optional, and items within resources, globals, and blocks can appear in any order. See Appendix B for the complete syntax.

Resources

```
resource identifier                  # general combined spec and body
   import or extend component_identifiers
   constant, type, or operation declarations
body identifier ( parameters )
   import component_identifiers
   declarations and statements
   procs, procedures, and processes
   final block end
end identifier


resource identifier ( parameters )   # simple combined spec and body
   resource body portion
end identifier


resource identifier                  # abstract spec
   resource spec portion
end identifier
```

```
resource identifier                      # separate concrete spec
   resource spec portion
body identifier ( parameters )  separate


body identifier                          # separate body
   resource body portion
end identifier
```

Globals

```
global identifier                        # combined spec and body
   import component_identifiers
   constant, type, variable, or operation declarations
body identifier
   import component_identifiers
   declarations and statements
   procs, procedures, and processes
   final block end
end identifier


global identifier                        # spec only; no body
   global spec portion
end identifier


global identifier                        # separate spec
   global spec portion
body identifier separate


body identifier                          # separate body
   global body portion
end identifier
```

Procs, Procedures, and Processes

```
proc identifier ( formal_identifiers )  returns result_id
   block
end identifier


procedure identifier ( parameters )  returns result_id : type
   block
end identifier
```

```
process identifier
    block
end identifier

process identifier ( quantifiers )
    block
end identifier
```

Blocks

declarations and statements (in any order)

Types, Constants, and Variables

```
bool                          # basic types
int
char
real
string[ maximum_length ]
file

enum ( enumeration_literals )        # user-defined types
rec ( field_definitions )
union ( field_definitions )
ptr type_definition or ptr any
cap resource_id, cap vm, cap operation_id, cap optype_id,
    cap operation_specification, or cap sem
[ ranges ] type_definition
type identifier = type_definition

const identifier[ subscripts ] : type := expression
var identifier[ subscripts ], ... : type
var identifier[ subscripts ] : type := expression
```

Operations and Operation Types

```
op identifier[ subscripts ] ( parameters )
    returns result_id : type { op_restriction }
op identifier[ subscripts ] : optype_identifier
sem identifier[ subscripts ] := expression
external identifier ( parameters ) returns result_id : type
```

```
optype identifier = ( parameters )
    returns result_id : type { op_restriction }
```

Quantifiers

bound_variable := start to finish by step st boolean_expr
bound_variable := start downto finish by step st boolean_expr

Assignment and Swapping Operators

variable := expression
variable +:= expression   # also -:=, *:=, ...
variable ++
variable --
++ variable
-- variable
variable :=: variable

Sequential Statements

expression   # such as an assignment
skip
stop (expression)
if boolean_expression -> block [] ... [] else -> block fi
do boolean_expression -> block [] ... [] else -> block od
fa quantifiers -> block af
exit
next
begin block end

Interaction Statements

call operation (actuals)
send operation (actuals)
forward operation (actuals)

receive operation (variables)
in (quantifier) operation_id (formal_identifiers)
    st synchronization_expr by scheduling_expr -> block
[] ...
[] else -> block
ni

```
V ( semaphore )
P ( semaphore )

return
reply

resource_capability := create resource_id ( actuals )  on vm_capability
vm_capability := create vm()  on physical_machine
destroy capability

co  ( quantifiers )  invocation  -> block  // ... oc
```

Keywords

af	global	receive
and	high	ref
any	if	reply
begin	import	res
body	in	resource
bool	initial	return
by	int	returns
call	low	sem
cap	mod	send
char	new	separate
co	next	skip
const	ni	st
create	noop	stderr
destroy	not	stdin
do	null	stdout
downto	oc	stop
else	od	string
end	on	to
enum	op	true
exit	optype	type
extend	or	union
external	P	V
fa	proc	val
false	procedure	var
fi	process	vm
file	ptr	xor
final	real	
forward	rec	

Collected Syntax

This appendix gives the complete grammar for SR. The parser in the SR compiler was generated using the **yacc** compiler-compiler program. The actual **yacc** grammar is stored in file `sr/grammar.y` in the SR distribution. We present a BNF version of the grammar here, with productions listed in the same order as in that file. However, we do not include several context-sensitive restrictions that appear as semantic actions in the **yacc** grammar.

Three standard suffixes are used in the names of many non-terminals. The suffix `_lp` stands for list plus and indicates a list of one or more items. Suffix `_ls` stands for list star and indicates a list of zero or more items. The name of an optional item has suffix `_opt`. As usual, epsilon (ε) represents an empty production.

The semicolon character is used as a separator or terminator in several places in the grammar. A semicolon can always be replaced by a newline character.

Components — Resources and Globals

component ::= spec_component ; | combined_component ; | separate_body ;

spec_component ::= comp_label spec_stmt_ls spec_body

combined_component ::= combined_specpart body_stmt_ls end_id

combined_specpart ::= comp_label comp_params

comp_label ::= comp_keyword identifier

comp_keyword ::= resource | global

spec_body ::= end_id | body identifier params_opt body_stmt_ls end_id |
              body identifier params_opt separate

params_opt ::= ε | parameters

separate_body ::= body identifier body_stmt_ls end_id

Component Spec and Body Contents

spec_stmt_ls ::= spec_stmt | spec_stmt_ls ; spec_stmt

spec_stmt ::= common_stmt | extend_clause

body_stmt_ls ::= body_stmt | body_stmt_ls ; body_stmt

body_stmt ::= common_stmt | expr | body_only

body_only ::= stmt | proc | process | procedure | final_block

common_stmt ::= ε | decl | import_clause

import_clause ::= import id_lp

extend_clause ::= extend id_lp

Top-Level Body Statements

op_decl ::= op_or_ext oper_def_lp

op_or_ext ::= op | external

oper_def_lp ::= oper_def | oper_def_lp , oper_def

oper_def ::= id_subs_lp op_prototype | id_subs_lp colon_opt qualified_id

colon_opt ::= ε | :

sem_decl ::= sem sem_def_lp

sem_def_lp ::= sem_def | sem_def_lp , sem_def

sem_def ::= id_subs sem_init

sem_init ::= ε | := expr

proc ::= proc identifier param_names block end_id

procedure ::= procedure identifier prototype block end_id

process ::= process identifier quantifiers_opt block end_id

final_block ::= final block end final_opt

final_opt ::= ε | final

Parameters

prototype ::= parameters return_spec_opt

parameters ::= (param_spec_ls)

param_spec_ls ::= ε | param_spec_lp

param_spec_lp ::= param_spec | param_spec ; |
                param_spec ; param_spec_lp

param_spec ::= param_kind_opt type | param_kind_opt id_subs_lp : type

param_kind_opt ::= ε | val | var | res | ref

return_spec_opt ::= ε | returns type | returns id_subs : type

param_names ::= (id_ls) return_name_opt

return_name_opt ::= ε | returns identifier

Declarations

decl ::= type_decl | obj_decl | optype_decl | sem_decl | op_decl

type_decl ::= type identifier = type

obj_decl ::= var_or_const var_def_lp

var_or_const ::= var | const

var_def_lp ::= var_def | var_def , var_def_lp

var_def ::= id_subs_lp var_att

var_att ::= : type | : type := expr | := expr

Type Specifications

type ::= subscripts unsub_type | unsub_type

unsub_type ::= basic_type | string_def | enum_def | pointer_def |
               record_def | union_def | capability_def | qualified_id

basic_type ::= bool | char | int | file | real

string_def ::= string [string_lim]

string_lim ::= expr | *

enum_def ::= enum (id_lp)

pointer_def ::= ptr type | ptr any

record_def ::= rec (field_lp)

union_def ::= union (field_lp)

field_lp ::= field | field ; | field ; field_lp

field ::= var_def_lp

capability_def ::= cap cap_for

cap_for ::= qualified_id | op_prototype | vm | sem

Optype Specifications

optype_decl ::= optype identifier eq_opt op_prototype

op_prototype ::= prototype op_restriction_opt

eq_opt ::= ε | =

op_restriction_opt ::= ε | { op_restriction }

op_restriction ::= call | send | call , send | send , call

Blocks and Statements

block ::= block_items

block_items ::= block_item | block_items ; block_item

block_item ::= ε | decl | stmt | expr | import_clause

stmt ::= skip_stmt | stop_stmt | exit_stmt | next_stmt | return_stmt |
reply_stmt | forward_stmt | send_stmt | explicit_call |
destroy_stmt | begin_end | if_stmt | do_stmt | for_all_stmt |
V_stmt | input_stmt | receive_stmt | P_stmt | concurrent_stmt

skip_stmt ::= skip

stop_stmt ::= stop | stop (**expr**)

exit_stmt ::= exit

next_stmt ::= next

return_stmt ::= return

reply_stmt ::= reply

forward_stmt ::= forward invocation

send_stmt ::= send invocation

receive_stmt ::= receive id_subs paren_list

V_stmt ::= V (**expr**)

P_stmt ::= P (id_subs)

explicit_call ::= call invocation

destroy_stmt ::= destroy expr

begin_end ::= begin block end

if_stmt ::= if guarded_cmd_lp else_cmd_opt fi

do_stmt ::= do guarded_cmd_lp else_cmd_opt od

guarded_cmd_lp ::= guarded_cmd | guarded_cmd_lp [] guarded_cmd

guarded_cmd ::= expr -> block

else_cmd_opt ::= ε | [] else -> block

for_all_stmt ::= fa quantifier_lp -> block af

Input Statement

input_stmt ::= in in_cmd_lp else_cmd_opt ni

in_cmd_lp ::= in_cmd | in_cmd_lp [] in_cmd

in_cmd ::= quantifiers_opt in_spec sync_expr_opt sched_expr_opt -> block

in_spec ::= id_subs param_names

sync_expr_opt ::= ε | and expr | st expr

sched_expr_opt ::= ε | by expr

Concurrent Statement

concurrent_stmt ::= co concurrent_cmd_lp oc

concurrent_cmd_lp ::= concurrent_cmd |
                      concurrent_cmd_lp // concurrent_cmd

concurrent_cmd ::= quantifiers_opt concurrent_invocation
                   post_processing_opt

concurrent_invocation ::= explicit_call | send_stmt | expr

post_processing_opt ::= ε | -> block

Quantifiers

quantifiers_opt ::= ε | (quantifier_lp)

quantifier_lp ::= quantifier | quantifier , quantifier_lp

quantifier ::= identifier := expr direction expr step_opt such_that_opt

direction ::= to | downto

step_opt ::= ε | by expr

such_that_opt ::= ε | st expr

Expressions

expr ::= identifier | literal | invocation | constructor | binary_expr |
          prefix_expr | suffix_expr | create_expr

literal ::=   # a token for one of the literals; see Chapter 2

binary_expr ::= expr operator expr   # see Appendix C for operators

prefix_expr ::= prefix_operator expr   # see Appendix C for operators
                | basic_type paren_expr | string paren_expr |
                type_opr (type)

paren_expr ::= (expr)

type_opr ::= new | low | high

suffix_expr ::= expr postfix_operator   # see Appendix C for operators
                | expr . identifier | expr [range_lp]

invocation ::= expr paren_list

paren_list ::= (paren_item_ls)

paren_item_ls ::= ε | expr_lp

expr_lp ::= expr | expr , expr_lp

constructor ::= (constr_item_lp)

constr_item_lp ::= constr_item | constr_item , constr_item_lp

constr_item ::= expr | [expr] expr

create_expr ::= create create_call location_opt

create_call ::= rsrc_name paren_list

rsrc_name ::= identifier | vm

location_opt ::= ε | on expr

Miscellaneous

qualified_id ::= identifier | identifier . identifier

end_id ::= end id_opt

id_opt ::= ε | identifier

id_ls ::= ε | id_lp

id_lp ::= identifier | identifier , id_lp

id_subs_lp ::= id_subs | id_subs , id_subs_lp

id_subs ::= identifier | identifier subscripts

subscripts ::= bracketed_list | bracketed_list subscripts

bracketed_list ::= [range_lp]

range_lp ::= range | range , range_lp

range ::= bound | bound : bound

bound ::= expr | *

Operators and Predefined Functions

SR provides a rich set of operators and predefined functions, both of which are used in expressions. This appendix summarizes the operators and describes the meaning and use of each predefined function.

Operators

The table on the following pages lists all of SR's operators. These are listed in groups based on precedence and associativity. The first two groups consist of the unary postfix and prefix operators. The other groups consist of binary operators. The table also indicates allowed operand types for each operator. See Chapter 2 for further details and examples (except for the ? operator, which was introduced in Chapter 11).

The operators within a group have the same precedence. The groups themselves are listed in *decreasing* order of precedence. Thus postfix operators have the highest precedence, followed by prefix operators, and so on; assignment operators have the lowest precedence.

The operators within a group of binary operators also have the same associativity. Most of the binary operators are left associative, which means that operands are evaluated left to right in an expression involving operators of the same precedence. For example, a*b/c is evaluated as (a*b)/c. The exponentiation and assignment operators are right associative.

Parentheses can, as usual, be placed around an expression to give it the highest precedence. Function invocations have precedence above the postfix operators. The dot "operator," which is used to reference fields of records and unions and to qualify imported names, has precedence equal to that of the postfix operators.

Operator	Operator Name	Operand Types
++	postincrement	ordered, real, pointer
--	postdecrement	ordered, real, pointer
^	pointer dereference	pointer
[...]	subscript or slice	array or string
not, ~	logical/bit-wise complement	boolean, integer
+	unary plus (no effect)	integer, real
-	unary negation	integer, real
++	preincrement	ordered, real, pointer
--	predecrement	ordered, real, pointer
@	address of	any variable
?	number of invocations	operation
**	exponentiation	integer, real
*	multiplication	integer, real
/	division	integer, real
%	remainder	integer, real
mod	modulus	integer, real
+	plus	integer, real, pointer
-	minus	integer, real, pointer
||	concatenation	string, character
<<	left shift	integer
>>	right shift	integer
=	equal	ordered, real, string, pointer, capability
!=, ~=	not equal	ordered, real, string, pointer, capability
>	greater than	ordered, real, string
<	less than	ordered, real, string
>=	greater than or equal	ordered, real, string
<=	less than or equal	ordered, real, string
and, &	logical/bit-wise and	boolean, integer
or, |	logical/bit-wise or	boolean, integer
xor	logical/bit-wise exclusive or	boolean, integer
:=	assign	all
:=:	swap	all

+:=	increment, then assign	integer, real, pointer
-:=	decrement, then assign	integer, real, pointer
*:=	multiply, then assign	integer, real
/:=	divide, then assign	integer, real
%:=	remainder, then assign	integer, real
**:=	exponentiate, then assign	integer, real
|:=	or, then assign	boolean, integer
&:=	and, then assign	boolean, integer
||:=	concatenate, then assign	string, character
<<:=	left shift, then assign	integer
>>:=	right shift, then assign	integer

Table C.1. Operators in decreasing order of precedence (by groups).

Basic Functions

The following functions can be applied to arguments having the types specified. (Strictly speaking, `low`, `high`, and `new` are not functions; their names are keywords and their arguments are type names, not expressions.)

```
abs(x)
```

The absolute value of x. Defined for integers and reals.

```
max(x1, ..., xn)
min(x1, ..., xn)
```

The maximum or minimum of the list of arguments. Defined for ordered types and reals. All arguments must be of the same type, except that integers and reals can be mixed (in which case the integers are implicitly converted to reals and the result is a real).

```
pred(x)
succ(x)
```

The predecessor or successor of x. Defined for ordered types.

```
low(T)
high(T)
```

The smallest or largest value of type T. Defined for ordered types and reals; `low(real)` is the smallest representable real value greater than 0.

```
lb(a,n)
ub(a,n)
```

The lower or upper bound of range `n` of array `a`. Argument `n` is optional; the default value is 1. If `n` is present, it must be an integer literal.

```
length(s)
```

The number of characters in string `s`.

```
maxlength(s)
```

The maximum number of characters that can be stored in string `s`.

```
new(T)
```

Allocates storage for a new object of type `T` and returns a pointer to it.

```
free(p)
```

Frees the object pointed to by pointer `p`; the object must have been allocated by `new(T)`.

Math Functions

The following functions take real arguments—or integers by the implicit conversion rule—and they return a real result. For the trigonometric functions, angles are measured in radians; the return ranges are consistent with ANSI C [ANSI 1989]. In most cases SR just calls C library routines directly, so the handling of erroneous arguments is system dependent.

```
sqrt(x)
```

The square root of `x`, for non-negative `x`.

```
log(x,b)
```

The logarithm of `x` with respect to base `b`, for $x > 0$ and $b > 1$. Argument `b` is optional; the default value is the base *e* of the natural logarithms (i.e., 2.7182...).

```
exp(x,b)
```

The value of `b` raised to the power `x`; this is equivalent to `b**x`, except that the result is always real. Argument `b` is optional; the default value is the base *e* of the natural logarithms (i.e., 2.7182...).

```
ceil(x)
floor(x)
```

The smallest integer not less than x or the largest integer not greater than x. Both functions return real results.

```
round(x)
```

The integer nearest to x (returned as a real). If x is halfway between two integers, the real equivalent of the even integer is returned.

```
sin(r)
cos(r)
tan(r)
```

The sine, cosine, or tangent of r.

```
asin(x)
acos(x)
atan(x,y)
```

The arc sine or arc cosine of x, or the arc tangent of x/y. For asin, x must be between -1 and 1, and the result is between $-\pi/2$ and $\pi/2$. For acos, x must be between -1 and 1, and the result is between 0 and π. For atan, argument y is optional (the default value is 1), either x or y can be zero (but not both), and the result is between $-\pi$ and π.

Random Number Generation

The following functions produce sequences of (pseudo-) random numbers. A sequence is not reproducible unless it is explicitly seeded with a nonzero value.

```
random()
random(ub)
random(lb,ub)
```

The first function returns a random number r such that $0.0 \leq r < 1.0$. The second returns an r such that $0.0 \leq r < ub$. The third returns an r such that $lb \leq r < ub$.

```
seed(x)
```

Seeds the random number generator with real value x. If x is zero, an irreproducible value is used.

Processes, Resources, and Virtual Machines

The following functions deal with process priorities, capabilities for resources and virtual machines, and the mapping from virtual to physical machines in a distributed program.

`setpriority(n)`

Sets the current process's priority to integer value `n`. This will cause the current process to relinquish the CPU to a higher-priority task.

`mypriority()`

Returns the executing process's current priority.

`myresource()`

Returns a capability for the resource in which the function is called.

`myvm()`

Returns a capability for the virtual machine on which the function is called.

`mymachine()`

Returns the integer number of the physical machine on which the function is called. By convention, program execution begins on machine 0. Numbers of other machines are installation dependent; see Appendix D for details.

`locate(x,s)`
`locate(x,s,p)`

Defines integer value `x` to be synonymous with the network node (machine) named by string `s` when used in `create vm()` on `x`. If argument `p` is present, it is a string specifying a pathname that will be used to load the executable program on machine `x`; see Appendix D for details.

Timing Functions

SR provides two functions that enable a program to determine how long it has been executing or to delay execution. The first is useful for timing program execution; the second is used to delay a process.

`age()`

Returns an integer that gives the elapsed time, in milliseconds, since the local virtual machine was created.

```
nap(msec)
```

Blocks the executing process for integer value `msec` milliseconds; has no effect if `msec` is non-positive.

Type Conversion Functions

SR provides several functions for converting (casting) values of one type into those of another. Values can be converted to and from types `int`, `real`, `char`, `enum`, `bool`, `ptr`, `string`, and `[]char` (array of `char`). All combinations are possible, although some (e.g., `bool` to `ptr`) make little sense.

Conversion functions are also associated with user-defined types that are equivalent to the above types. In addition, a record constructor function is implicitly associated with each user-defined record type.

The conversion functions have no effect when given an argument of the same type as that returned by the function; e.g., `int(5)` returns 5. In a conversion from `string` or `[]char` to anything other than `string` or `[]char`, both leading and trailing whitespace are discarded before interpretation; the whitespace characters are blank, tab, newline, return, vertical tab, and formfeed. When converting to and from ordered types, values of type `char` are viewed by the conversion functions as small integers, not as short strings.

```
int(x)
```

The return value depends on the type of `x`, as follows:

real	integer portion of `x`, which must not cause overflow
char	integer value of `x`, with no sign extension
bool	1 for true, 0 for false
enum	integer value of `x`; enumeration literals start at 0
ptr	integer value of the address of `x`
string	converted value; string must be a valid integer literal, possibly with a leading – or + sign; octal and hexadecimal literals are allowed
[]char	same as for `string`

```
real(x)
```

The return value depends on the type of `x`, as shown in the table at the top of the next page.

`int`	real equivalent of x
`char`	real equivalent of `int(x)`
`bool`	real equivalent of `int(x)`
`enum`	real equivalent of `int(x)`
`ptr`	real equivalent of `int(x)`
`string`	converted value according to rules of C's `scanf("%lf")`
`[]char`	converted value according to rules of C's `scanf("%lf")`

`char(x)`

The return value depends on the type of x, as follows:

`int`	character constructed from low order 8 bits of x; the discarded bits must be all 0 or all 1
`real`	same as `char(int(x))`
`enum`	same as `char(int(x))`
`bool`	same as `char(int(x))`
`ptr`	same as `char(int(x))`
`string`	first non-whitespace character in x; returns `\0` if there is no such character
`[]char`	same as for `string`

`bool(x)`

The return value depends on the type of x, as follows:

`int`	true if $x \neq 0$; false otherwise
`real`	true if `int(x)` $\neq 0$; false otherwise
`char`	true if `int(x)` $\neq 0$; false otherwise
`enum`	true if `int(x)` $\neq 0$; false otherwise
`ptr`	true if $x \neq$ `null`; false otherwise
`string`	true if x is `"t"` or `"true"`; false if x is `"f"` or `"false"`; fatal error if x is any other value the comparison is case insensitive
`[]char`	same as for `string`

`string(x)`

Returns a string formatted according to the following rules, which depend on the type of x:

[]char	the equivalent string
char	a one-element string containing the character
int	a string consisting of the equivalent decimal number
enum	a string consisting of an integer literal that specifies the position of enumeration literal x in the type
real	a string consisting of an equivalent real literal
bool	returns "true" or "false", depending on the value of x
ptr	if x is a null pointer, returns "==null=="; otherwise returns the address of x as a string of eight hexadecimal digits

chars(x)

Returns the same result as string(x), but the result is an array of characters instead of a string. Note that chars is a true predefined function, not a language keyword like previous conversion functions.

T(x)

T is the name of a user-defined type. If T names a type equivalent to one of the following, the effect is as indicated:

int	same as int(x)
real	same as real(x)
char	same as char(x)
bool	same as bool(x)
enum	same as e(int(x)), where e is the name of the equivalent enumeration type; x must be a number, not an enumeration literal
string	same as string(x); resulting length must be legal for T
[]char	same as chars(x); resulting length must be legal for T
rec	constructs a record of type T; in this case, the conversion function has one argument for each field of type T

If T names a type equivalent to a pointer type p, the effect depends on the type of x, as follows:

string	if x is equal to "==null==" (ignoring whitespace), then return null; otherwise interpret x as a string of hexadecimal digits and cast that number to type T
[]char	same as for string
others	return int(x) converted to an address

File Access Functions

The following functions are used to open, close, or remove a file; to flush a file buffer; or to adjust the read/write pointer on a random access file.

open(pathname,mode)

Opens file `pathname` and returns a file descriptor, which is a value of type `file`. Returns `null` if the file cannot be opened. The value of `pathname` is a string containing an absolute or relative file name. If `mode` is READ, an existing file is opened for reading. If `mode` is WRITE, a new file is created, or an existing file is truncated. If `mode` is READWRITE, an existing file is opened for both reading and writing. In all cases, the read/write pointer starts at the beginning of the file. For files opened in READWRITE mode, `seek` must be used when switching access modes. (Files corresponding to terminals that are to be read and written should be opened twice: once for reading from the keyboard and once for writing to the display.)

flush(f)

Flushes the output buffers of file `f`, which should be open for writing. An unsuccessful `flush` is a fatal error. Output statements implicitly flush output buffers, so `flush` is not actually needed.

close(f)

Closes file `f`, which should be open. Open files are implicitly closed when a program terminates. An unsuccessful `close` is a fatal error.

remove(pathname)

Removes file `pathname` from the file system and returns true if successful, false if not. The value of `pathname` is a string containing an absolute or relative file name. If the file is open, its contents will not disappear until the file is closed.

seek(f,stype,offset)

Seeks in file `f` and returns the new position of the read/write pointer. The type of seek is determined by the value of `stype`. If `stype` is ABSOLUTE, then the read/write pointer is set to `offset`. If `stype` is RELATIVE, then `offset` is added to the read/write pointer. If `stype` is EXTEND, then the read/write pointer is set to the end of the file plus `offset`.

where(f)

Returns the current position of the read/write pointer in file `f`.

Input/Output Functions

SR provides three groups of input/output functions. The first treats a file as a stream of characters, the second provides implicit type conversions and formatting, the third supports user-specified formatting. With the formatting functions, if a particular formatting specification is not supported by the underlying C implementation, the mismatch is not detected and program behavior is unpredictable. Strings (and character arrays) used with formatted I/O may not contain the ASCII NUL character ($\backslash 0$).

When an SR process calls an input function, it delays until the function returns; however, another process may execute in the meantime. On the other hand, when a process calls an output function, it retains control of the processor. A process is not preempted when doing output, so write statements added for debugging will not affect the order in which processes execute. The -A option to the SR linker **srl** makes output asynchronous; in this case a process might be preempted while waiting for output to complete.

```
get(str)
get(f,str)
```

Reads characters from `stdin` or file `f` and stores them in `str`. Argument `str` is either a string variable or an array of characters. If `str` is a string and the input file contains at least `maxlength(str)` more characters, that many are read. Otherwise, all remaining characters are read. If at least one character was read, `get` returns a count of the number of characters that were read and sets the length of `str` to that value. If end-of-file is encountered immediately, no characters are read and `get` returns `EOF`. The argument to `get` can also be a character array, in which case the entire array is filled (unless `EOF` is encountered).

```
put(str)
put(f,str)
```

Writes `length(str)` characters to `stdout` or file `f`. Argument `str` can also be an array of characters, in which case the entire array is written.

```
read(x,...)
read(f,x,...)
```

Reads values from `stdin` or file `f`, stores them in the arguments, and returns the number of values successfully read. If end-of-file is encountered before any value is read, `read` returns `EOF`. It returns 0 if there is an error reading the first value.

The arguments are assigned values in order. The value assigned to argument `x` depends on its type. If `x` is a string or array of characters, the next input line is read into `x`. The newline at the end of the line is discarded, not stored. If the line is too long, it is truncated, and the rest of the line remains unread. If x is a string, its length is set. If x is of type []char and the input line is shorter than the length of the array, extra elements of x are filled with blanks.

If x is any other type T, the next token is read as a string s and converted to T using type-conversion function T(s). A token is defined as a sequence of non-whitespace characters terminated by whitespace. Leading whitespace characters are skipped; trailing whitespace characters are consumed and discarded up to and including the first newline character. If the conversion T(s) succeeds, read continues with the next argument (if any). If the conversion fails, read returns immediately and x is not modified.

```
write(x,...)
write(f,x,...)
writes(x,...)
writes(f,x,...)
```

Formats and writes the arguments to stdout or file f. For each argument x, the value written is string(x). For write, one space is written between each pair of output values and a newline is written after the last value. No implicit spaces or newline characters are written by writes.

```
printf(format,x,...)
printf(f,format,x,...)
```

Prints its arguments on stdout or file f using the format specified by string value format. The format specification must be acceptable to C's printf function, except that a new specification has been added for SR's boolean type. An argument x of the correct type must be supplied for each conversion character. The format characters and corresponding argument types are

%d, %i, %o, %q, %x, %X, %u	int **or** enum
%b, %B	bool
%c	char
%s	string **or** []char
%f, %e, %E, %g, %G	real (**or** int, by conversion rules)
%p	any pointer
%n	not allowed by SR
%%	(no argument)

Format %q is an alternate form of %o. Format %b writes true or false, and %B writes TRUE or FALSE; width and precision are interpreted as with %s. Pointers are written in hexadecimal using %08X format because %p is not yet supported by all C implementations.

All of the ANSI C "flags" ("`-+ 0#`") are allowed and have the same meanings. None of the word size modifiers ("`hlL`") is allowed, however. Use of `*` as a width or precision specifier is also not allowed. Each conversion is limited to a maximum of 509 characters (as in ANSI C).

```
sprintf(buffer,format,x...)
```

Formats and writes its arguments like `printf`, but the output is placed in string variable `buffer`. The length of `buffer` is set to the length of the output string; it is an error if `buffer` is too small.

```
scanf(format,x,...)
scanf(f,format,x,...)
```

Reads formatted input from `stdin` or file `f`, stores it in arguments `x`, and returns the number of items converted and assigned. If end-of-file is reached before a successful conversion is performed, `EOF` is returned. The input format is specified by string value `format`, which must be acceptable to C's `scanf` function.

Field specifiers in `format` are of the form "`%[*][digits]$`", where `$` is one of the formats described below. None of C's word size modifiers ("`hlL`") is allowed. The optional *digits* field specifies the maximum number of characters to be scanned for this field. The optional `*` indicates suppression; the input will be read but no assignment will be made. Even if assignment is suppressed, format checking still occurs, so invalid input will cause a failure.

An argument `x` of the correct type must be supplied for each conversion character in `format` not accompanied by the `*` assignment-suppression flag. Arguments must be SR variables, not pointers to variables as in C. The format characters and corresponding types are

`%d, %i, %o, %q, %u, %x`	`int`
`%b`	`bool`
`%e, %f, %g`	`real`
`%c, %[...], %s`	`string` or `[]char`
`%c, %[...]`	`char` if field width is 1
`%p`	any pointer (default input format `%8x`)
`%n`	not allowed by SR
`%%`	(no argument)

The input expected for each kind of format is:

`%d, %u`	decimal integer
`%i`	SR integer literal (decimal, octal, or hexadecimal)
`%o, %q`	octal integer, with or without a trailing `q` or `Q`
`%x`	hexadecimal integer, with or without a trailing `x` or `X`

%b   true, false, TRUE, or FALSE
%p   an address specified by a string of hexadecimal digits,
            or the special string ==null== for a null pointer

Each of the above formats may have an optional field-width specifier. If a field width is specified, up to that many characters are read. For example, given a format of %6s and input string "abraham", the argument string will be assigned "abraha". The next character read will be "m".

The default field width for the integer, real and s formats is the ANSI limit of 512. For the p format, the default is 8. For c, it is 1. The b format has a variable default length: 4 characters for "true" and 5 for "false".

For each argument, scanf consumes input until the field width is exhausted or a character is read that is not part of a legal value. For example, consider the string "3BAGELS" scanned using a "%i" format. This reads 3BA because 3BA is an initial substring of the legal value 3BAx. But because 3BA is not legal by itself, nothing is assigned to the corresponding variable, and scanf returns on the mismatch. Subsequent reads begin at the letter G.

If argument x is a string variable and the scanned input string is longer than the maximum length of x, then the input string is truncated before being assigned to x. No warning is given of this, so if in doubt use the optional field width specifier.

sscanf(buffer,format,x...)

Reads and formats input like scanf, but the input is read from string value buffer.

Accessing Command-Line Arguments

Two operations provide access to the arguments of the UNIX command that invoked execution of an SR program.

getarg(n,x)

Reads argument n into variable x. If n is 0, x is assigned the command name itself (argv[0]). If argument n does not exist, getarg returns EOF.

If x is of type string or []char, getarg copies argument n into x until either the argument is consumed or x is filled. In this case getarg returns the number of characters that were copied. If x is a string, its length is set to this same value.

If x is of any other type T, the command-line argument is read as a string s, converted to type T using the rules for conversion function T(s), and then assigned to x. If conversion succeeds, getarg returns 1. If it fails, getarg returns 0 and x is not modified.

```
numargs()
```

Returns the number of command-line arguments, not counting the command name.

External Operations

As described in Section 6.4, external operations provide access to procedures or functions written in C or a language compatible with the C calling sequence. (The name of an external should not begin with `sr_` since names of that form are used by the SR implementation.) Like an `op`, an external may be invoked by either call or send statements. An external may also have a return specification and hence may be used to invoke a C function.

The declaration of an external specifies the type of each argument and how it is passed. An invocation block is allocated to pass parameters to and from an external. Before an external is invoked, `val` and `var` parameters are copied into the invocation block; for `ref` parameters, a pointer to the parameter is copied into the invocation block. If an external is called (not sent), `var` and `res` parameters are copied back when the call completes.

The following table indicates the SR data types that can be passed to an external only by value or by reference; these should not be declared as `var` or `res` parameters.

SR type	Passed by val as	Passed by ref as
bool	int	(char *)
char	int	(char *)
int	int	(int *)
enum	int	(int *)
real	double	(double *)
file	(FILE *)	(FILE **)
ptr	(char *)	(char **)

All four parameter passing modes may be used for `string`, `rec`, and array types. To an external, they always appear to be passed by reference using a `(char *)` pointer. For a string declared as a `val` or `var` parameter, SR ensures that the string is terminated by a `'\0'` character before the external is invoked.

Care should be taken when passing an external an array of strings or array of records because individual elements are not converted. In this case the programmer needs to determine the internal representation used by the SR implementation.

For externals that have return specifications, the allowed SR return types and the corresponding C function types are as follows:

SR type	C function type
bool	int
char	int
int	int
enum	int
real	double
file	(FILE *)
ptr	(char *) **or** (void *)
string	(char *)

If a C function returns a pointer to a null-terminated character string, it may be described in SR as returning string[n] as long as n is large enough to accept the largest string ever expected. (If n turns out to be insufficiently large, the returned string will be silently truncated.) If the C function returns a null pointer, an empty string will be returned to the SR program. For return values—and var or res parameters—declared as string, the C strlen() function is called implicitly to set the SR string length after the C function returns.

Program Development
and Execution

This appendix provides a brief overview of the components of the SR system and the way they are used to develop and execute SR programs. Detailed descriptions of commands and tools are contained in the manual pages that are part of the SR distribution.

Basics of Compilation and Execution

An SR program is contained in one or more source files. The names of these files must have a `.sr` suffix, e.g., `matrix.sr`. Source files can contain entire programs, individual components (resources or globals), component specs, component bodies, or any combination of these. However, the spec of a component has to be compiled before its body and before it is imported. If two components import each other, their specs may be compiled in either order (before either body is compiled).

The SR compiler, **sr**, takes a set of source files and makes two passes over them. First it processes information in the spec parts of globals and resources. Assuming no errors were encountered during this pass, the compiler then processes component bodies, translates the SR source code into a C program, and calls the C compiler to create a separate `.o` file for each global and resource in the program.

Linking is directed by **srl**, which acts as a front end to the UNIX linker **ld**. The SR linker combines one or more `.o` files with the SR and C run-time libraries to produce an executable program. The last resource specified on the command line to **srl** is taken to be the main resource of the program. By default, **sr** calls **srl** implicitly. In this case the last resource compiled by **sr** is taken to be the main resource.

Compilation and linking take place in the context of an `Interfaces` directory, which is used by the compiler and linker for storing `.o` files and information about component specs. The programmer can control where the `Interfaces` directory is created; the default location is the current working directory.

Additional Tools

Although only **sr** and **srl** are needed to run SR programs, other tools assist with related tasks. One, **srm**, creates a makefile that assists with compiling and executing complex SR programs. Two commands, **srtex** and **srgrind**, format SR programs for typesetting.

There are also three preprocessors for use with SR. The first, **ccr2sr**, converts source code written using a form of conditional critical regions (CCRs) into SR code. The second, **m2sr**, converts source code written using a form of monitors into SR code; it also supports several different monitor signaling disciplines. The third preprocessor, **csp2sr**, converts source code written in a variant of Communicating Sequential Processes (CSP) into SR code. See the UNIX man pages for descriptions of the preprocessors. See [Andrews 1991] for descriptions of CCRs, monitors, and CSP.

Multiprocessor Programs

When an SR program is executed on a single processor, SR processes are executed one at a time in an interleaved fashion. However, on some shared-memory multiprocessors—such as a Sequent Symmetry—the SR implementation supports true concurrency. In particular, there are a number of so-called job servers, and each executes SR processes. (See Appendix E for an overview of the implementation.)

The SR programmer uses an environment variable `SR_PARALLEL` to specify the number of job servers and hence how much actual parallelism there will be in an SR program that is executed on a multiprocessor. With the C shell, **csh**, this variable is set by executing

```
setenv SR_PARALLEL 4
```

With the Bourne shell, **sh**, or the Korn shell, **ksh**, it is set by executing

```
export SR_PARALLEL; SR_PARALLEL=4
```

If `SR_PARALLEL` is set as above, the next time an SR program is executed, four job servers will be created. Thus up to four SR processes will execute concurrently. The default value for `SR_PARALLEL` is 1, in which case a program is executed as if it were on a uniprocessor system.

On some multiprocessors, processes are not able to share files that are opened after the program begins execution in multiprocessor mode. (This is true in Sequent's DYNIX system, for example.) In this case the SR implementation creates one I/O server in addition to `SR_PARALLEL` job servers. Most I/O operations are handled by the I/O server, which unfortunately increases the overhead for doing I/O. Details on multiprocessor versions of SR are in the `doc` directory in the SR distribution.

Distributed Programs

An SR program is treated as a distributed program if it makes explicit use of virtual machines. In this case it executes in cooperation with an execution-time manager, **srx.** Execution of **srx** starts automatically when an SR program first creates an instance of the predefined `vm` resource, or when it calls the predefined `locate` operation.

The **srx** program is not contained within the SR program; instead, it is loaded from a predetermined location (which can be overridden by the environment variable `SRXPATH`). If a new version of the SR system is installed, existing programs may need to be rebuilt to be compatible with the new **srx.** An incompatible version of **srx** aborts with an error message.

A new virtual machine is created on physical machine X by executing `create vm() on X`. Machine X can be specified in either of two ways. The simplest way is to use a string expression that gives the symbolic name of a machine; this is of course installation dependent.

Machines can also be specified using integers. By convention, program execution commences on machine 0. Other integers have default meanings that depend on the local network configuration. To avoid installation-dependent meanings, it is best to associate machine numbers with machine names by calling `locate`. For example,

```
locate(n,hostname)
```

associates integer n with string `hostname`, which is the symbolic name of some host machine. The `locate` function thus provides an indirect way to specify remote machines by name. This association between n and `hostname` affects the subsequent meaning of machine n on *all* virtual machines.

A distributed SR program can use only those hosts on a network to which a user has access. A user's login name must be the same on all these hosts. In general, SR programs should be distributed only over machines with compatible CPU architectures, such as SPARCs or MIPS, but not both. However, it is possible under some circumstances, and with some trickery, to run a distributed program over machines with different architectures or different versions of UNIX. It is usually necessary to compile the identical programs separately under all the different environments and to arrange (by calling `locate` if necessary) to execute the correct versions. (Sometimes, however, different C compilers generate code that is not compatible; e.g., they may allocate storage for fields in structures in different ways.)

When an SR program creates a virtual machine on a host, the **srx** manager uses the UNIX **rsh** command to initiate execution of the SR program on the remote host. A problem is specifying the program's location from the remote host's viewpoint.

An automatic solution is available on systems that support remote disk access with a systematic naming scheme, e.g., NFS. The SR installer configures an `srmap` file containing rules for locating and naming files. This file is read from a known location by **srx**; an alternate file can be substituted by defining the environment variable `SRMAP`. The automatic scheme can be overridden by using a third parameter on a `locate` call:

```
locate(n, hostname, pathname)
```

This specifies that `pathname` is the file to be executed by **rsh** when a virtual machine is created on host `n`.

On systems without remote disks, some sort of manual action is usually needed to copy the executable SR program to remote machines. The UNIX **rcp** or **rdist** command can be used for this. The remote location will depend on the `srmap` file. Typically this would be the same location relative to the login directory, e.g., `~mike/test/a.out` on all machines. Be sure to recopy the file each time it is rebuilt; mixing old and new versions can lead to disaster. If the automatically generated file name is unsuitable, again an explicit path in a `locate` call can be used to override it.

Cautions and Pitfalls

We have tried to make the error messages and warnings issued by the SR compiler and run-time system as descriptive as possible. However, like any programming language, SR gives the programmer plenty of rope to hang him- or herself. Here we describe a few things that might cause surprises.

When a block is entered, storage for scalar variables is allocated before any statements in the block are executed. However, storage for arrays is allocated dynamically when the declaration is encountered. Allowing statements to appear before array declarations provides very useful functionality since it allows the size of an array to depend on input values. However, it gives rise to a somewhat strange problem. For example, the following program will crash (typically with a segmentation fault):

```
resource main()
  op foo()
  call foo()
```

```
        var a[10]: int
        proc foo()
          a[1] := 3
        end
      end
```

This program crashes because `foo` is called before storage has been allocated for `a`, and the body of `foo` accesses `a`.

A similar problem occurs in the program in Section 14.1. The global `sizes` is imported by the resource `mult` before array `c` is declared. If the global calls `stop`, then the finalization code in the resource will crash since `c` has not yet been allocated. This problem can be remedied by adding the following statement to the start of the finalization code in resource `mult`:

```
      if N mod PR != 0 -> stop fi
```

The programmer should also be careful when destroying resources because there might be active procs or processes that should not be destroyed. For example, suppose a proc in one resource calls a proc in a second resource. An error will result if the second proc destroys the first resource because the second proc will no longer have a place to which to return.

When an SR program executes `create vm()`, the new virtual machine executes in the context of the user's *current* directory and environment on the machine that executes the create statement. However, when a program executes `create vm() on X`, the virtual machine executes in the context of the user's *home* directory and *initial* environment on machine `X`, even if `X` happens to be the same machine. As an example, Chapter 17 presented a simple distributed file system that allows one to create files on remote machines. There, instances of resource `DirServer` open a file of accounts by executing the following:

```
      var f := open("dfs/Accounts", READ)
```

Suppose that the following statements are executed on machine `ivy`:

```
        var vmcap := create vm() on "ivy"
        var dscap := create DirServer() on vmcap
```

For these SR uses **rsh** to start up the virtual machine, and the location of file `dfs/Accounts` is relative to the user's home directory. Suppose instead that the following statements are executed on machine `ivy`:

```
        var vmcap := create vm()
        var dscap := create DirServer() on vmcap
```

For these SR uses **fork** and **exec** to start up the new virtual machine, and the location of `dfs/Accounts` is relative to the user's current working directory. We could avoid this difference by having SR always use **rsh** for virtual machine creation, but that would increase overhead for the local case. Moreover, the programmer is most likely to expect a virtual machine that is created locally to execute in the context of the current directory and environment.

The output from a virtual machine is subject to network delays before it reaches its ultimate destination on the disk or terminal. Thus if several machines write to `stdout` or `stderr`, the ordering may be unexpected even if properly synchronized at the SR level.

As in many other languages, misusing pointers in SR can sometimes lead to strange results in program execution. For example, execution of erroneous user code can overwrite run-time system (RTS) data structures, which can result in unexpected error messages from the RTS. So check pointer use in such cases before yelling "SR bug!" In addition, errors that cause a virtual machine to crash can cause **srx** to lose a connection to the virtual machine.

Implementation and Performance

The SR implementation has three major components: the compiler, linker, and run-time system (RTS). Appendix D described the compiler and linker. This appendix gives an overview of the RTS, focusing on how it implements the concurrency features of SR.

As mentioned in Appendix D, the SR compiler generates C code, which is in turn passed through the C compiler to produce machine code (MC). The SR linker combines the MC from a specific SR program with the program-independent RTS to produce an executable image.

The RTS provides the environment in which the MC executes. In particular, it provides primitives for creating and destroying resources and globals, invoking and servicing operations, memory allocation, input/output, virtual machines, timing functions, and various miscellaneous functions. (The doc directory in the SR distribution contains a description of all the RTS primitives.) Internally, the RTS contains a small collection of indivisible process management and semaphore primitives. This comprises a light-weight threads package that multiplexes execution of SR processes (threads) on a single processor or a shared memory multiprocessor.

When a user starts execution of an SR program, the RTS creates one virtual machine (VM) on the local physical machine. After initializing the VM, the RTS then creates one instance of the program's main resource and creates a process to initialize that resource. Each VM executes as a single UNIX process in which concurrency is simulated by the RTS. VMs exchange messages using UNIX sockets.

The RTS hides the details of the network from the MC; i.e., the number of machines and their topology is transparent. When the RTS receives a request for a service that is provided on another machine—e.g., creating a

315

resource or invoking an operation—it simply forwards the request to the destination machine. Upon arrival at the destination, the RTS on that machine services the request just as though it had been generated locally. Results from such requests are transmitted back in a similar fashion.

The remainder of this appendix describes how the RTS implements resources, operations, invocation statements, and input statements. We first describe the single-processor implementation and then give an overview of the multiprocessor implementation. The last section discusses the relative performance of the various process-interaction mechanisms.

Resource and Global Creation and Destruction

On each VM the RTS maintains a table of active resource instances.* A resource capability consists of (1) a VM identity, a pointer into the resource instance table, and a sequence number, and (2) an operation capability for each of the operations declared in the resource's spec (operation capabilities are described below). The sequence number for a resource is assigned when the instance is created; it is stored in the resource instance table. The RTS uses sequence numbers to determine whether a resource capability refers to a resource instance that still exists, i.e., whether the referenced resource instance has been destroyed.

The MC for the create statement builds a creation block that contains the identity of the resource to be created, the VM on which it is to be created, and the values of any parameters. This block is passed to the RTS, which transmits it to the designated VM. When the creation block arrives at the designated VM, the local RTS allocates a table entry for the instance and fills in the first part of the resource capability accordingly. The RTS then creates a process to initialize that resource. The create statement terminates and returns a resource capability when this process terminates or executes a reply statement.

The resource-initialization process does several things before executing user-specified initialization code. First, a resource-variable structure is allocated. This structure contains storage for the resource capability, simple resource constants and variables (e.g., integers), and pointers to other resource variables (e.g., arrays). Second, class descriptors are created for the operation classes in the resource. Third, a descriptor is created for each operation that is declared in the spec or that is implemented by a proc or external, and the resource capability is initialized. (Operation classes and operation descriptors are described below.) Finally, the resource-initialization process executes user-specified initialization code. This includes assignments in variable declarations, dynamic allocation of arrays, state-

---

*All RTS table entries are allocated dynamically, so tables are represented by linked lists.

ments in the top level of the resource body, and code to create background processes. This code is executed in the order in which items appear in the spec and body of the resource.

To destroy a resource instance, the MC passes the RTS a capability for the instance. The RTS first creates a process to execute the resource's final code. (To avoid special cases, this process is always created.) When the finalization process terminates, the RTS uses the resource instance table to locate processes, operations, and memory that belong to the resource instance. The RTS then kills the processes, frees the entries in the resource and operation tables, and frees the resource's memory. The sequence number in each freed entry is altered so that future references to a resource that has been destroyed, or to one of its operations, can be detected as being invalid.

Globals are created and destroyed in a similar way. On each VM the RTS maintains a table of active globals. When an import clause is processed, for each global named in the clause, the RTS on the current VM checks to see if the global has already been created. If not, a process is created to initialize the global. Since globals have nearly the same contents as resources, they are initialized in nearly the same way. When the global initialization process terminates or executes a reply statement, it returns a pointer to the structure containing the global's exported objects.

Globals are destroyed in the same way as resources. The only difference is that sequence numbers are not needed since global table entries cannot ever be reused. (A global is created at most once per VM, and it is destroyed only if its VM is explicitly destroyed.)

Operations

The RTS also maintains an operation table on each VM. This table contains an entry for each operation that is serviced on that VM and is currently active. The entry indicates whether the operation is serviced by a proc or by input statements. For an operation serviced by a proc, the entry contains the address of the code for the proc. For an operation serviced by input statements, the entry points to its list of pending invocations. Operations that are serviced by input statements are also grouped into *classes*, which are sets of operations serviced by the same input statement(s). Classes are described in detail in the section below on input statements.

An operation capability consists of a VM identity, an index into the operation table, and a sequence number. The sequence number serves a purpose analogous to the sequence number in a resource capability: It enables the RTS to determine whether an invocation refers to an operation that still exists. (An operation exists until its defining resource is destroyed or its defining block terminates.)

Invocation Statements

To invoke an operation, the MC first builds an invocation block, which consists of header information and actual parameter values. The MC fills in the header with the kind of invocation—call, send, concurrent call, or concurrent send—and a capability for the operation being invoked. The MC then passes the invocation block to the RTS. If necessary, the RTS transmits the invocation block to the VM on which the operation is located. The RTS then uses the index in the operation capability to locate the entry in the operation table and thus to determine how the operation is serviced.

For an operation serviced by a proc, the RTS creates a process and passes it the invocation block. (In some cases the RTS can avoid creating a process; this is discussed in the section below on optimizations.) For an operation serviced by input statements, the RTS places the invocation block onto the list of invocations for the operation; then it determines if any process is waiting for the invocation and, if so, awakens such a process. Independent of how an operation is serviced, if it is invoked by a call statement, the RTS blocks the calling process. When the operation has been serviced, the RTS awakens that process; it retrieves any results from the invocation block and then deallocates the block.

The implementation of the concurrent statement builds on the implementation of call and send statements. First, the MC informs the RTS when it begins executing a `co` statement. The RTS then allocates a structure in which it maintains the number of outstanding call invocations (i.e., those that have been started but have not yet completed) and a list of call invocations that have completed but have not yet been returned to the MC. Second, the MC performs all the invocations without blocking. For each call invocation the MC places an arm number—the index of the concurrent command within the `co` statement—in the invocation block. Third, since send invocations complete immediately, the MC executes the postprocessing block (if any) corresponding to each send invocation. The MC then repeatedly calls an RTS primitive to wait for call invocations to complete.

For each completed call invocation, the MC executes the postprocessing block (if any) corresponding to the invocation; specifically, it uses the arm number in the invocation block as an index into a jump table of postprocessing blocks. When all invocations have completed—or when one of the postprocessing blocks executes `exit`—the MC informs the RTS that the `co` statement has terminated. The RTS then discards any remaining completed call invocations and arranges to discard any call invocations for this `co` statement that might complete in the future. The infrequent situation in which a postprocessing block itself contains a `co` statement is handled by a slight generalization of the above implementation.

Input Statements

Input statements are the most complicated statements in the language and hence have the most complicated implementations. In its most general form, a single input statement can service one of several operations and can use synchronization and scheduling expressions to select the invocation it wants. Moreover, an operation can be serviced by input statements in more than one process, which then compete to service invocations. However, as we shall see, the implementation of simple, commonly occurring cases is quite efficient.

Classes are fundamental to the implementation of input statements. They are used to identify and control conflicts between processes that are trying to service the same invocations. Classes have a static aspect and a dynamic aspect. A static class of operations is an equivalence class of the transitive closure of the relation "serviced by the same input statement." At compile time, the compiler groups operations into static classes based on their appearance in input statements. All operations exported by a global are placed in a single class per global since they can be serviced in arbitrary combinations inside resources that import the global.

At run-time, actual membership in the dynamic classes depends on which operations in the static class are extant. For example, an operation declared local to a process joins its dynamic class when the process is created and leaves its dynamic class when the process completes execution. The RTS represents each dynamic class by a *class structure*, which contains a list of pending invocations of operations in the class, a flag indicating whether or not some process has access to the class, and a list of processes that are waiting to access the class. Each operation table entry points to its operation's class structure.

At most one process at a time is allowed to access the list of pending invocations of operations in a given class structure. That is, for a given class at most one process at a time can be selecting an invocation to service or be appending a new invocation. Processes are given access to both pending and new invocations in a class structure in first-come/first-served order. Thus a process waiting to access the invocations in a class will eventually obtain access as long as all functions in synchronization and scheduling expressions terminate eventually.

The RTS provides several primitives that the MC uses to implement input statements. These primitives are tailored to support common cases of input statements, and they have straightforward and efficient implementations. The key primitives are the following:*

---

*For simplicity, we have omitted the `sr_` prefix that is common to the names of all RTS functions.

`access(class, else_present)`

Acquires exclusive access to `class`, which is established as the current class for the executing process. That process blocks if another process already has access to `class`. After gaining exclusive access, a process releases access when it blocks trying to get an invocation, or when it executes `remove` (see below). Parameter `else_present` is true if the input statement has an else clause; it is false otherwise.

`get_anyinv()`

Returns a pointer to the invocation block the executing process should examine next. This invocation will be on the invocation list in the current class of the executing process; successive calls of this primitive return successive invocations. If there is no such invocation, the RTS releases access to the executing process's current class and blocks that process.

`get_myinv(op_cap)`

Returns a pointer to the next invocation of the operation named by `op_cap` (an operation capability). If there is no such invocation, the RTS releases access to the executing process's current class and blocks that process.

`chk_myinv(op_cap)`

Returns a pointer to the next invocation of the operation named by `op_cap`. This primitive is identical to `get_myinv`, except that the RTS does not block the executing process; instead the RTS returns a null pointer. This primitive is used when an input statement contains a scheduling expression.

`remove(invocation)`

Removes the invocation block pointed at by `invocation` from the invocation list of the executing process's current class. The RTS also releases exclusive access to that class.

`finished_input(invocation)`

Informs the RTS that the MC has finished executing the command body in an input statement and is therefore finished with the invocation block pointed at by `invocation`. If that invocation was called, the RTS passes the invocation block back to the invoking process and awakens that process.

```
receive(class)
```

Gets and then removes the next invocation in `class`. This primitive is a combination of `access(class)`, `inv := get_myinv(op_cap)`, and `remove(inv)`; hence it returns a pointer to an invocation block. It is used for receive statements and for simple input statements that are like receive statements.

Below are four examples that illustrate how these primitives are used by the MC. More complicated input statements are implemented using appropriate combinations of the primitives.

First consider the simple input statement:

```
in q(x) -> ... ni
```

This statement delays the executing process until there is some invocation of q and then services the oldest such invocation. (Receive statements expand into this form of input statement.) For this statement, if q is the only operation in class c, the MC executes `inv := receive(c)`. Otherwise the MC executes `access(c)`, `inv := get_myinv(q)`, and `remove(inv)`. In either case the MC then executes the command body associated with q, with parameter x bound to the value of x in the invocation block. When the command body terminates, the MC calls `finished_input(inv)`.

Second, consider the following two-armed input statement:

```
in q(x) -> ... [] r(y,z) -> ... ni
```

This statement services the first pending invocation of either q or r. Since q and r appear in the same input statement, they will be placed in the same class c. For the above statement, the MC first calls `access(c)` and then it calls `inv := get_anyinv()` to look at each pending invocation in class c to determine if it is an invocation of q or r (there might be additional operations in the class). If the MC finds an invocation of q or r, it calls `remove(inv)`, then executes the corresponding command body with the parameter values from the selected invocation block, and finally calls `finished_input(inv)`. If the MC finds no pending invocation of q or r, the executing process blocks in `get_anyinv` until an invocation in the class arrives. When such an invocation arrives, the RTS awakens the process, which then repeats the above steps.

Next consider an input statement with a synchronization expression:

```
in q(x) st x > 3 -> ... ni
```

This statement services the first pending invocation of q for which parameter x > 3. If q belongs to class c, the MC first uses `access(c)` to obtain exclusive access to c. The MC then uses either `inv := get_anyinv()` or `inv := get_myinv(q)` to obtain invocations of q one at a time. The first primitive is used if q is the only operation in class c; otherwise the second is used. For each such invocation, the MC evaluates the synchronization expression using the value of the parameter in the invocation block. If the synchronization expression is true, the MC notifies the RTS of its success by calling `remove(inv)`, executes the command body associated with q, and calls `finished_input(inv)`. If the synchronization expression is false, the MC repeats the above steps to obtain the next invocation.

Finally, consider an input statement with a scheduling expression:

```
in q(x) by x -> ... ni
```

This statement services the oldest pending invocation of q that has the smallest value of parameter x. The MC uses the same steps as in the previous example to obtain the first invocation of q. It then evaluates the scheduling expression using the value of the parameter in the invocation block; the MC saves this value and a pointer, `psave`, to the invocation block. The MC then obtains the remaining invocations one at a time by repeatedly executing `inv := chk_myinv(q)`. For each of these invocations, the MC evaluates the scheduling expression, compares it with the saved value, and updates the saved value and pointer if the new value is smaller. When there are no more invocations (i.e., when `chk_myinv` returns a null pointer), `psave` points to the invocation with the smallest scheduling expression. The MC acquires that invocation by calling `remove(psave)`, executes the command body associated with q, and finally calls `finished_input(psave)`.

Note that synchronization and scheduling expressions are evaluated by the MC, not the RTS. We do this for two reasons. First, these expressions can reference objects such as local variables for which the RTS would need to establish addressing if it were to execute the code that evaluates the expression. Second, these expressions can contain invocations; it would greatly complicate the RTS to handle such invocations in a way that does not cause the RTS to block itself. A consequence of this approach to evaluating synchronization and scheduling expressions is that the overhead of evaluating such expressions is paid for only by processes that use them.

Optimizations

The SR compiler optimizes special uses of operations. The first optimization applies to calls of procs that are in the same resource as the caller or are in a global imported by the caller. If the proc does not contain a reply or forward statement and does not call `setpriority`, then the compiler generates conventional procedure-call code instead of going through the RTS. In particular, the compiler generates code that allocates and initializes an invocation block and passes the block's address to the called proc. Thus the code in the proc is independent of whether it is executed by the calling process or as a separate process.

A similar optimization is performed for a call of a proc that is located on the same VM as the caller and that does not contain `reply`, `forward`, or `setpriority`. The RTS must be entered, however, because the compiler cannot in general determine whether an operation is implemented by a proc—due to separate compilation of specs and bodies—or whether that proc is in the same VM—due to dynamic resource creation.

A third optimization is that operations that are used like semaphores are implemented directly by the RTS's semaphores rather than by the general mechanisms described above. The main criteria that an operation must satisfy to be implemented by semaphores are that it (1) is invoked using send, not call, (2) has no parameters or return value, (3) is serviced by input (or receive) statements in which it is the only operation and in which there are no synchronization or scheduling expressions, and (4) is declared at the global or resource level. Note that these criteria are relatively simple to check. Programmer-declared semaphores (`sem`) that are invoked only using P and V will be implemented as true semaphores if they are declared at the global or resource level.

Processor Scheduling

Processes are created and destroyed dynamically during execution of an SR program. At any point in time, each existing process is either executing, ready to execute, or blocked (e.g., waiting for a remote call to complete or waiting to receive a message). On a single-processor architecture, at most one process is executing at a time within each virtual machine. Other ready processes are stored on the ready list. A blocked process is stored on a list that depends on what the process is waiting for.

The ready list is implemented as a priority queue. The highest priority ready process is at the front of the queue. When a blocked process is awakened, its descriptor is inserted in the ready list after processes of higher or equal priority and before processes of lower priority. Thus, the ready list is a FIFO queue in an SR program that does not call the `setpriority` function. The RTS keeps track of the priority of the process at the end of the ready list to facilitate rapid insertion in this common case.

In general, the executing process continues until it voluntarily enters the RTS, e.g., when it invokes an operation. A process is never preempted at an arbitrary point. However, there is a run-time limit on the maximum number of consecutive loop iterations a process can execute before it will be forced to enter the RTS. This limit is set using the `-L` option to the SR linker **srl**. (The `-l` option of **srl** displays the defaults for all run-time limits.)

The primary computation in an SR program executing on a single virtual machine terminates when the ready list is empty, no processes are napping, and there is no pending I/O. The RTS then creates a process to execute the final code in the main resource. The next time the RTS detects termination, it exits.

A distributed program executing on more than one virtual machine terminates when every ready list is empty, no processes are napping, there is no pending I/O, and there are no messages in transit between virtual machines. The distributed termination detection algorithm is coordinated by SR's remote execution manager **srx**, with input from the RTS on each virtual machine. After the primary computation terminates, the RTS on the main virtual machine creates a process to execute the final code in the program's main resource. The next time the program terminates, **srx** kills all virtual machines and then exits.

Multiprocessor Implementation

The implementation of SR that executes on shared-memory multiprocessors is called MultiSR. The essential functional difference between MultiSR and regular SR is that up to SR_PARALLEL processes can execute concurrently in each virtual machine. However, this true concurrency has several implications, the most important of which is the need to lock critical RTS data structures such as various descriptors and queues. Locks that protect critical sections in the RTS are implemented using busy waiting.

Before executing code in a user's program, MultiSR forks SR_PARALLEL job servers. Each executes one SR process at a time. The job servers share a single ready list, which is locked when a process descriptor is inserted or removed. If SR_PARALLEL is unset or is 1, then MultiSR uses only one job server; hence that server will never have to wait to acquire a lock.

When a job server finds that the ready list is empty, it executes an instance of a special idle process. That process first loops for a short while, repeatedly checking to see if an SR process is inserted on the ready list by another job server. If the ready list remains empty, the idle process goes to sleep for a few milliseconds; when it awakens, it again checks the ready list. (One instance of the idle process has responsibility for checking for program termination.) We have idle processes spin for a while to facilitate efficient barrier synchronization, but we then have them sleep as a courtesy to other users of a timeshared multiprocessor. On a stand-alone machine, we would most likely want idle processes to continue checking the ready list.

On the Sequent DYNIX implementation of MultiSR, a file opened by one job server (e.g., in response to an SR process calling open) cannot be accessed by any other job server. Rather than force all operations on a file to be executed on the job server that opened it, we have chosen to employ a separate I/O server. When an SR process invokes an I/O operation, that

Experiment	SGI 340	HP 720	Sun IPX	Sequent
loop control overhead	0.39	0.48	0.51	4.61
local call, optimized	1.70	1.98	2.65	16.90
interresource call	15.00	23.60	26.00	120.00
interresource call, new process	50.00	60.70	197.90	357.00
process create/destroy	45.00	53.20	171.90	307.00
semaphore pair	1.45	1.33	1.57	13.30
semaphore, context switch	10.50	9.30	52.70	74.50
asynchronous send/receive	21.00	28.20	34.80	155.00
message passing, context switch	35.00	33.35	122.50	229.50
rendezvous	54.00	52.20	202.90	350.00

Figure E.1. Performance measurements (in microseconds).

operation is put on a queue for the I/O server, and the SR process blocks. (The exceptions are writes to `stdout` and `stderr`.) The I/O server repeatedly executes I/O operations; when it finishes one, it awakens the SR process that invoked the operation. An I/O server is not needed, or used, if job servers can share all file descriptors.

Performance

SR provides a variety of communication and synchronization mechanisms, which facilitates its use for writing concurrent programs for a variety of applications and hardware architectures. However, the different mechanisms have significant differences in performance. Naturally, it takes longer to communicate using message passing—especially across a network—than it does using shared variables. But there are also major performance differences between the various message-passing mechanisms. This in turn affects the performance of applications.

Figure E.1 lists the execution time, in microseconds, of different combinations of process-interaction mechanisms on different processors. The first column of numbers reports tests on a Silicon Graphics Iris 4D/340 processor, which has a 33 MHz clock and a MIPS R3000 chip. The second column is for a Hewlett-Packard 9000/720 ("Snake"), which has a 50 MHz clock and an HP PA-RISC chip. The Sun Microsystems IPX has a 40 MHz clock and a SPARC chip. The final column of numbers is for a Sequent Symmetry 81, which has a 16 MHz clock and an Intel 386 chip.

The main process in each test program consisted of a control loop that exercised a single mechanism from 10,000 to a million times.* The execution time of the control loop was measured using SR's `age` function. Each test program was run ten times in a single virtual machine on an unloaded processor. There were occasional perturbations, but each test produced quite consistent results. The numbers in Figure E.1 are the median values from the ten tests. All performance numbers include the loop control overhead, which is reported in the first line of the figure.

An optimized local call is very fast. It is not, however, as fast as a null C procedure call, because an SR call contains four hidden arguments that are used to address variables and arguments and to handle the general case that a call might be remote. Also, the SR procedure entry and exit code saves and restores values that are used for run-time tracing and error reporting.

As noted earlier, an interresource call has to be handled by the RTS. If the RTS determines that the operation is serviced by a procedure and is in the same virtual machine, then the RTS simply jumps to the procedure. Such an interresource call takes an order of magnitude longer than an optimized call due to this overhead of entering the RTS and due to the need to allocate storage for the arguments. If an interresource call requires creating a new process—and hence also requires two context switches—the time increases by about another factor of three. (The context-switching overhead is much greater on the SPARC architecture because of the SPARC's register windows.) The actual time to create and destroy a process—without returning results, as in a call—is reported on the fifth line.

The semaphore-pair test program did repeated V and P operations, in that order, so that the main process never blocked. The execution time is less than for an optimized call because only one argument has to be passed to the RTS. When a semaphore operation causes a context switch, the execution time is much greater, as shown on the next line. Again the SPARC architecture has a large overhead.

Asynchronous message passing is more costly to use than semaphores because the RTS has to manipulate message queues. It is also somewhat more costly to use than an interresource procedure call because the message has to be copied from the invocation block into the variables in a receive statement. The asynchronous send/receive times listed in Figure E.1 are the cost of a send/receive pair with no arguments and no blocking, and hence no context switching. Message passing, like semaphores, takes longer when a context switch occurs, as shown in the next line. Both sets of execution times increase slightly for non-null messages, depending, of course, on the number of values in the message.

---

*The test programs and shell scripts to run them are included in the SR distribution.

Rendezvous is more costly than message passing because communication is two-way and because there have to be two context switches to complete a rendezvous. Rendezvous is, however, less costly than two send/receive pairs with context switches because the same invocation block is used for both the value and result arguments. The reported times are for a simple rendezvous with no synchronization or scheduling expressions.

We have also run the message-passing tests on our local network, with the main process executing on one workstation and the server process on another. When the test program executes on top of UNIX, communication is about two orders of magnitude slower. However, there is an experimental stand-alone implementation of SR that employs a customized communication kernel. In this case intermachine communication is only two or three times slower than intramachine communication.

To summarize, using shared variables is always less expensive than using message passing. This is hardly surprising since it takes less time to write into shared variables than it does to allocate a message buffer, fill it, and pass it on to another process. On a shared memory machine, the programmer would most likely not want to use message passing unless that is the most natural way to structure the solution to a problem.

On a distributed memory architecture, message passing of some form has to be used, either explicitly or implicitly. If information flow is one-way—e.g., in a network of filters—then asynchronous message passing is the most efficient mechanism. Asynchronous message passing is also the most efficient, as well as the easiest to use, for interaction patterns such as those in heartbeat algorithms. For client/server interaction, however, rendezvous and RPC are more convenient to use. The choice between rendezvous and RPC depends on whether the programmer wants to have an existing or a new process service the client's call. SR's input statement is very powerful—and hence very useful at times—but it should be apparent from the description of its implementation that using synchronization or scheduling expressions decreases performance.

History of SR

The basic ideas in SR—resources, operations, input statements, and asynchronous (send) and synchronous (call) invocations—were conceived by Andrews in 1978 and written up in early 1979; that paper eventually appeared in late 1981 [Andrews 1981]. The initial version of a full SR language was defined in the early 1980s and implemented by the authors and several graduate students [Andrews 1982]. That version is now called SR_0 ("SR naught"). Based on local experience with SR_0, the authors designed a new version in the mid 1980s; it added RPC, semaphores, early reply, and several additional mechanisms. Andrews and Olsson [1986] describe the evolution of SR, explaining what was changed and why, as well as what was not changed and why not (also see Olsson's Ph.D. dissertation [1986]). After using and testing the new version locally, we began distributing SR in March 1988. Andrews et al. [1988] describe SR version 1.0, explain the implementation, and compare SR with other languages.

Feedback from users of SR 1.0—and contributions from many of them—led to version 1.1, which was released in May 1989 [Andrews & Olsson 1989]. Further experience, plus the desire to provide better support for parallel programming using shared variables and operations, led to the design of version 2.0, which is the version described in this book.

Several papers and theses evaluate aspects of SR and report on experiences using SR for various applications. Purdin [1987] presents a novel design for a distributed file system and describes a prototype implementation written in SR. Atkins and Olsson [1988] describe experiments to measure the performance of SR's (version 1.0) concurrency, communication, and synchronization mechanisms; they compare the results with those for Ada reported in Clapp et al. [1986]. The experiments reported in Appendix E are designed similarly to these earlier ones. Atkins [1988] describes experiments using different upcall program structures for implementing network communications software. Coffin and Olsson [1989] show how to use SR to program multiway rendezvous, which is a generalization of rendezvous in which more than two processes participate. Finley [1989] describes a multiprocessing implementation of SR 1.1 for the Encore Multimax. Herman [1989] shows how to use SR to program a variety of synchronization mechanisms, such as conventional and distributed CCRs and monitors; his technique for monitors is used in the preprocessor mentioned in Appendix D. Olsson and Whitehead [1989] describe the **srm** tool for generating "makefiles" for SR programs (see Appendix D) and show how their techniques can automate and avoid unnecessary recompilation in any modular language. Huang and Olsson [1990] define an exception-handling mechanism for the language. Coffin [1990] introduces Par, an object-oriented language that draws from SR, as part of a methodology that attacks the problem of separating the algorithmic concerns of writing a concurrent program from the details of scheduling, placement, and synchronization. McNamee and Olsson [1990, 1991a, 1991b] present a collection of program transformations—and techniques for applying them automatically within a compiler—that improve the performance of synchronization mechanisms. The transformations are illustrated using SR; they employ the technique of passing the baton described by Andrews [1991]. Bal [1992] evaluates the design of SR version 1.1 based on experience using SR to implement several parallel algorithms. Hartley [1992] reports on experience using SR in an undergraduate operating systems course. Finally, Atkins and Coady [1992] show how to implement adaptable concurrency control for atomic data types; they used SR to implement their adaptable servers.

SR is but one of the concurrent programming languages available today, although we tend to favor it! The September 1989 issue of *ACM Computing Surveys* contains three papers that consider many concurrent programming languages: Bal et al. [1989] survey concurrent functional and logic languages as well as those based on explicit message passing, Hudak [1989] surveys functional languages (one section considers concurrency), and Shapiro [1989] surveys the family of concurrent logic languages. Andrews [1991] also compares and contrasts several concurrent programming languages and their uses.

Bibliography

Andrews, G. R. 1981. Synchronizing resources. *ACM Trans. on Prog. Languages and Systems 3*, 4 (October), 405-430.

Andrews, G. R. 1982. The distributed programming language SR—mechanisms, design, and implementation. *Software—Practice and Experience 12*, 8 (August), 719-754.

Andrews, G. R. 1991. *Concurrent Programming: Principles and Practice*. The Benjamin/Cummings Publishing Co., Redwood City, CA.

Andrews, G. R., and Olsson, R. A. 1986. The evolution of the SR language. *Distributed Computing 1*, 3 (July), 133-149.

Andrews, G. R., and Olsson, R. A. 1989. Report on the SR programming language, version 1.1. TR 89-6, Dept. of Computer Science, University of Arizona, May.

Andrews, G. R., Olsson, R. A., Coffin, M., Elshoff, I., Nilsen, K., Purdin, T., and Townsend, G. 1988. An overview of the SR language and implementation. *ACM Trans. on Prog. Languages and Systems 10*, 1 (January), 51-86.

ANSI. 1989. *ANSI X3.159-1989. Programming Language—C*. American National Standards Institute, NY.

Atkins, M. S. 1988. Experiments in SR with different upcall program structures. *ACM Trans. on Computer Systems 6*, 9 (November), 365-392.

Atkins, M. S., and Coady, Y. M. 1992. Adaptable concurrency control for atomic data types. *ACM Trans. on Computer Systems 10*, in press.

Atkins, M. S., and Olsson, R. A. 1988. Performance of multi-tasking and synchronization mechanisms in the programming language SR. *Software—Practice and Experience 18*, 9 (September), 879-895.

Bal, H. E. 1992. Parallel programming in SR. *Proc. IEEE International Conference on Computer Languages*, San Francisco, April, 310-319.

Bal, H. E., Steiner, J. G., and Tanenbaum, A. S. 1989. Programming languages for distributed computing systems. *ACM Computing Surveys 21*, 3 (September), 261-322.

Bruno, G. 1984. Using Ada for discrete event simulation. *Software—Practice and Experience 14*, 7 (July), 685-695.

Chandy, K. M., and Misra, J. 1984. The drinking philosophers problem. *ACM Trans. on Prog. Languages and Systems 6*, 4 (October), 632-646.

Clapp, R. M., Duchesneau, L., Volz, R. A., Mudge, T. N., and Schultze, T. 1986. Toward real-time performance benchmarks for Ada. *Comm. ACM 29*, 8 (August), 760-781.

Coffin, M. H. 1990. Par: an approach to architecture-independent parallel programming. TR 90-28. Doctoral dissertation, Dept. of Computer Science, The University of Arizona, August.

Coffin, M. H., and Olsson, R. A. 1989. An SR approach to multiway rendezvous. *Computer Languages 14*, 4, 255-262.

Courtois, P. J., Heymans, F., and Parnas, D. L. 1971. Concurrent control with "readers" and "writers." *Comm. ACM 14*, 10 (October), 667-668.

Dijkstra, E. W. 1968a. The structure of the "THE" multiprogramming system. *Comm. ACM 11*, 5 (May), 341-346.

Dijkstra, E. W. 1968b. Cooperating sequential processes. In *Programming Languages*, F. Genuys (ed.), Academic Press, NY, 43-112.

Dijkstra, E.W. 1976. *A Discipline of Programming*. Prentice-Hall, Englewood Cliffs, NJ.

Finley, C. M. 1989. A multiprocessor SR implementation. Master's thesis, Dept. of Computer Science, University of California, Davis, March.

Hartley, S. J. 1992. Experience with the language SR in an undergraduate operating systems course. *Proc. SIGCSE Technical Symposium*, Kansas City, March, 176-180.

Hensgen, D., Finkel, R., and Manber, U. 1988. Two algorithms for barrier synchronization. *Int. Journal of Parallel Prog. 17*, 1 (January), 1-17.

Herman, J. S. 1989. A comparison of synchronization mechanisms for concurrent programming. Master's thesis, CSE-89-26, University of California at Davis, September.

Hill, M. D., and Larus, J. R. 1990. Cache considerations for multiprocessor programmers. *Comm. ACM 33*, 8 (August), 97-102.

Hillis, W. D., and Steele, G. L., Jr. 1986. Data parallel algorithms. *Comm. ACM 29*, 12 (December), 1170-1183.

Hoare, C. A. R. 1974. Monitors: an operating system structuring concept. *Comm. ACM 17*, 10 (October), 549-557.

Hoare, C. A. R. 1978. Communicating sequential processes. *Comm. ACM 21*, 8 (August), 666-677.

Huang, D. T., and Olsson, R. A. 1990. An exception handling mechanism for SR. *Computer Languages 15*, 3, 163-176.

Hudak, P. 1989. Conception, evolution, and application of functional programming languages. *ACM Computing Surveys 21*, 3 (September), 359-411.

INMOS Limited. 1984. *Occam Programming Manual*. Prentice-Hall Int., Englewood Cliffs, NJ.

Johnson, D. S. 1990. Local optimization and the traveling salesman problem. *Proc. 17th Colloquium on Automata, Languages, and Programming*, Springer-Verlag, Berlin, 446-461.

Lawler, E. L., Lenstra, J. K., Rinnooy Kan, A. H. G., and Shmoys, D. B. 1985. *The Traveling Salesman Problem*. John Wiley & Sons, Chichester.

Manber, U. 1989. *Introduction to Algorithms: A Creative Approach*. Addison-Wesley, Reading, MA.

May, D. 1983. OCCAM. *SIGPLAN Notices 18*, 4 (April), 69-79.

McNamee, C. M., and Olsson, R. A. 1990. Transformations for optimizing interprocess communication and synchronization mechanisms. *Int. Journal of Parallel Programming 19*, 5 (October), 357-387.

Mellor-Crummey, J. M., and Scott, M. L. 1991. Algorithms for scalable synchronization on shared-memory multiprocessors. *ACM Trans. on Computer Systems 9*, 1 (February), 21-65.

Olsson, R. A. 1986. Issues in distributed programming languages: the evolution of SR. TR 86-21. Doctoral dissertation, Dept. of Computer Science, The University of Arizona, August.

Olsson, R. A. 1990. Using SR for discrete event simulation: A study in concurrent programming. *Software—Practice and Experience 20*, 12 (December), 1187-1208.

Olsson, R. A., and McNamee C. M. 1991a. An overview of compiler optimization of interprocess communication and synchronization mechanisms. *Proc. 1991 International Conf. on Parallel Processing*, Vol. II, St. Charles, IL, 31-35.

Olsson, R. A., and McNamee C. M. 1991b. Inter-entry selection: non-determinism and explicit control mechanisms. *Computer Languages 16*, in press.

Olsson, R. A., and Whitehead, G. R. 1989. A simple technique for automatic recompilation in modular programming languages. *Software—Practice and Experience 19*, 8 (August), 757-773.

Purdin, T. 1987. Enhancing file availability in distributed systems (the Saguaro file system). TR 87-26. Doctoral dissertation, Dept. of Computer Science, The University of Arizona, August.

Shapiro, E. 1989. The family of concurrent logic programming languages. *ACM Computing Surveys 21*, 3 (September), 412-510.

Wirth, N. 1982. *Programming in Modula-2*. Springer-Verlag, Berlin.

Index

Obtaining the SR Implementation

The SR Project at The University of Arizona distributes a public-domain implementation of the SR programming language. The implementation can be configured to run on a variety of hardware platforms, some of which are described at the start of the Preface.

This book describes SR Version 2.0, which was released in August, 1992. We continue to work on the design of SR and its implementation and anticipate making further releases. Several other people also continue to make contributions, such as porting SR to additional platforms and operating systems. For information on the latest release of SR, contact us at the addresses or phone numbers listed below.

SR is available by anonymous FTP from `cs.arizona.edu`. The SR distribution is located in subdirectory `sr` of the anonymous FTP area.

SR is also available on diskettes, magnetic tape, or cartridge tape for a nominal charge to cover our media and shipping costs. For further information and an order form, send electronic mail to

`sr-project@cs.arizona.edu`

send regular mail to

SR Project
Department of Computer Science
The University of Arizona
Tucson, AZ   85721
USA

or call

(602) 621-8448 — ordering information
(602) 621-4246 — FAX

We also maintain a mailing list for discussion of SR-related topics. Electronic mail sent to `info-sr@cs.arizona.edu` is automatically forwarded to people on this list. To join, send a request including your email address to `info-sr-request@cs.arizona.edu`.